# Intelligence and Strategic Surprises

# Intelligence and Strategic Surprises

Ariel Levite

Columbia University Press
New York    1987

Library of Congress Cataloging-in-Publication Data

Levite, Ariel.
  Intelligence and strategic surprises.

  Bibliography: p.
  Includes index.
  1. Military intelligence.  2. Surprise.  3. Preemptive
attack (Military science).  4. Pearl Harbor (Hawaii),
Attack on, 1941.  5. Midway, Battle of, 1942.  I. Title.
UB250.L48   1987        355.3'432        86-17401
ISBN 0-231-06374-1


Columbia University Press
New York     Guildford, Surrey
Copyright © 1987 Columbia University Press
All rights reserved

Printed in the United States of America

This book is Smyth-sewn.
Book design by J. S. Roberts

For my parents
with love and gratitude

# Contents

# Preface

To catch one's rival(s) by surprise is commonly considered a desirable feat. Surprise, in these instances, is seen as a factor that could significantly diminish costs and risks and enhance chances for success of whatever initiative one is contemplating. On occasion, surprise assumes even greater importance, being (or at least perceived to be) the *sine qua non* for success. This happens when one attempts action that is a long shot with the odds very much against him. Such is the case when a rescue mission is attempted (e.g., the Israeli rescue mission in Entebbe, the German in Mogadishu, the American in Teheran) and more generally, when an inferior force strikes a superior one. The Japanese attack on Pearl Harbor (1941), the American landing in Inchon (1950), the Arab attack on Israel (1973), and the Israeli attack on the Iraqi nuclear reactor (1981) are just a few cases in point. The overall importance of the surprise phenomenon is further enhanced by the traumatic experience associated with it, the public perception of its consequences, the widespread belief in the frequency of its occurrence, and the extensive (and costly) measures commonly taken to guard against it.

All in all, surprise appears to play a role of some significance in international affairs. It is, therefore, no wonder that the element of surprise and the ways to attain it have long preoccupied statesmen and military strategists (e.g., Sun Tzu 1971:53; Clausewitz 1968:269-74; Mahan 1957:466-67). In the past quarter century the surprise phenomenon has also attracted a considerable amount of academic research, which has made a truly significant contribution to our understanding of the surprise phenomenon. Yet, for all its numerous merits, the existing body of academic

research on surprise is ridden with problems of both concep-
tualization and methodology. It is these problems, rather than that
the study of surprise has reached a point of marginal utility, as
some argue (e.g., Handel 1979:26), that stand in the way of further
progress in the field.

In view of all of the above, this study pursues three
primary goals. The first is to provide a substantive (as distinguished
from chronological) review and synthesis of roughly half a decade
of research into the surprise phenomenon. The second is to
diagnose the weaknesses of the existing literature and to offer
some remedies. And the third goal is to make some theoretical
contribution to the study of surprise and national security decision
making on the basis of empirical research as well as deductive
reasoning.

The first chapter reviews the literature on strategic
surprise, highlights its merits and weaknesses, and proposes an
alternative approach for studying the surprise phenomenon. Chapters 2 and 3 present two longitudinal case studies, one of a
successful surprise attempt—Pearl Harbor (1941)—and another of
a surprise attack that failed—the Battle of Midway (1942). Chapter
4 then attempts to put the surprise phenomenon in perspective,
integrating explanations of surprise into a broader policy-related
theory of warning, threat perception, and response (action). Finally,
chapter 5 draws some theoretical and methodological lessons from
the case studies, and offers some thoughts on the probability of
surprise in the present and near future.

# Acknowledgments

In the fall of 1977, I took a job as a research assistant to Dr. Uzi Arad of Tel Aviv University. Early on, while discussing various research topics, Dr. Arad suggested that I look into a subject that until then had received only limited attention and seemed well worth further investigation. The subject he mentioned was strategic surprise. It was a subject I had always found fascinating, but I had never given it any systematic attention until I began to work for Dr. Arad.

The theory laid out in the memos I wrote for Dr. Arad, and the much more elaborate work he produced on its basis is, in certain respects, similar to the one presented in this study. However, there are many differences; and without a doubt, this final product is a vast improvement over that initial effort. Although I bear full responsibility for this work, I could not have taken this study of intelligence and surprise as far as I have without the initial encouragement and support of Dr. Arad, as well as the assistance of several individuals and institutions, to all of whom I owe a great debt of gratitude.

My greatest debt is to Professor Alexander L. George of Stanford University. His constant encouragement and support, his sound advice, and his many detailed and most helpful remarks on everything I have written, from the early draft of the first chapter to the final draft of the entire work, have greatly influenced the final product. He also deserves much credit for pushing me to get the work published. My dissertation committee at Cornell University, Professors George H. Quester, T. J. Pempel, and especially Peter J. Katzenstein provided me with invaluable assistance from the inception of this project to its successful completion.

They also provided the ideal amount of guidance; I never felt stifled by their demands or forsaken. I have thoroughly enjoyed working on this study and that is largely the result of the excellent relationship I had with my committee.

Other individuals have carefully read chapters of this study and offered many helpful comments: Admiral Bobby R. Inman, Joseph F. Bouchard, Professor Sidney Drell, Dr. Bruce Jentleson, Dr. William Perry, Athanassios Platias, Ted Ralston, Professor Judy Reppy, Dr. Jon Wiant, and Dr. Dore Gold. Joseph Bouchard deserves special thanks for his help in incorporating in this work the graphs appearing in chapter 4. John E. Taylor of the Modern Military Section of the National Archives in Washington, D.C., proved invaluable in locating the primary documents extensively used in this study. His generous assistance is also gratefully acknowledged.

While working on this study I received financial support from various sources. The Cornell Peace Studies Program supported me during my stay at Cornell and provided funds for me to do research at the National Archives in Washington. I also received support from the Government Department and the Graduate School of Cornell University (Summer Research Fellowship), and from the Center for International Security and Arms Control, Stanford University. The Jaffee Center for Strategic Studies at Tel Aviv University has generously provided me with the time and facilities to revise this manuscript for publication. Without their generous support, this study could not have been written.

From September 1982 to 1983, I was a research fellow at the Center for International Security and Arms Control, Stanford University, where most of the book was written. I would like to thank the many individuals at this institution who were helpful to me, as well as all of those who have talked to me at length about the various subjects encompassed within this study. Many thanks are also due the staff of Columbia University Press, especially to Kate Wittenberg. Their guidance and cooperation in the entire publication process has been truly exceptional.

Finally, anyone who has written a book-length study knows the value of moral encouragement and support. In this regard it is to my wife, Ziva, that I owe the greatest debt, for her confidence in me and ever-present willingness to support me.

# Intelligence and Strategic Surprises

# Chapter 1

# The Study
# of Strategic Surprise

**Explicit, detailed, and** cogent definitions of the phenomenon under discussion here—strategic surprise—are hard to come by in the existing literature. Some important differences exist between the few definitions that are available. Since quite a few of the problems with the surprise literature can be traced back to this weakness, a definition of strategic surprise is clearly worth dwelling on at some length.

As defined here,[1] strategic surprise is a sudden realization that one has been operating on the basis of an erroneous threat perception. It occurs through failure to predict, much less anticipate, an acute and immediate foreign threat to the "vital" national interests.[2] Based on this definition, strategic surprise has *all* of the following features:

1. It is a discrete case, rather than a continuous development, composed of a fairly clear-cut series of events. Yet, it is a matter of degree, and can occur on one or several dimensions (see below). Strategic surprise, strictly defined, is not mere over- or underestimation of an opponent's capabilities.

2. Since strategic surprise affects the core interests of the target country, that country and its leadership can derive considerable benefits from averting a strategic surprise, and conversely, can suffer equally considerable penalties for failing to do so. Consequently, senior government officials, including po-

litical leaders, play an important role in the assessment of strategic warning, and in the recognition
of and reaction to strategic threats.

3. Strategic surprise occurs through failure to anticipate immediate (as distinguished from potential)
threats posed by hostile as well as peaceful actions.
Furthermore, failure to recognize the opponent's
hostile intentions can take place in the transition
from peace to war and from war to peace, as well
as within war. The difference between the three
cases is essentially quantitative (i.e., a matter of
degree) rather than qualitative.

4. Surprise is strategic only when the perpetrator *deliberately* intends and designs his actions to catch
his target by surprise. The term "strategic" is therefore used here with the same connotation it has in
game theory. The deliberate intention to surprise
is important because it has considerable impact on
the problem faced by both the perpetrator and the
target. It also distinguishes strategic surprise from
other types of erroneous threat perception.[3]

5. Another similarity to game theory is that the interaction leading to strategic surprise is essentially
a dyadic quarrel in which each participant is aware
of the values at stake. While each side to the quarrel
may be one state or a coalition thereof, each side
shares at least one joint purpose—to catch by surprise or to avert a surprise action against itself.

6. Strategic surprise may occur on one or more of
the following dimensions: (a) identity of the perpetrator (who?); (b) type of action involved (what,
how?); (c) timing of action (when?); (d) location of
action (where?); and (e) motivation for taking the
action (why?). As a practical matter, however, perhaps the most critical dimension of surprise is not
*who* will initiate *what* kind of action, *when*, *where*,
and *why*, but rather *whether* or not an antagonist

will act, and/or act in a certain manner, at a given time, etc. Here I should point out that in the transition from peace to war surprise can occur on all the five dimensions presented above, while surprise in war can occur only on dimensions b through d. After all, in war the general identity of the opponent and at least his general motivation for taking action are known.

7. Strategic surprise may take place at either of two stages: (a) acquisition, transmission, evaluation, and dissemination of the strategic warning by the intelligence community, and (b) perception (recognition) of the strategic threat by the national policymakers. Whereas failures at either or both of these stages that result in erroneous threat perception produce surprise when the threat materializes, accurate threat perception by policymakers (irrespective of the quality of the warning available to them) rules out, by definition, the possibility of strategic surprise. One must be careful, however, not to confuse surprise with unpreparedness. While the two phenomena are obviously related, they are not identical; surprise is not necessarily met by unpreparedness, nor is unpreparedness necessarily preceded by surprise (see chapter 4).

Now that we are familiar with the definition and main features of strategic surprise, we may proceed to consider the importance of the phenomenon. Previously, it was suggested that strategic surprise is not only a salient event, one that attracts the interest of the leadership and captures the imagination of the public, but also that it is a momentous event. When successful, it imposes devastating, although not necessarily fatal, consequences on the victims of surprise and provides considerable, although not always decisive, benefits to its perpetrator (Knorr 1982; Whaley 1975; Clausewitz 1968:269–73). Furthermore, strategic surprise is a stunning and humiliating experience for its victims. Its impact far transcends the immediate role it plays in the specific context in which it occurs, which in itself is far from negligible (Clausewitz 1968:269–73). This is the case because such surprise frequently reveals weaknesses, vulnerabilities, and pathologies that might not have otherwise become apparent. The overall impact of a successful surprise attempt is, therefore, enhanced and magnified by diverse developments which it does not directly cause, but nonetheless dramatically exposes.

The memory of a strategic surprise does not quickly fade away. It continues to haunt its victims and perpetrators alike long after the event. The immediate experience as well as its memory influences the behavior of the nations immediately in-volved for extended periods of time. It intrudes on their domestic politics and affects the fortunes of the leadership on both sides. Yet it also leaves its mark on other nations not directly involved in the confrontation—the bystanders. Abortive surprise attempts, i.e., strategic initiatives which bargain for surprise but are pre-maturely exposed by the target state, whether leading to their cancellation or reducing their effectiveness, have similar, although perhaps more subtle, consequences. Much more than a loss of face or gain of prestige is at stake even when a planned action is forfeited due to its premature disclosure. The impact of strategic surprises can thus be said to be psychological as much as it is political, military, and economic, extensive as well as intensive, immediate and also long-lasting. Several examples will illustrate these points.

The strategic surprise experienced by the United States in Pearl Harbor is by far the best-known instance of such surprise and is, therefore, particularly well-suited to illustrate the points made above. The element of surprise was critical for the success of the Japanese assault and was recognized by them as such. When it was achieved, it provided the Japanese with a decisive military advantage that they did not fail to exploit, at least not initially—witness the devastation of the U.S. Pacific Fleet at Pearl Harbor. The attack also did much to alter the heretofore prevailing image of Japan and the Japanese, at least in the United States, as a weak power and inferior people. The shock and concomitant outrage at the Japanese move, at the action itself and no less so at the way it was carried out ("sneak" attack), not only triggered the United States' entry into World War II, but also consolidated the American people behind President Roosevelt, perhaps more so than any other form of aggression would have done. The surprise and unpreparedness of the United States at Pearl Harbor subsequently led to the establishment of numerous commissions of inquiry, cost some distinguished military commanders their careers, and provided the United States with an incentive for establishing, for the first time in its history, a peacetime intelligence organization—the CIA.

The Pearl Harbor incident continued to leave its mark on the United States as well as other nations well beyond the immediate post-World War II period. During the Cuban Missile Crisis, for example, the analogy of a surprise U.S. air strike against the Soviet missiles to the Japanese attack on Pearl Harbor was apparently instrumental in convincing President Kennedy to abandon the air strike option (Allison 1971:60, 123–24, 133–34, 203). When Israel was caught unprepared in the Yom Kippur War (1973), the lessons of Pearl Harbor were carefully studied by a member of the official commission of inquiry that was established by the government to study the causes of the debacle (Laskov 1976). Finally, the reception that Roberta Wohlstetter's study on the Pearl Harbor surprise received when it came out in 1962, and even more so the attention that several recent books and articles dealing with the same issue (Costello 1981; Prange 1982, 1985; Toland 1982; Bratzel and Rout 1982; Layton et al. 1985) managed to attract—over forty years after the event—only serve to demonstrate the mark that strategic surprises leave in the minds of men and the lives of nations.[4]

The surprise of the German attack against the Soviet Union in June 1941 ("Operation Barbarossa") not only provided the Germans with a significant military advantage, but also served to bolster Hitler's standing among his generals, some of whom previously doubted the wisdom of the operation and its timing. Stalin apparently managed to escape politically unharmed from the debacle, at least in the short run, although he did collapse physically and disappeared from the helm for ten days or so. After Stalin's death, however, the blame for the surprise became a hot and extremely sensitive political issue. Khrushchev, for example, used the incident in his "secret speech" (1956) to discredit Stalin. The official Soviet history of the event was revised on a couple of occasions, with the degree of responsibility for the surprise attributed to Stalin and other key figures varying from one version to another and reflecting the political needs of the ruling elite at each point in time (Petrov 1968).

Unlike their apparent failure to catch Israel by surprise in mid-1973, when the Israelis detected Arab military preparations and mobilized their troops (the cancellation of the planned attack, however, was not caused by the Israeli mobilization but rather by Soviet pressure on Egypt and Syria), the Egyptians and Syrians did manage to catch the Israelis off-guard in the opening day of the Yom Kippur War (October 1973). This Arab success was a major military setback for Israel, whose defense doctrine was based on the premise that a 48-hour advance warning prior to an enemy attack would always be available. While Israel, like the United States in the case of Pearl Harbor and the Soviet Union in "Operation Barbarossa," managed to regain the initiative in later stages of the Yom Kippur War and was close to achieving an overwhelming military victory before a cease-fire was imposed, the cost of reversing the initial setback was extremely high.

The full political and psychological repercussions for Israel of the Yom Kuppur debacle only became evident after the war was over. The episode, publicly referred to as the "Mechdal" (roughly meaning dereliction of duty) caused a mass protest movement to erupt and led to the establishment of an official commission of inquiry (the Agranat Commission), which later forced the firing of several top military commanders including the Chief of the General Staff. The Yom Kuppur experience also brought a major reassessment of Israeli military doctrine that culminated in an increase in the size of the standing Israeli military. And the political leadership was also eventually forced to pay the price of failure—Prime Minister Golda Meir and Defense Minister Moshe Dayan resigned from the cabinet. And Dayan, who until the 1973 war enjoyed the status of a national hero, largely due to his association with two Israeli surprise attacks, 1956, 1967), continued, until his recent death, to be haunted by the public perception of his responsibility for the Mechdal. The repercussions, however, did not end with internal Israeli politics. The Arabs, and especially the Egyptians, quickly and skillfully translated their military success in the early stages of the war into a significant political and psychological victory.

Finally, and most recently, Argentina, in a surprise move, took over the Falkland Islands from Britain (April 1982). In this case, surprise provided the Argentinians with enough of a military advantage to capture the islands with little initial re-sistance, in sharp constrast to an earlier incident (1977) when timely detection by Britain of the Argentinian intentions enabled the British to pre-position naval forces around the Islands (FCR 1983:17–19). The Argentinian surprise invasion also dealt a severe blow to the prestige of Britain and its government, forced the resignation of several high-ranking British officials, including the foreign and defense ministers, and, above all, exacted a heavy price from Britain in the recovery of the Islands and their defense thereafter. In Argentina, on the other hand, the successful invasion of the Falklands had the immediate effect of shoring up a politically unpopular, ineffective, and fragile regime (by diverting attention from domestic problems and inspiring a nationalistic fervor), an effect that only evaporated when the Argentinian military proved incapable of holding on to the Islands.

With so much at stake in strategic surprise for the perpetrator, the target, and possibly also for many others, it is hardly surprising that over the years the phenomenon has attracted much scholarly and professional interest. What follows below is, therefore, a concise review and evaluation of twenty-five years of research on strategic surprise. This review, which examines both the methodology and theory of the existing literature, is designed to serve a dual purpose. First, it will introduce the reader to the literature on the topic, and acquaint him with its characteristics as well as its achievements and problems. Second, it will lay the groundwork for the presentation of my own research which will be made in a subsequent section.

Systematic study of strategic surprise did not begin, at least not in academic circles, until the late 1950s, and found its first major expression in 1962 with the publication of Roberta Wohlstetter's path-breaking book on Pearl Harbor. Several additional articles on the topic by Wohlstetter herself (1965), Klaus Knorr (1964), and others were published by the mid-1960s when the interest, at least the academic interest, in the phenomenon seems to have subsided, only to pick up again in the mid-1970s. Since then, however, the interest in the phenomenon has remained at quite a high level, something which is clearly reflected in the amount of work on the topic published in recent years. In fact, most of the literature on strategic surprise, at least in terms of quantity, is a product of the last decade.

Despite the great diversity in interests, background, and purpose of the scholars researching strategic surprises, their work has a great deal in common in terms of both theory and methodology. While some deviations from and exceptions to this pattern obviously exist, they are neither very common nor always significant. The premise shared by most students of strategic surprise is that the phenomenon is ubiquitous, namely both very common and universal (e.g. Knorr 1976, 1979; Handel 1976:7). Such a premise rules out either sheer coincidence or idiosyncracies of certain individuals as causes of surprise (Whaley 1973:7; Wohlstetter 1962:392).

The overwhelming majority of scholars also believe (this will be discussed and challenged throughout this study), that warning is (was) almost always available to the surprise victims prior to the event (e.g. Handel 1981:144n; Betts 1980). Consequently, they feel that what needs to be explained is the failure of a surprise target to utilize the warning at his disposal to prevent surprise. The various scholars approach this issue by pointing to pathologies inherent in the processing of information in general, and the production and consumption of intelligence in particular, which downgrade and distort any warning that reaches the target, and preclude the acquisition of any more conclusive and timely warning.

The broad consensus among the scholars in the field regarding the general causes of surprise leaves as a major bone of contention only a question of specifics—the relative importance of each factor in determining the outcome (i.e., causing surprise) either in general or in one or another historical instance of surprise. In the review of the literature which follows, I therefore attempt to cover all of the specific factors suggested by various studies as causes of surprise. These factors belong to two major clusters, one of general pathologies in information processing, the other of problems unique to intelligence. Within the first cluster the order of discussion of the various factors will be according to the setting in which the pathologies operate: individuals, small groups, complex organizations, and government bureaucracies.

## General Pathologies[5]

### Individuals

Having ruled out idiosyncracies of certain individuals as a "cause" of surprise, the emphasis of many scholars is on various mechanisms associated with individual psychology that narrow, curtail, and distort the processing of information by both intelligence analysts and policymakers. Following the extensive literature adapting and applying social psychology theories to the study of foreign policy, and especially the seminal studies by Jervis (1968, 1970), De Rivera (1968) and Steinbruner (1974), many of the writings on strategic surprises regard cognitive perceptual factors in the form of beliefs, images, expectations, desires, and the need to maintain consistency (i.e., avoid cognitive dissonance) as the most crucial barrier to accurate and timely threat perception. These factors are believed to raise the standard of evidence required of discrepant information before it gains acceptance, forcing such information to pass stricter tests than information that is congruent with beliefs, perceptions, etc. (George and Smoke 1974:514). Such a biased screening process of incoming information is said to increase considerably the likelihood of strategic surprise. The sharpest enunciation of this argument comes from Richard Betts, who observed that "the ultimate causes of error have been wishful thinking, cavalier disregard of professional analysts, and above all, the premises and preconceptions of policy-makers" (1978:61; see also Knorr 1977:193).

It is worth noting that the impediments to accurate threat perception discussed above are essentially those referred to by Klaus Knorr (1976:97–98) as "predispositional," meaning that they are subjective and are introduced by the actor's intervening attitudes. These are distinguished from "intrinsic" or "intellectual" impediments which are objective and are inherent in the nature of the international environment. The latter type of impediment will be discussed in the next section.

### Small Groups

The psychologist Irving Janis (1972) has introduced an explanation of strategic surprise which is derived from experimental work in social psychology on the dynamics of small groups. The structure, internal process, and management of small groups of decision makers are said to provide a clue to the causes of the failure of decision makers, in some instances, to reach an accurate appraisal of the situation on the basis of the information (warning) available to them. These factors, argues Janis, can also explain the occasional selection by policy makers of highly inappropriate and extremely risky courses of action. Janis identifies a small group phenomenon which he labels "groupthink" that produces these kinds of results. According to Janis the phenomenon is characteristic of cohesive groups, isolated from the outside world, in which strong pressures for conformity exist.

*Complex Organizations*

Another strain of explanations on strategic surprises draws on theories of complex organization. Harold Wilensky (1967) and Graham Allison (1971), among others, have followed the pathbreaking works by Herbert Simon (1957) and Charles Lindbloom (1959) on complex organizations, and applied insights borrowed from that area to the analysis of foreign and defense policymaking. Observing that modern governments consist of numerous such complex organizations, each of which functions along the lines portrayed by Simon and the organizational theorists, they have highlighted some key features of such organizations which impinge on the way they, and consequently also a government as a whole, process information and make decisions. In the specific context of strategic surprises, hierarchy, specialization, centralization, and regularized patterns of behaviors (standard operating procedures, or SOPs) are commonly suggested as the organizational features that play a particularly important role in causing surprise. These are believed to impede and distort the acquisition, evaluation, dissemination, and consumption of strategic warning, thereby contributing to the occurrence of surprise.

*Governmental Politics*

Governmental politics explanations of strategic surprises have been developed on the basis of models developed by Roger Hilsman (1967), Graham Allison (1971), and Morton Halperin (1974) for the analysis of foreign and defense policymaking. These explanations have two specific strains that are worth noting. The first strain bears great similarity to the cognitive-perceptual explanation noted above, with one fundamental difference. Unlike the simple cognitive perceptual explanation, in the governmental politics explanations top policymakers are not looked upon as "plain" individuals but rather as political animals, with their outlook, perceptions, and expectations largely (though not totally) determined by their political commitments and administrative positions. These perceptions, although different in origin, function in the same manner as other types of preconceptions, at least as far as the processing of information is concerned. It is argued that they predispose the policymakers, and consequently also their subordinates (both political appointees and civil servants), toward incoming information, thereby introducing a systematic bias in its interpretation and dissemination. This bias, in turn, is believed to result in failure to recognize impending threats.

A second strain of governmental politics explanations of strategic surprise focuses on bureaucratic politics, namely self-serving organizational parochialism and the concomitant interpersonal and interagency as well as intra-agency competition and rivalry. Bureaucratic politics is said not only to reduce the efficiency in allocation of resources for both acquisition and interpretation of warning, but also to introduce serious distortions in the efforts which are still carried out. Delays, lack of coordination and sharing of information, and significant biases in interpretation are thought to be some of the most acute problems that arise from bureaucratic politics and affect strategic warning.


### Cybernetics

Another source of explanations of strategic surprise is the cybernetic theory of decisions most coherently presented in the work of John Steinbruner (1974). What this type of explanation has in common with the others is that it also emphasizes deviations from rationality in processing of information as a major factor contributing to failures to reach a realistic threat perception. Unlike the other explanations, however, "cybernetic distortions" are not said to operate only on one or another level of decision making. Instead, they are presented as a comprehensive alternative model of decision making, believed to be equally applicable to the behavior of individuals, complex organizations, and government bureaucracies. Certain features of cybernetic decision making, such as narrow input channels, low and highly structured receptivity to incoming information in the form of both stimuli and feedback, limited repertoire of responses attempted sequentially, and a slow and cumbersome learning process, are believed to hinder accurate threat perception and implementation of response.

Having thus far discussed explanations of strategic surprise that are based on *general* pathologies in information processing, I now turn to review another cluster of explanations of the surprise phenomenon. These are based on barriers to analytic accuracy and impediments to information processing that are *unique* to production and consumption of intelligence. The barriers under discussion here are primarily, although not entirely, those considered by Knorr as intrinsic or intellectual difficulties involved in international threat perception. Richard Betts (1980) has recently compiled a remarkably comprehensive and probably exhaustive list of such barriers, and also provided vivid illustrations for most of them. The discussion below, therefore, draws in the main from Betts' most insightful work, although it also uses the work of various other scholars who base their explanations of surprise on many of the same pathologies.

## Intelligence-Related Pathologies and Obstacles

### Noise

As Roberta Wohlstetter originally suggested (1962:3), the information reaching the intelligence services of the target country rarely, if ever, comes in a pure form. It consists of "signals" (accurate and relevant information) as well as "noise" (inaccurate, incorrect, and/or irrelevant information); the signals are not only embedded in the background noise but usually also vastly outnumbered by it. Sifting the signals from the noise thus becomes an extremely difficult, arduous, and time-consuming process which can be done with great ease only in retrospect (with the benefit of hindsight), and is therefore a formidable obstacle in the way of reaching accurate and timely threat perception. It should be noted that almost every student of strategic surprise since Roberta Wohlstetter has attributed great significance to this obstacle and incorporated it in her explanation of a strategic surprise episode.

*Cover and Deception*
    The background noise, as Barton Whaley has persua-
sively argued (1973:244), frequently consists not only of irrelevant,
inaccurate, and simply incorrect information, but also of deliberately planted false and misleading information, namely the opponent's deception. Planting or leaking misleading information
(i.e., generating noise) is commonly a part of a broader effort by
the perpetrator to manipulate the information reaching his target
in order to secure the element of surprise, an effort that typically
includes also the use of *cover*, i.e., concealment of one's true
intentions and actions through secrecy, compartmentation, etc.
(i.e., suppressing signals). The purpose of the overall cover and
deception effort may be either to confuse a surprise target or,
alternatively, to steer him in the wrong direction. Either way, the
practice of cover and deception fundamentally alters both the
composition of noise and the signal to noise ratio, thereby enhancing the prospects for achieving surprise.
    While explanations of surprise based on deception are
not new, they have grown in popularity in recent years, especially
since the appearance of several studies on deception and surprise
by Barton Whaley (1969, 1973, 1975). This trend finds its most
recent expression in two major research programs on strategic
deception, one sponsored by the CIA (1979-80), the other by the
Naval Postgraduate School (Daniel and Herbig 1982), as well as
in several other publications on the issue (e.g., Heuer 1981b;
Perlmutter and Gooch 1982). As Heuer points out (1981b:319),
part of deception as an explanation for otherwise incongruous
events is that it "imposes order on an otherwise disorderly set of
data, and it enables us to attribute deviousness and malevolence
to our enemies."


*Structural Disadvantage*
    Intelligence production is by definition the art of fig-
uring out what an actual or potential opponent is up to on the
basis of the available information on his capabilities, intentions,
and actions. The opponent contemplates or initiates certain de-

cisions or actions, and it is the job of the intelligence services of the other side to overcome the perpetrator's cover and deception and determine what he is capable and likely to do. It is, therefore, a sequential process in which intelligence services are always at a structural disadvantage—they have to catch up with an opponent who, as far as they are concerned, always has the initiative. The structural disadvantage in which intelligence services of the target country find themselves entails, at the very minimum, a time lag in determination of the opponent's intentions. This time lag may prove at times critical, as it may be sufficiently long to permit the perpetrator to catch his target by surprise. This holds particularly true in situations where the transition from a routine posture to one posing an ominous threat is rather swift, thanks to technological advances in communications, transportation, and capabilities of weapons systems.

There is at least one more way in which the time lag stands in the way of accurate and timely threat perception. Accurate information collected on the opponent's intentions and capabilities may become rapidly outdated by developments of which the intelligence services of the target are not immediately aware. The outdated information then serves as another screen of noise which warning has to penetrate for accurate threat perception to be reached. It thus increases the likelihood that surprise will ensue.[6]

### Inherent Uncertainty

Another dimension of the structural disadvantage which is inherent in intelligence work is the ever-present possibility that the perpetrator may be indecisive or reverse himself on one or more occasions. Such incoherence or inconsistency by the perpetrator obviously makes a determination of his true intentions by a foreign intelligence service all the more difficult. As Betts (1980:557) puts it, "the victim's intelligence is always at the mercy of the attacker to change his plans." What makes matters worse is the fact that intelligence services are sometimes required, usually expected, and almost always pressured by their consumers to extract certainty from situations in which the course of events, much less the outcome, is inherently uncertain, and/or in which they possess only fragmentary, ambiguous, or equivocal information on the adversary's intentions. In both types of cases the pressure is to produce much more conclusive estimates than the data would permit, and this pressure creates additional barriers to analytical accuracy. It should be realized that resistance by intelligence analysts to pressure to produce conclusive estimates, reflected in the preparation of indecisive or cautious estimates that hedge against all possibilities, runs the grave risk of alienating the consumers and/or losing their ear, penalties that are quite strong incentives for compliance.

*Influence on Policy*
Since the process of intelligence production is not, and should not be, completely isolated from the policymaking process, intelligence regarding enemy intentions can actually affect the outcome. The target country may make decisions and take action on the basis of intelligence that will lead the perpetrator to modify his original intentions. This dynamics suggests the serious possibility of "self-fulfilling" and "self-negating" prophecies, both of which are barriers to analytical accuracy. The latter is also a potential source for surprise.

*Policy Influence*
The complex relationship between intelligence authorities and policymakers is the source of additional distortions in information processing, and consequently also the basis for one more explanation of strategic surprise. Intelligence production may be more or less isolated from the policymaking process. Either way, the ultimate subordination of intelligence to operational authorities introduces some distortions in the evaluation of incoming information on an impending threat. The more intelligence is involved in policymaking, the more it is relevant and geared to its needs, and the better informed are the decision makers. But such involvement also generates pressures on the intelligence

authorities to supply "intelligence to please"—provide estimates which contain little uncertainty and support existing policy and policymakers' preferences—or face demotion (isolation). Conversely, isolation of intelligence production from policymaking contributes to less biased but also more sterile intelligence and more ignorant policymakers. Furthermore, it also enables the policymakers to interpret incoming information erroneously, either inadvertently, as a result of their ignorance and inexperience in intelligence matters, or deliberately to fit their predilections.

## Compartmentation

Compartmentation—limitation of access to classes of data—is another feature of intelligence work that accounts for underutilization of strategic warning that does reach the target state. Here the emphasis is on neither the impact of specialization (which is a feature of any complex organization) nor that of inter- or intraorganizational rivalry (which is a feature of governmental politics), although the latter can definitely lead to abuse of compartmentation. Instead, the focus is on intrinsic pathologies in the processing and consumption of information, when restrictions on pooling and sharing information and consulting experts are introduced to satisfy security requirements for protection of sources and methods.

## "Cry 'Wolf' Syndrome"

The "cry 'wolf' syndrome"—repeated false warnings which erode the target's receptivity to authentic warning—provides the basis for another common explanation of strategic surprise. Students of strategic surprise have uncovered some evidence for the existence of the "cry 'wolf' syndrome" in almost every historical instance of surprise. Intelligence services are always at pains to avoid both strategic surprises and false alarms. The latter mandates raising the standard of evidence required for threat indicators to be acknowledged and institutional warning issued, thereby increasing the likelihood that the former will take place. Conversely, preventing strategic surprise requires, among other things, issuing institutional warning even on the basis of fragmentary and ambiguous threat indicators, thereby risking false alarms. To make matters worse, repeated false alarms undermine the credibility of the source or the intelligence service that provides or issues them, and erode the receptivity and response to future warning by intelligence analysts, operational authorities, and field units. The trade-off between false alarms and strategic surprises is therefore inescapable and is widely believed to erect another major hurdle in the way of timely recognition of and response to threat (see chapter 4).


Scholars who have conducted, over the years, empirical studies of strategic surprise (see Appendix A) suggest that they have found evidence to support all of the aforementioned explanations of strategic surprise. In particular, they submit that in the cases they have studied they have been able to document the availability of adequate warning to intended surprise targets, as well as to establish the existence of some or all of the pathologies and obstacles discussed above. Consequently, these scholars conclude with some confidence that the occurrence of surprise can be attributed to obstacles to and pathologies in acquisition, processing, and consumption of warning.

Furthermore, despite the persistence of much disagreement between the various scholars in the field over the importance of certain factors in causing surprise, both in general and in some specific instances, a broad consensus among them exists regarding several other key points. First, failures (i.e., strategic surprises) are not the exception but rather the rule—practically every strategic surprise attempt is said to succeed (Handel 1976:9; Knorr 1977:193, 1979:72, 1983:286; Betts 1978:88, 1980:572). Second, such failures are inevitable, unavoidable, and even natural, as a result of obstacles in the way of accurate and timely threat perception that are both profound and numerous, and therefore also practically insurmountable (Betts 1978:88; Knorr 1979:72; Handel 1980:105). And third, reforms of various kinds designed to reduce the likelihood of surprise usually have only marginal utility, their costs frequently exceed their benefits, and in any case, they almost always atrophy over time (Betts 1978). According to the existing literature, therefore, there is also little hope that surprise attempts will be any less likely in the future than they have been in the past (e.g., Knorr 1982, 1983).

Such pessimistic conclusions as the literature provides do not leave much room for policy prescription, something which is indeed reflected in recent surprise studies that have largely given up hope on averting strategic surprises altogether. Instead, these studies, in their policy prescriptions, seek to reduce somewhat their likelihood, diminish their scope, and limit the impact of those strategic surprises that do take place. The most common (if not the most useful) recommendations to emerge from this literature, therefore, suggest "learning to live with fatalism," "developing tolerance for disaster," and maintaining a higher level of preparedness on a routine bases.

How does one appraise the strategic surprise literature surveyed thus far? Reflecting on its numerous achievements, one must conclude that it has certainly made a most valuable contribution to our understanding of the phenomenon. Attention has been drawn not only to the importance of the phenomenon but also to its universality. Many surprise cases worldwide have been identified and studied in detail. Even more important, the literature has provided interesting and often original insights into and explanations of some of the better known historical instances of surprise. In the process it has identified significant pathologies in information processing in general, and intelligence production and consumption in particular, and developed a most useful terminology for characterizing these pathologies.

If one were to conclude that the explanations of surprise and the conclusions regarding its causes and likelihood that are found in the literature are basically valid, then additional studies of the phenomenon are largely superfluous, lacking either theoretical or practical importance. Such an argument is, in fact, explicitly made by Handel, who argues that the study of military surprise has reached the point of diminishing returns (1979:26).

It is doubtful, however, that this is indeed the case. While I am persuaded that the existing body of literature on strategic surprises provides us with an excellent base from which to proceed in the construction of a theory of strategic surprise, I contend that it by no means exhausts the topic. It also leaves much to be desired in other respects as well. The discussion that follows therefore explicates the deficiencies of the existing surprise literature. As will become apparent later in the study, it does so not in an effort to discount all its claims and detract in any way from the significance of its contribution to our understanding of the phenomenon. Rather it is done out of a conviction that a detailed exposition of the shortcomings of existing studies is a necessary first step toward refining their findings and expanding on them.

One problem with many of the explanations of specific instances of surprise is that they are not fully warranted on the basis of the empirical evidence. This becomes clearly evident when one examines relevant government documents that have been declassified in recent years. A second problem is that at least some of the general explanations of strategic surprise and the generalizations regarding its likelihood that are provided by the literature are suspect of being systematically biased, if not altogether flawed. Finally, the utility of the policy prescriptions advanced by many of the scholars either to avert strategic surprises or to diminish their impact is very limited, and certainly highly disproportionate to the importance of the phenomenon. Moreover, it can be argued that some (although by no means all—see chapter 4) of the policy prescriptions that have been offered are counterproductive, possibly even dangerous, as they may actually increase the likelihood of surprise.[7]

The next section elaborates further on these points, thereby providing the rationale for this study. The remainder of the chapter presents my research goals and outlines the way I proceed to meet them.

The weaknesses of the surprise studies noted above can be traced back to some underlying methodological and conceptual problems. Since these problems are common and their implications truly profound, I shall examine them here in some detail.

In the existing empirical studies of surprise (see Appendix A) there are at least four methodological deficiencies that account for observable distortions in their findings. These deficiencies can be summarized as those having to do with the research strategy, the type of data, the operationalization of the concepts, and the selection of cases. Let me elaborate on each of these factors.

One type of research strategy, namely case studies, and especially single case studies,[8] virtually dominates the empirical research of strategic surprise. The various advantages of case studies notwithstanding, they do have some important shortcomings, the most critical of which is, perhaps, that they are *inherently difficult to generalize from* (Eckstein 1975; George 1979b, 1982). Overcoming this difficulty requires great care in designing the research program,[9] rigor and consistency in carrying it out, and considerable caution in drawing conclusions from it. Yet most case studies of surprise fall short of satisfying these requirements, but hardly acknowledge that this is the case. In consequence, we are faced with a problem of generalizability of the findings of the individual studies, and as a result also the cumulativeness of the research in the field as a whole.[10]

Another prominent shortcoming of the empirical studies of surprise stems from the type of data used in the various case studies. The overwhelming majority of case studies in the field rely *exclusively* on secondary sources for their data, frequently, but not always, due to a lack of other sources. The use of secondary sources is problematic in any historical research due to their inherently uncertain reliability. But this practice seems particularly troublesome for the study of surprise, since the especially strong self-serving interests and requirements of secrecy in this area combine to produce fragmentary, inaccurate, and frequently outright misleading accounts of events. This state of affairs obviously casts a doubt on the findings of surprise studies that make exclusive use of secondary sources (Chan 1979:174–75).

The empirical studies of surprise are further jeopardized by a validity problem stemming from their operationalization of the surprise concept. These studies use only one (implicit) criterion for classifying historical cases as strategic surprise—being caught unprepared by a major foreign initiative. Such an operationalization, however, is both too broad and too narrow. On the one hand, it is too broad because it includes cases where strategic surprise does not occur, as unpreparedness may occur in the absence of surprise. Failure to formulate and/or implement adequate policy for tackling an opponent's initiative, or else inability to apply adequate precautionary measures (due to scarcity of resources) are independent causes of unpreparedness (see chapter 4). On the other hand, this operationalization is too narrow since it excludes one specific type of strategic surprise—surprise that is not met by unpreparedness. By sheer luck, intuition, or coincidence the defender may be prepared to counter an opponent's initiative of which he has no positive foreknowledge (see chapter 4).

Another interesting problem with the operationalization of surprise is the number of countries that may be involved in a strategic surprise. Abiding by the definition, a strategic surprise is not necessarily limited to events where only two countries, the initiator (offender) and the target (defender), are involved. While the more trivial cases are those in which the target country and the immediate victim of the initiator's move were one and the same, another case is also possible. We may conceive of historical cases where the target country was also, and perhaps even primarily, a third country that was not even bordering the country that was the immediate victim. But for such cases to qualify as strategic surprise for the third country we must establish the fact that the third country indeed had considerable values at stake in the victim county (as well as satisfy all the other requirements of the definition).[11] If we fail to acknowledge this requirement and demonstrate that it was indeed satisfied in the context of a case under consideration (a common practice in the field), we cannot consider such a case as one more example of a strategic surprise, as it is qualitatively different from the cases we have studied so far. Let me illustrate the point.

Numerous scholars have considered the invasion of South Korea by the North (1950), leading to the Korean War, to be a strategic surprise for the United States. Prior to the war, however, South Korea was not defined as a strategic asset to the United States, and consequently received very little attention from either U.S. intelligence or its policymakers. There is a striking qualitative difference between this case (which I reject as a strategic surprise for the United States) and the Chinese intervention in the Korean War, which was also suggested as a strategic surprise for the United States. Since the United States established considerable interest in Korea and the Korean War in the interim period, the latter may certainly qualify as a strategic surprise for the United States, if it can be demonstrated convincingly that the United States was indeed caught by surprise.

The common operationalization of surprise in existing studies therefore shakes our confidence in the reliability of their findings. It also raises some doubts regarding the suitability for study of the strategic surprise phenomenon of some of the historical cases heretofore chosen for that purpose. The exposition of these weaknesses here, however, is intended first and foremost as a practical guide for future research.

Finally, probably the most striking methodological problem with the existing studies of surprise is that they examine only successful surprise attempts[12] (i.e., cases of erroneous threat perception) while completely ignoring abortive surprise attempts.[13] Why strategic surprise does not occur, despite a deliberate attempt to achieve it, is no less scientific a question than why strategic surprises occur when they do. Just as Sherlock Holmes found a clue in the fact that the dog did not bark, so do we have to focus on the nonoccurrence of surprise, and it is only when we study the two phenomena side by side that we are likely to derive valid generalizations regarding the cause and likelihood of surprise. The failure to consider abortive surprise attempts, which unfortunately characterizes virtually the entire literature on strategic surprise,[14] amounts therefore to more than mere neglect of a valuable research tool—a quasi control group. It also introduces into the findings of the studies a systematic "availability bias" toward the inevitability of successful surprise, a bias that is indeed reflected in the conclusions of these studies. In short, only the empty part of the glass is examined.[15]

The various methodological deficiencies of surprise studies are compounded by several theoretical problems. Previous studies have suggested explanations of strategic surprise based on distortions in information processing that are introduced by the setting in which information is processed (i.e., individuals, small groups, complex organizations, and government bureaucracies) or by the process of intelligence production. In the existing literature, the various distortions are either provided as an inductively derived inventory of potential barriers to accurate and timely threat perception (e.g., Betts 1980) or used in an ad hoc fashion to explain one or another instance of strategic surprise (as in most of the studies). While both of these approaches are useful and important, their utility as building blocks of a theory of strategic surprise is rather limited. For what the development of an inductively derived theory of strategic surprise requires is a serious systematic effort aimed at determining the conditions under which the various distortions are likely to manifest themselves, and influence/determine the outcome.

Specifically, what is called for is a typological theory of surprise—conditional generalizations regarding the circumstances in which various causal patterns leading to surprise occur. These, however, are painfully missing from most of the existing work, the studies by George (1979a) and by George and Smoke (1974) being notable exceptions. The way in which the failure to proceed in this direction stands in the way of theory development can be illustrated by two specific problems which it creates—nonfalsifiability and overdetermination.

Recall that the crucial barriers to accurate threat perception, according to the existing literature, are distortions in processing and consumption of strategic warning. These distortions are said to be inherent in the process and therefore always present, yet they produce surprise only on occasion. Thus, it is necessary to specify either a threshold beyond which individual distortions will have decisive impact on the outcome, or alternatively to classify the distortions as either necessary and/or sufficient conditions for surprise. Unless this is done—which is not the case with existing studies—the explanations are *nonfalsifiable* and cannot be evaluated. Furthermore, when the studies offer (which they commonly do) *multivariable* explanations of surprise, namely explanations based on the combined operation of some or all of the distortions and obstacles noted above, they again have to suggest necessary and sufficient conditions or assign separate weight to each factor. Since they do not, we are faced not only with the nonindependence of explanations but also with a severe problem of overdetermination.

The last, but definitely not the least, problem with the literature is the attempt by quite a few scholars to derive generalizations regarding the probability of success of strategic surprise attempts. Such probabilistic generalizations are unwarranted on the basis of the small number of cases examined by the scholars in the absence of any reliable method of establishing the universe of cases of strategic surprise attempts or a representative sample thereof. Moreover, as was already noted, a strong bias exists in the selection of cases for study since no abortive surprise attempts are considered.[16] These flaws obviously detract from the validity of the generalizations regarding the likelihood of surprise that were offered in the literature.[17]

Having discussed the importance of strategic surprises, reviewed the existing literature and explored its deficiencies, I will now proceed with my own study, first presenting the argument in brief, then describing the study's outline and its operationalization.

Recall that earlier research on strategic surprise created an impression, one that by now is commonly shared and deeply rooted, that surprise occurs *despite* warning (Handel 1976:7; Knorr 1979:74; Betts 1980). The "ultimate" cause of surprise is believed by these scholars to be poor receptivity to the warning that is available, a situation that is itself a product of numerous pathologies in information processing in general, and in intelligence production and consumption in particular. These types of explanations of strategic surprise are vulnerable on at least two points. First, it is not clear how one can validly determine causes, much less "ultimate" causes of surprise. And while the various scholars do not hesitate to suggest causal links and point out "ultimate" causes, a discussion of the procedure by which these are determined is nowhere to be found. It is the second area of vulnerability of these explanations, however, that is of even greater importance and it is to this that I shall devote most of my attention.

The second area of vulnerability arises from the fact that the face validity of the explanations of strategic surprise based on pathologies in information processing rests on one common premise—that warning is indeed available to the target prior to a strategic surprise attempt, but he somehow fails to make use of it. Since this premise is so crucial for all the explanations, it would seem to warrant a close scrutiny. The urge to reexamine it is reinforced by an observation made in my earlier study (1981) that the barriers to receptivity seem to be present not only in historical instances of strategic surprise, but also in instances in which surprise was attempted but failed (see chapter 3). This observation suggests that the pathologies mentioned above are not, at least in some cases, the actual cause of surprise, and that one or more other factors are responsible for the difference in outcome between some surprise and nonsurprise cases. The form and quality of the available warning (although not necessarily its quantity) seem plausible candidates for such independent variables.

A tentative reexamination of the historical cases of surprise that have been studied by other scholars, as well as the preliminary study of several other cases that I have recently carried out (1981), demonstrate that *no* credible or conclusive warning (operationalization of this concept is provided later in chapter) was available prior to many historical cases of strategic surprise, arguments to the contrary notwithstanding.[18] The study also points out that many cases in which such warning was available frequently did not result in surprise, despite the presence of severe barriers to receptivity. Both of these findings enhance the plausibility of our proposition that the availability of warning is potentially a most useful independent variable for explaining success or failure of strategic surprise attempts.[19]

It is, therefore, hypothesized that strategic warning originating in reliable source(s),[20] possibly even in the form of a single report, has a demonstrated capacity to overcome barriers to receptivity, force its way to and impose itself on policymakers, thereby potentially preventing surprise (although not unpreparedness) from taking place.[21] Warning of a strategic surprise attempt is believed to have some unique features that make it less vulnerable, although by no means immune, to structural, cognitive, and political distortions than other forms of intelligence. Among the features that make such warning so unique are the relative transparency, saliency, and incontroversiality of the national interest at stake, the short maturation time of the threat, and the concomitant urgency and time pressure, as well as the high rewards associated with its timely detection and recognition, and the correspondingly large penalties for failure. These rewards and penalties apply not only to the nation as a whole but also to the people directly involved—civil servants, political appointees, and elected officials alike.

All of these features of strategic warning allow for less slippage in its processing and transmission, and make for its relatively uninterrupted and undistorted flow to the policymakers. These features also induce policymakers to recognize and acknowledge the impending threat and consider (though not necessarily also initiate) some response to it (see chapter 4). And the preference of policymakers to err on the side of safety in such issues (Art and Jervis 1973:4) only accentuates these tendencies. Thus, if a surprise target is able to obtain high-quality warning (see chapters 4 and 5)—which I definitely believe to be possible[22]— then it is likely, although by no means certain, that he would not be caught by surprise.

To sum up the argument, I suggest, and intend to test in this study, the following propositions:

1. that strategic surprises often happen exactly because no reliable early warning is available to the target; and

2. that high-quality strategic warning is, as a practical matter, attainable, and when it is available, chances are that it will not be overlooked (because of its unique traits) and surprise will therefore be avoided; but also

3. that even when a surprise attempt is foiled, the target may still be caught, for a variety of reasons, unprepared by the perpetrator's action.

It ought to be emphasized that I do not deny in any way the existence, noted by other scholars, of any or all of the diverse obstacles to acquisition of adequate early warning and generation of accurate threat perception and corresponding response. Nor do I mean to imply either that high-quality warning is always available to surprise targets or that in every case in which such strategic warning is available surprise does not follow. This clearly is not the case. I do, however, reject the opposite arguments that high-quality warning is rarely if ever available, or that surprise always or almost always happens despite the possession by the defender of high-quality warning, because the barriers to accurate threat perception are virtually insurmountable. The point is that the various barriers (e.g., cognitive biases) are at most a matter of tendency, not a black and white rule that applies to all at all times with a decisive impact.[23]

What this study aims for is, therefore, to assess, refine, and expand on the theoretical insights of earlier studies by determining under what conditions warning is likely to be available, penetrate the barriers, and prevail over policymakers' readings of the situation. It also seeks to identify and assess the impact of other factors that affect threat perception and response. These, to repeat what I have suggested earlier, are the major goals of this book.

To test my three hypotheses—to be able to correlate various levels of the independent variable (quality of warning) with different levels of the dependent one (degree of surprise)—I need to examine historical instances of both surprise and abortive surprise. This shall be done in chapters 2 and 3. These chapters provide what approximates a "structured, focused comparison"[24] between one instance of surprise (chapter 2) and another of abortive surprise (chapter 3).

I have selected the Japanese attack on Pearl Harbor (December 7, 1941) as the surprise case study, and the Battle of Midway (June 4, 1942) as the abortive surprise case study. The selection of these specific historical instances was governed by three primary considerations: (a) that primary sources that exhaust the issues of warning and the reaction to it are fully available in unclassified form for both cases; (b) that the two cases involve only two countries (the perpetrator, Japan, and the target, the United States) of which one clearly sought to catch the other by surprise in both instances; and (c) that the instances not only concern the same two countries but are also drawn roughly from the same period, thereby providing a somewhat greater degree of control over exogenous variables than would have otherwise been possible.

But while the selection of Pearl Harbor and Midway for in-depth study avoids some of the most glaring problems in existing empirical studies of surprise, it does, nonetheless, raise some specific concerns that must be addressed and convincingly put to rest before we proceed to conduct the case studies. The first of these concerns has to do with the need to restudy the surprise at Pearl Harbor in view of Roberta Wohlstetter's classical study on the issue (1962) as well as some more recent books dealing with the subject (Costello 1981; Prange 1981; Toland 1982). The other concern centers around the validity of the comparison between Pearl Harbor and Midway, since one was a strategic surprise attempt that occurred in wartime while the other took place in the transition from peace to war. It has been argued that these are two distinct types of strategic surprise, with the difference in the environment in which they occur said by some to account for the difference in the relationship between the pertinent variables (Betts 1982a). Studying the two instances thus opens one to the charge of comparing apples with oranges. Let me address both of these concerns.

My case for replicating Wohlstetter's study of Pearl Harbor is built on four main pillars. First, Wohlstetter's study, for all its merits (and they are definitely numerous) is plagued by serious conceptual and methodological problems (Levite 1981: Appendix C) which lead to rather significant empirical errors. That some of these problems beset, no doubt, the advent of any new area of substantive inquiry does not make them any less detrimental. Second, the unique status that Wohlstetter's study enjoys in the field—it is considered a landmark in rigor and insight and is used as the model for many similar studies—makes its deficiencies all the more meaningful and their expositon all the more important. Thus, even if it could be persuasively argued that the restudy of Pearl Harbor has little inherent interest in and of itself (for there are quite a few other instances that could be studied with equal or greater profit), the standing of the existing study on the topic makes the reinvestigation of significance within the context of strategic surprise literature.

The third pillar is the conceptual and methodological progress made in the field since Wohlstetter's original study was conducted (the 1950s), as well as the accumulation of new, heretofore classified, data on the warning prior to Pearl Harbor. Both of these developments make the replication of Wohlstetter's study seem even more desirable and promising. Finally, the fourth pillar on which my case for replicating Wohlstetter's study is based is that a focused comparison of the Pearl Harbor surprise with the abortive surprise at Midway promises not only to generate new theoretical insights but also to improve our understanding of the Pearl Harbor (as well as the Midway) case, thereby further enhancing the attractiveness of the enterprise.

Putting to rest also the second and more formidable objection to the selection of my case studies—the one based on the distinction between strategic surprises (or failures thereof) that occur in war and those that take place in the transition from peace to war—requires discussion on two levels. It calls for discussion of the importance of the distinction in principle (in the abstract), as well as of its relevance in the context of the specific case studies, namely Pearl Harbor and Midway. Here I shall deal only with the first of these levels. The discussion of the importance of the context (i.e., war or peace) in accounting for the difference in outcome between the surprise attempts at Pearl Harbor and Midway will have to await my in-depth analysis of both instances, and will therefore be presented in the concluding section of chapter 3.

Those who emphasize the theoretical importance of the distinction between surprise attempts that occur in wartime and those that take place in the transition from peace to war (e.g. Betts 1982a) build their case on two basic claims. First, it is assumed that "strategic conditions and political context in wartime are entirely different" (from those in the transition from war to peace) and that "there are no political, psychological or strategic incentives to disbelieve threatening tactical intelligence" (ibid.). Second, it is claimed that the involvement of political leaders in assessing the indicators regarding the opponent's intentions in wartime is either nil or negligible (ibid.). I largely disagree with both arguments, and submit that at least for the purposes of this study the distinction between strategic surprises occuring in war and those taking place in the transition from peace to war is neither very significant in principle, nor very meaningful in the context of the historical instances under discussion here.

As for the first of these claims, the key question seems to be whether the rewards and costs associated with recognizing warning signals or failing to do so are any lower in wartime than in peacetime. Betts (1982a), for example, contends that in wartime at least the costs are lower as there are no political, psychological, and strategic incentives to disbelieve threatening intelligence. If this argument is correct, then intrawar strategic surprises should be rather rare events. But we know of numerous such episodes, something which is difficult to reconcile with this argument. Moreover, one can think of important disincentives for believing incoming warning in wartime of exactly the same types that Betts tends to discount. Such a disincentive, apart from the "cry wolf syndrome," which Betts acknowledges, is the scarcity of resources that makes it difficult to accept warning without the capacity to do anything about it. And if these two disincentives are not enough to prove the point, some intrinsic characteristics of battle conditions, such as lingering fatigue (psychological as well as physical), extreme time constraints, strict discipline and hierarchy, rapid developments (from policy formulation to implementation) and heavy burden on the intelligence and decision systems, are all sources for serious and diverse barriers to analytical accuracy and distortions in the processing of information and the consumption of warning.

Nor do other pathologies in information processing, such as bureaucratic politics, misperceptions, and resistance to cognitive dissonance, which exist in peacetime, disappear in wartime. Since there are no arguments to suggest that the rewards of detecting a strategic surprise attempt in wartime are any lower than in the transition from peace to war, and the costs and difficulties have also been demonstrated to be rather similar, it would seem that the response at least to the first question is a negative one. Many similarities between peacetime and wartime exist in the cost/benefit ratio and in the barriers to analytical accuracy.

The second of the claims centers on the involvement of political leaders in the recognition of warning which is said to be minimal or zero in the former case. One can bring up the examples of Churchill, Stalin, or Hitler in World War II, John and Robert Kennedy in the Cuban Missile Crisis, Moshe Dayan and Golda Meir in the Yom Kippur War, and Margaret Thatcher in the Falkland Islands crisis, to demonstrate that this argument is not fully convincing. While the involvement of the National Command Authority (NCA) and the political leadership may be very limited in tactical battles, they are quite often actively involved in issues pertaining to strategic campaigns.

Perhaps the strongest objection to the analogy is that in the case of a transition from peace to war the identity of the opponent may not be clear, which definitely does not hold true for intrawar confrontation. This difference is definitely meaningful provided the identity of the opponent indeed is not obvious prior to the breakout of hostilities. For under such circumstances the defender has to determine the identity of the opponent on top of the questions regarding the nature, timing, and place of his initiative which he also needs to answer in wartime; that is, in the transition from peace to war surprise can occur on one additional dimension. As a practical matter, however, the target state is usually familiar with the identity of its opponent(s) either because that opponent has been a traditional rival, or else because he has been in the process of becoming one for quite some time prior to the actual transition from peace to war.

Finally, the great similarities between strategic surprises (or failures thereof) in war and in transition from peace to war may make it fruitful and practical, at least in some cases, to consider the elements common to both rather than to emphasize their differences and unique traits. To return to the apples and oranges analogy, at times it is beneficial to remember that both are fruit and study them as such. As Przeworski and Teune (1970:34–39) have already persuasively argued with respect to the "most different design," as long as the initial assumption that systemic factors do not play any role in explaining the observed behavior holds, there is no need to consider systemic factors. In my case, this logic would imply that as long as there is no need to distinguish between strategic surprise attempts occurring in wartime and those occurring in the transition from peace to war in order to explain the outcome (surprise/no surprise), it is indeed profitable to refrain from making the distinction. I shall, therefore, attempt to explain the difference in outcome between the Japanese strategic surprise attempts at Pearl Harbor and Midway without resorting to the distinction between wartime and peacetime conditions.

Thus far I have considered the importance of the strategic surprise phenomenon, reviewed the existing literature on the subject, observed its merits, and highlighted its weakness, proposed an alternative explanation for the phenomenon, and suggested a new research strategy for studying it. Here I wish to elaborate further on the last theme.

As I hope to have made clear in the earlier discussion, the basis for any explanation of surprise is an assessment of the quality of warning available to the target prior to the event. Since so much hinges on the determination of whether warning was available to the target prior to the surprise attempt, it is absolutely essential to exercise great caution in defining, operationalizing, and ultimately also measuring warning so as not to predetermine the findings. Furthermore, in order to enhance the reliability of the study, it is also important to make the definition, operationalization, and measurement procedure as explicit as possible. It is to this task that I now turn.

The common practice in the existing surprise literature has been to make use of a rather loose and extremely broad definition of warning, one that essentially incorporates every possible indicator of the perpetrator's intentions and capabilities, from the most tangible and explicit to the most amorphous and implicit. It thus includes, among other things, raw as well as processed intelligence, rumors and newspaper stories, and even the "logic of the situation" and "lessons of the past." Such a definition is so broad and ambiguous that it is highly susceptible to subjective interpretation. As such it can hardly serve as the basis for rigorous and systematic measurement of warning.[25] From this point in the study onwards, I therefore opt for a much more restrictive definition of warning, one including only threat indicators obtained and processed intelligence. However, in assessing the information available to a surprise target prior to the event, I will take into account other threat indicators as well.[26]

In reconstructing the information picture available to a surprise target prior to the event I follow the example provided in Wohlstetter (1962:3) and take into consideration the signals as well as the noise. Yet, I incorporate not only positive but also negative types of evidence; in other words, the absence of warning and other threat indicators, when they are reasonably expected to be present in the event of an impending threat, is considered an important type of evidence.[27] Unlike Whaley (1973), however,

I classify as "signals" or "noise" only reports that can be *documented* to have reached the government of the target state (its intelligence services and/or its policymakers).

Another probem that I attempt to deal with in my assessment of warning is that of analysis in retrospect, i.e., with the benefit of hindsight. The problem that warning (as well as other threat indicators) seems much clearer with the benefit of hindsight was originally recognized by Wohlstetter (1962:387–88). Yet neither Wohlstetter nor any of her followers managed to tackle it systematically. The procedure they used—classifying the information available to the target prior to the event into signals and noise followed by a determination of a signal to noise ratio (S/N)—is obviously illuminating. But in its *simple* form it is also uniquely susceptible to distortions introduced by analysis in retrospect (Chan 1979:174–75).

Recall that the quality of warning and for that matter any other information as well is a function of two factors: its relevance and accuracy (signal or noise), and the known reliability of its source. This known reliability of the source determines to no small degree the treatment the report receives and the impact it has in real time (ibid.:172). Consequently, it is inappropriate to assume, as Wohlstetter and others have done, that each report is essentially equal in weight to any other at the point of entry into the system, and to represent the warning picture available to the defender at the time in terms of a *simple* S/N, merely counting the numbers of signals as well as noise reports. Thus, in this study, when reconstructing the warning picture, I opt, at least implicitly, for a *complex* S/N, one in which the reports of each type are weighed by the known reliability of their sources.

An additional feature of my operationalization of warning is that it considers warning, like surprise, to be a matter of degree. Following the example provided by Alexander George (1979a), I consider warning as well as surprise as continuous variables on an ordinal level of measurement. Their values range from no warning (complete surprise) to perfect warning (no surprise or threat perception) respectively, on each of five complementary dimensions (who, what, where, when, and why).

Finally, to overcome the problems commonly stemming from the use of unpreparedness as the sole empirical indicator for the presence of surprise, I employ four separate empirical indicators for surprise. Each of these indicators can take a positive or negative value (anticipation/lack of anticipation of the move by the opponent, respectively). While any single one of these indicators may take a positive value even when surprise is present, positive value on all four provides unmistakable evidence that surprise is absent.[28]

Before closing, a final word is in order regarding the research design, the falsifiability of our hypotheses, and the interpretation of the findings that this study is expected to generate. Recall that the main preoccupation of this study is with an empirical examination of competing explanations of surprise in an endeavor to establish its proximate causes. As I have already suggested in my critique of the existing literature, it is essential for any such research project to include, among other things, an analysis of instances of abortive surprise as well as an effort to overcome the generalizability limitations inherent in single case studies. In this study I meet these requirements by examining the abortive surprise at Midway (chapter 3) as well as by conducting a structured focused comparison between the Midway and Pearl Harbor cases. My effort to establish proximate causes of surprise is thus based on the combination of a controlled comparison (following Mill's logic of elimination in controlled experiments of small "n,") and process tracing (i.e., tracing through the historical sequence to discover a cause and effect chain).[29]

How confident can I be of the findings that emerge from this study and the inference derived therefrom? The explanations of the two historical instances (Midway and Pearl Harbor) that form the basis for assessing/refining/elaborating the surprise theory will be necessarily provisional, as is the case with any historical research (George 1982:31), let alone one comprising of a small number of cases. Yet the nature of my research design, coupled with the fact that I am testing deductively derived hypotheses, does enhance the plausibility of my explanations. And as George has already argued (ibid,), "the utility of explanations developed in the case studies for theory development rests on their plausibility (definitive historical explanations, assuming that such are possible, are not necessary for theory development)." Finally, the relative confidence in each specific inference necessarily depends on whether it contradicts a given hypothesis (which can be invalidated by a single inconsistent datum) or is consistent with it (which is insufficient by itself to validate a theory but can enhance its plausibility). It is, therefore, necessary to consider several alternative findings that can emerge from this study and their potential significance.

      An observation that high-quality warning *was* available to a surprise victim prior to the event but was not heeded by his policymakers would clearly be incompatible with my hypotheses.The opposite, however, is not equally true, since an observation that such a warning was *not* available prior to a strategic surprise, while congruent with my hypothesis, would not be particularly meaningful. This is the case because it is not totally incompatible with alternative explanations of surprise. Findings along these lines (no warning prior to surprise) would, therefore, assume somewhat greater weight only if it could be conclusively demonstrated that they also hold true for surprise instances that were heretofore attributed by other scholars to pathologies of intelligence and information processing rather than lack of warning (e.g., Pearl Harbor).

      Still, only abortive surprise instances are likely to provide a more difficult and therefore more potent test of my hypotheses. Confidence in the validity of my explanation would be greatly enhanced should I uncover evidence in abortive surprise attempts to suggest that both high-quality warning and significant barriers to analytical accuracy were present. This is the case because such findings would impinge directly on the core of my hypotheses, which is also what distinguishes them from other explanations of surprise. It is, however, possible that in these abortive cases the presence of both high-quality warning and barriers to analytical accuracy could not be adequately documented, in which case the significance of the findings would be greatly diminished.

Here I wish to introduce two caveats. First, although we may not encounter in the case studies instances where warning is received but leaders are nevertheless surprised, such cases can not be ruled out altogether. They will therefore be discussed in some detail in chapter 4, when I explore the impact of other variables that intervene between warning and threat perception. Second, even in the event that the case studies would appear to lend strong support to my hypotheses, it is unlikely that we would be able to rule out all alternative explanations of the outcome(s), not in the least those that suggest that the consistency between predictions and outcomes is fortuitous, i.e., that the supportive observations are merely an artifact of other causes that happen to point in the same direction as my hypotheses.[30]

In addition we must also consider whether the surprise phenomenon is subject to "plurality of causes" so that the case outcomes can also be predicted and explained by some theories other than the one I am attempting to test (George 1982:34). Thus, even under the best of circumstances, the findings that emerge from this study will only strengthen confidence in my explanation of surprise and detract from the plausibility of other explanations, but by no means dispense with them altogether.

This is the time to reiterate that the explanation of strategic surprise I put forward in this study *does not deny* the existence of numerous and diverse pathologies in the processing of information and barriers to analytical accuracy which other scholars have emphasized so strongly. To suggest that this is the case is to misconstrue my argument. However, I would contend that while these various pathologies and obstacles are very real, they are less applicable to strategic warning than are other forms of information and intelligence, and are therefore less important as causes of strategic surprise. The picture portrayed by many other scholars, I submit, is incomplete and partially biased (and therefore distorted) but in no way unfounded or irrelevant.

# Chapter 2

# Pearl Harbor
# Revisited

**The Japanese surprise** attack on Pearl Harbor on December 7, 1941, has been the subject of numerous studies and investigations, and has been discussed, in one form or another, in an almost endless number of publications. So much, in fact, has already been written about the Pearl Harbor episode that one is intuitively inclined to doubt the utility of any new examination of the case, and with good reason, I might add. Few of the more recent studies of the Pearl Harbor surprise have contributed much to our understanding of either the episode itself or the surprise phenomenon. Some have added to our knowledge of the historical background to Pearl Harbor (i.e., the developments in Japanese-American relations preceding the war between the two countries). To suggest that some skepticism about the value of additional research on the Pearl Harbor surprise or, for that matter, any similarly well-researched historical episode, is healthy and warranted is not, however, tantamount to saying that we already possess the "definitive word" on it and should therefore refrain from studying it any further. Such a view is not unjustified but even dangerous, as it reflects a basic misunderstanding of the nature of historical research.

History, as E. H. Carr has so aptly reminded us, "is a continuous process of interaction between the historian and his facts, an unending dialogue between the present and the past" (1961:35). Even if it can never proceed on the basis of complete and definitive knowledge of all the facts on a given subject (which in itself is highly questionable), historical study necessarily entails

selection of the facts deemed relevant, as well as their interpretation—two dynamic, iterative, and above all subjective processes.
If this holds true of "configurative idiographic" historical research,
it is doubly so in the case of "nomothetic" historical and political
study which does not look at a historical case as an end in itself
but rather as a means for understanding a broader phenomenon,
such as, in this case, strategic surprise.

What I would therefore like to suggest is that existing
studies have by no means exhausted the Pearl Harbor episode.
There are still many important insights into the surprise phenomenon that can be derived from the study of the Pearl Harbor
case, insights which have either been overlooked or misinterpreted
in earlier studies. This is not to deny any utility or validity to
those studies. Rather, it is to suggest that theoretical advances in
the study of strategic surprise over the last two decades and
methodological advances in the field of political science, coupled
with new evidence based on recently declassified documents, seem
to put us in a position to select and interpret the facts in the
Pearl Harbor episode in a way that would further enrich our
understanding of the surprise phenomenon. In the process it can
also provide us with a more satisfactory explanation of the Pearl
Harbor surprise.


In view of the proliferation of studies on Pearl Harbor
I find it prudent to start off by delineating the specific, not to
say unique, theoretical concerns of this study. These are a function
of the theoretical interests of the author as well as the availability
of other studies that cover similar and related ground. I shall
therefore deal at the outset, albeit briefly, with some of the more
prominent works on the Pearl Harbor surprise. By way of focusing
attention on the merits and shortcomings of those other studies
I also hope to lay the groundwork for my own analysis.

At the outset I would like to make it clear that my
study addresses itself only to one rather specific question, namely
the extent to which the United States was surprised (in the sense
of lack of foreknowledge) by the Japanese attack on Pearl Harbor

and the causes of this surprise. I will therefore touch upon, but refrain from discussing at any great length, a related question— the causes of the appalling state of unreadiness of U.S. forces in Hawaii on December 7, 1941, this being, at least analytically, a separate question. For as I have already suggested earlier and will discuss at some length below, the almost complete state of un- preparedness of U.S. forces in Hawaii, and therefore also its devastating consequences, need not have been inevitable even in the event that the Japanese action had come as a total surprise to the U.S. military authorities in both Washington and Hawaii. After all, different standard operating procedures, or more com- prehensive precautionary measures activated on a basis other than positive knowledge of the Japanese intent, could have significantly altered the fate of Pearl Harbor on that day of infamy.

While I focus on only one element of the Pearl Harbor episode, I approach it from a perspective that is both historical and comparative in nature. This chapter, which discusses only the Pearl Harbor case, is immediately followed by a similarly structured chapter considering the Battle of Midway. The many similarities between the two cases, coupled with their sharply contrasting outcomes, provide us with an interesting comparison, one enabling us to better understand both cases as well as reach more valid conclusions regarding the surprise phenomenon in general. In this sense the study seeks to satisfy the requirements and therefore reap the benefits of both scientific rigor and historical richness. I thus combine a research method known as a "structured focused comparison" (George 1979a) with an historical approach that seeks in "history not merely what happened but rather what happened in the context of what could have happened" (Trevor-Roper 1980).

Having explicated my main theoretical and method- ological concerns, I would now like to proceed with a brief and highly selective review of the literature on the Pearl Harbor surprise. Of the voluminous literature that discusses in one form or another the Pearl Harbor attack, most studies do not address either specifically, analytically, or in any great length the surprise issues, failing by and large to distinguish between surprise and unprepa  dness. Most of the literature is purely descriptive, fre-

quently jounalistic in nature, and in many cases seems also pro-
grammatic and biased. Even the better studies of this genre have
become largely outdated by the recent declassification of much
relevant historical material shedding new light on the Pearl Harbor
case. The existing body of literature, with only a few notable
exceptions (see below) is therefore of very limited utility for our
purposes here.

The exceptions are primarily of two types: skillful
analytical studies of the surprise issue, the primary example of
which is Roberta Wohlstetter's classical *Pearl Harbor: Warning
and Decision* (1962); and up-to-date historical essays tapping some
of the recently declassified documents, the most important of
which are John Costello's *The Pacific War* (1981) and Gordon
Prange's *At Dawn We Slept* (1981) and *Pearl Harbor: The Verdict
of History* (1985).[1] Only Wohlstetter's study, however, is both
relevant and useful for my entire discussion here and will therefore
be referred to throughout the chapter. The historical essays, on
the other hand, are neither primarily interested in the issues of
concern to me here, nor sufficiently rigorous and consistent in
their standards of admissibility of evidence. They will therefore
be used here only as secondary sources for discussion at one point
or another.

Underlying any explanation of a strategic surprise is
an assessment of the quality of the threat indicators possessed by
the victim prior to the event.[2] This assessment is of critical
importance since it determines whether we ought to look for the
roots of failure to anticipate the threat in either the acquisition
of threat indicators or, alternatively, in their processing and consumption. It is therefore quite self-evident, but nonetheless worth
emphasizing here for reasons that will be become immediately
apparent, that only once we have conclusively established that
advance threat indicators of his oponent's intent were available
to the surprise victim can we proceed to search for the causes of
surprise in factors that hinder or impede the evaluation, dissemination, and consumption of warning. The first step, then, in my

study of the Pearl Harbor surprise ought to be a reassessment of the quality of threat indicators possessed by the United States prior to the event. I begin my analysis by reviewing the views on the issue of Wohlstetter and others, and then proceed to examine it myself.

Roberta Wohlstetter has indeed examined with great care the threat indicators available to the United States prior to the Japanese attack on Pearl Harbor. Although she did not enjoy access to many important documents pertaining to the case, most of which have been declassified over the last few years, she was nonetheless able to reconstruct a fairly accurate (if incomplete) picture of the threat indicators possessed by the U.S. authorities both in Washington and Hawaii prior to December 7, 1941. She did so primarily on the basis of the thirty-nine volumes of the congressional hearings on the Pearl Harbor attack (PHA 1946), as well as memoirs of statesmen and military commanders, secondary accounts by historians, some private documents, and extensive interviews with key participants which she conducted herself (Wohlstetter 1962:xi). Thanks to her extensive research, Wohlstetter is rarely wrong in any *factual* matters of any significance. Consequently, Wohlstetter's data base, once expanded and updated to include information ignored by her or unavailable to her at the time, can serve as a solid foundation for my analysis. The same, however, does not necessarily hold true of Wohlstetter's conclusions, which may not have been fully justified on the basis of her original data base, let alone the updated one. In my discussion, I therefore draw a clear distinction between *facts* presented by Wohlstetter and her *interpretation* of these facts.

Wohlstetter summarizes her assessment of the threat indicators obtained by the United States prior to the Pearl Harbor attack as follows: "At the time of Pearl Harbor the circumstances of collection in the sense of access to a huge variety of data were, at least in Washington, close to ideal" (ibid.:70). Wohlstetter continues to argue that "if our intelligence systems and all our other channels of information failed to produce an accurate image of the Japanese intentions and capabilities, *it was not for want of the relevant materials.* Never before have we had so complete an

intelligence picture" (ibid.:382, emphasis added). Wohlstetter con-
cludes: "It is apparent that our decision makers had at hand an
impressive amount of information on the enemy" (ibid.:386–87)
and the United States therefore "failed to anticipate Pearl Harbor
not for want of the relevant materials but because of a plethora
of irrelevant ones" (ibid.: 387).

The above quotes clearly reflect Wohlstetter's assessment that the U.S. possessed excellent threat indicators prior to
the Pearl Harbor attack. Wohlstetter's assessment is shared by the
overwhelming majority of students of the Pearl Harbor episode
(see, for example, Critchley 1978:47–52; Janis 1972:4; Barnes 1972:21
ff.; Cline 1976:17; Millet and Moreland 1976:17–18, 246). Most of
these scholars, however, have either endorsed Wohlstetter's conclusions outright or expressed similar views independently but
without actually examining closely Wohlstetter's data base or
extensively consulting any other sources. A partial exception is
Richard Betts, who in a recent study did consult some other
secondary sources, though no primary ones, and has, nonetheless,
reached very similar conclusions. Betts suggests that "warning
indicators were abundant" (1982b:42) and that indications of the
*ultimate* intentions of the Japanese government were plentiful
(ibid.:44, emphasis added). Probably the most extreme recent
expression of this view, though certainly not the most convincing
one (Kahn 1982) is contained in a new book on Pearl Harbor by
John Toland (1982).

Let us now try to determine whether sufficient evidence
exists to support the catgorical conclusions reached by Wohlstetter
and the others regarding the quality of threat indicators obtained
by the United States prior to Pearl Harbor. Wohlstetter, as well
as the other subscribers to this school of thought, base their
assessment of the quality of the threat indicators implicitly or
explicitly on one or two criteria: the sources of information in
Japan (collection assets) at the disposal of the United States and
the actual signals acquired (concrete threatening reports received,
threat indicators detected) by the United States prior to the attack.
I shall consider one at a time starting with the collection assets.

As for the collection assets, Wohlstetter as well as Betts seemed to be particularly impressed by both their quality and variety. Aerial reconnaisance, (radio) traffic analysis, British and Dutch intelligence, the American embassy in Tokyo, the military observers and attachés throughout the Far East, and above all Magic (the generic name for the deciphering of Japanese *diplomatic* communications worldwide) constituted, according to Roberta Wohlstetter, a magnificent, in fact close to ideal, collection of sources which the United States would unlikely be able to master again in the future (1962:70, 382). Magic, in particular, struck Wohlstetter as the ultimate intelligence source: "Magic was the most important single device for listening in on secret Japanese communications and was, therefore, one of the key guides to detection of Japanese intentions. But American policymakers had many other guides at their disposal" (ibid.:228). "The ability to read these [Japanese ciphers and] codes gave the U.S. a remarkable advantage over the enemy—an advantage not likely to be repeated" (ibid.:170). Betts clearly concurs with this assessment of Magic when he writes that "Magic exposed the innermost thoughts and instructions of the government in Tokyo" (1982b:45).

Surprisingly enough, neither Wohlstetter nor Betts present much in the way of solid evidence to support their enthusiastic appraisal of U.S. collection assets. There simply is no such evidence around. So how did such a rosy assessment of U.S. collection assets emerge? To no small degree it stemmed from the application of inadequate criteria for the measurement of sources' quality. One yardstick used by Wohlstetter for the purpose—comparison to the quality of sources possessed by the United States at earlier times—is meaningless. The United States simply did not have any peacetime intelligence organization to speak of prior to 1947. Another yardstick used by Wohlstetter—comparison to the quality of sources that are at all feasible or that the United States is likely to possess in the future—is misleading. It is misleading on methodological grounds because Wohlstetter had no valid way of predicting the quality of sources the United States was likely to have at its disposal in the future. It is also misleading on empirical grounds since better sources are not only feasible but were actually possessed by the United States after Pearl Harbor and by other countries both before and after that time (see chapters 3 and 4).

A third and final yardstick used by Wohlstetter, Betts, and others for measurement of the source's quality was the threat indicators they were actually able to generate on the eve of the Pearl Harbor attack. This yardstick is no less problematic than the other two. For one thing the performance of an intelligence source in a single instance, important as it may be, provides only shaky grounds for assessing its overall quality. For another thing, even this yardstick when applied systematically and rigorously to the Pearl Harbor context fails to sustain a favorable appraisal of the collection sources at the disposal of the United States prior to December 7, 1941. To underline this point I now proceed to review all the sources of intelligence on Japan possessed by U.S. intelligence prior to that day.[3]

## Overt Sources

These are the most important and abundant sources for every intelligence service, especially so when it deals with open societies. This, however, was not the case with Japan prior to the Pearl Harbor attack. Both the Japanese media and the American press corps in Tokyo were gravely affected by the tightening of Japanese security measures throughout 1941.[4] As for the Japanese press, in 1941 it was tightly controlled by the government, much more so than in earlier periods, as a result of a series of stringent security measures taken by the government to control the mass media (May 1973:525). Thus, for example, "in December 1940 the Cabinet Information Division was elevated to the status of a bureau responsible for dissemination of information and propaganda and overall control of the mass media (Tomiko 1973:548). This new bureau was modeled on Joseph Goebbels' propaganda ministry in Berlin and was staffed with some full-time military officers in its key sections (May 1973:525). In January 1941, the government further extended its press control by "an imperial edict giving the prime minister (and therefore the Information Bureau) the power to restrict or prohibit, by issuance of directives, publication of any article bearing upon the execution of national policies, whether financial, economic, diplomatic, etc." (Tomiko 1973:548). Finally, in March 1941 "the national defence security law stipulated extremely severe punishments for anyone found guilty of violating the restrictions on speech and publications" (ibid.).

As a result of the numerous measures taken by the Japanese government to control the mass media, news reporters were relegated "to serving merely as messengers for the military and government authorities" (ibid.). The independent English language press completely disappeared with the only remaining newspaper in English published with government subsidy and under its control (May 1973:525). The foreign correspondents in Tokyo did not fare any better. They encountered growing difficulties in obtaining any original information from any sources in Japan. Press conferences for foreign correspondents by the Army, Navy, and the Foreign Ministry were eliminated. These correspondents received no printed material in English other than emissions from the government, and the material in Japanese was hardly more useful. Furthermore, the Japanese government went to great lengths to discourage correspondents from making efforts to obtain news other than that officially handed out by its officials. Consequently, they had only minimal sources open to them (ibid.:526). The foreign correspondents were also subjected to tight police surveillance. They were frequently stopped and harassed, some were even arrested and tried on espionage charges (ibid.). They also encountered numerous difficulties in relaying their stories to the United States; their outgoing dispatches and telephone calls were heavily censored, long delayed, and frequently interrupted (ibid.).

To all the obstacles put in the way by the Japanese the American correspondents added a few of their own making. By the summer of 1941 the American press corps in Tokyo were mostly new and had no background for interpreting Japanese affairs (May 1973:526-30). Most of them "went to Japan ignorant of the country's history, culture and language. For the most part they remained ignorant." (ibid.:530). It is therefore hardly surprising that Ernest May concluded on the basis of his impressive study of U.S. press coverage of Japan that the communications of these journalists "contributed relatively little to the understanding of their American readers" (ibid.:526) and their reportage "was superficial, fragmentary, insensitive and, in the end, misleading" (p. 530). Roberta Wohlstetter, in her more superficial study of the issue, generally tended to give the reports of the American correspondents in Japan much higher grades, but she conceded that "for the last few weeks before the Pearl Harbor strike . . . the public newspaper accounts were not very useful" as a result of the "very tight control over leaks exercised during this crucial period" in Tokyo and Washington (1962:384). Consequently, these journalists, even according to Wohlstetter, "had to limit their accounts to speculation and notices of diplomatic meetings with no exact indication of the content of the diplomatic messages (ibid.). As for the Japanese press itself, Wohlstetter maintains that it was "an important public source" (ibid.).

## Semi-Covert Sources

Semi-covert intelligence sources usually provide abundant information on countries with which one maintains commercial and diplomatic ties. Ambassador Grew and his staff in Tokyo were indeed an invaluable source of intelligence on Japan, producing in 1940 and 1941 not only perceptive and detailed factual reports but also sophisticated interpretations of developments in the Japanese scene. General Sherman Miles, the head of Military Intelligence (G-2) at the time of Pearl Harbor, testified that this was the most important source of information on Japan available to him (PHA 1946, 27:57). But even this source was severely affected by the Japanese security arrangements in late 1941—so much so, in fact, that Ambassador Grew felt the need, on November 17,

1941, to explain the situation to his superiors in Washington and warn them that neither he nor his military attachés would be able to perform what they considered their most important duty, namely "to detect any premonitory signs of naval or military operations and guard against surprise" (ibid.:58). Ambassador Grew then went on to disclaim any responsibility for providing advance warning of Japanese military operations. His explanation, contained in the November 17 message, is worth quoting at some length.

". . . you are advised of not placing the major responsibility in giving prior warning upon the Embassy staff, the naval and military attaches included, since in Japan there is extremely effective control over both primary and secondary military information. We would not expect to obtain any information in advance either from personal Japanese contacts or through the press; the observation of military movements is not possible by the few Americans remaining in the country, concentrated mostly in three cities (Tokyo, Yokohama, Kobe); and with American and other foreign shipping absent from adjacent waters the Japanese are assured of their ability to send without foreign intervention their troop transports in various directions." (ibid.)

Thus, while Ambassador Grew continued until the outbreak of war to provide Washington with his perceptive analysis of Japanese affairs and his reading of the situation proved (in retrospect) accurate and prescient, at the time he had very little evidence on which to base his analysis, and the authorities in Washington were fully aware that this was the case.

To elaborate further on one of the key points made by Grew, the United States traditionally acquired much valuable information on movements of the Japanese fleet through shipping intelligence—sighting of Japanese vessels by Allied commercial ships sailing in the Pacific. The rerouting of all U.S. and most Allied trans-Pacific shipping in mid-October 1941 practically eliminated this source of information (PHA 1946, 14:1402-3).

Another semi-covert source of intelligence was U.S. military attachés and observers throughout the Far East.[5] The American military observers and attachés scattered throughout the Far East provided Washington with much useful information which

they collected first hand or obtained through American business-
men, journalists, commercial attachés and consuls, employees of
American companies, and some local contacts. But their ability to
engage in straightforward intelligence collection activity (and consequently to obtain highly sensitive information) was severely
restricted by scarcity of funds, strong opposition from the State
Department for any activity that would compromise U.S. neutrality,[6] and above all, Japanese security measures. While they were
fairly successful in obtaining valuable information on the Japanese
military in China, where the access was relatively easy, their
performance in Japan itself—where conditions were much less
favorable—was rather disappointing and reached a low ebb in late
1941. The deteriorating American-Japanese relations and the concomitant suspension of commercial ties, as well as the tightening
Japanese security measures (including restrictions on travel) deprived them of virtually any access to sensitive Japanese military
information.

### Clandestine Sources

With the overt and semi-overt intelligence sources being what
they were, much, if not all, of the United States' capacity to
obtain advance warning of Japan's intentions depended on the
quality of its covert collection assets. These, however, were not
in much better shape than the more overt sources.

One critical covert source, human intelligence (Humint), otherwise known as espionage, was practically nonexistent.
In sharp contrast to Great Britain, Germany, Japan, and the Soviet
Union, which were investing, at the time, a lot of resources in
espionage (and with rather impressive results), the United States
deliberately refrained from engaging in this type of intelligence
activity due to moral, political, and budgetary considerations (PHA
1946 2:899; Hilsman 1956:85; Cline 1976:13; Dorowart 1983; ch.
12). At the time the United States possessed, according to General

Miles, only "a nucleus of what might be called a secret service under Colonel Clear in Singapore," to which very little money was allocated, and Clear's progress was confined to "tying in with the British Secret Service in the Far East" (PHA 1946 2:785). Thus, as a result of its deliberate decision not to make any more concerted efforts in the development of Humint, the United States effectively deprived itself of the source of intelligence that is best suited for detection of enemy intentions, and has traditionally been recognized as such.

Aside from Humint, the only other sources of intelligence commonly capable of providing strategic warning are Sigint (signal intelligence) and, especially, Comint (communications intelligence). But Comint at the time was only making its first steps and the United States was by no means at the forefront of research, development, production, and deployment of Comint assets (Safford 1952). The technical deficiencies of Comint were exacerbated, at the time, by a severe shortage of resources (skilled and trained manpower, money, and equipment), much of it having to do with the low priority assigned to this field of activity until late 1941 (Friedman 1945; Safford 1952; Farago 1967:55, 61). These problems were compounded by legal constraints imposed by Section 605 of the Federal Communications Act of 1934, which explicitly prohibited wiretaps or the interception of messages to and from foreign countries. One of the consequences of the act was the sustained refusal of the commercial cable companies (RCA, Mackay, Globe Wireless, etc.) to cooperate with U.S. intelligence services and provide them with copies of messages sent to and from Japan (Prange 1981:79–80). Objective topographical limitations on interception of Japanese radio communication, coupled with Japanese communications security and deception, made the dismal situation even worse.

The only glimmer of hope in this area was some success in the field of cryptanalysis, namely in breaking and reading several Japanese cryptographic systems (codes and ciphers). Here it must be emphasized, however, that this success, which received so much public attention in the Pearl Harbor investigations and the ensuing literature, was largely confined, in the year prior to December 7,

1941, to the Japanese *diplomatic* systems, i.e. Magic (see below). The recovery of numerous Japanese cryptographic systems, including the sophisticated top security system (Purple) serving the communication needs of the Japanese diplomatic heads of mission was indeed a remarkable cryptanalytical achievement (Safford 1952; Farago 1967: ch. 13; Kahn 1967: ch. 1). Magic certainly provided the United States with much useful information of extremely high reliability, but its importance and potential value were highly exaggerated both by its consumers at the time (McCollum 1973:275–76) and most students of the Pearl Harbor episode thereafter.

As the producers of Magic at the time, and particularly Captain McCollum and Lieutenant Commander Kramer, emphasized all along, Magic did not represent much "of what these little people are going to do" (ibid.). Most of the information obtained through Magic pertained either to countries other than Japan (through detailed reports that Japanese diplomats stationed in those countries sent to their Foreign Ministry), or to the state of negotiations with the United States. And while it did reveal in ample detail Japan's negotiating strategy with the United States, it offered only a few clues to the thinking of the Japanese cabinet which was shaping this strategy, and hardly any information of operational value on the Japanese armed forces. It is quite clear why this was the case: the Japanese Foreign Ministry in general, and the Japanese diplomats in Washington in particular, were victims of tight compartmentalization (ibid.; Kirkpatrick 1969:87–89; Wohlstetter 1962:202).

The Japanese diplomats abroad were kept in the dark about major decisions of the Japanese cabinet and were completely ignorant of the operational planning and preparations for war of the Japanese armed forces. This was clearly evident in the numerous misunderstandings and clashes between the negotiators in Washington and their superiors in Tokyo over the proposals submitted to the United States (Chihiro 1973:165–88). As a result, the worldwide communications of the Japanese diplomats, authentic as they may have been, could not reveal "the inner-most thoughts and instructions of the government in Tokyo," Betts'

claim to the contrary notwithstanding (1982b:45), and the producers of Magic were fully aware that this was the case (McCollum
1973:274-75).

Only one small part of the Japanese diplomatic communications network, that between their consulate in Hawaii and
Tokyo, was somewhat more promising as a source of information
on the operational planning of the Japanese Navy, although this
was far from clear at the time. With the benefit of hindsight, we
now know that the Japanese naval intelligence was occasionally
using this channel to communicate with the Japanese consulate
in Hawaii regarding the collection of information on U.S. military
installations in Hawaii. At the time, however, U.S. intelligence
was not aware that this was the case. For one thing, Japan's
communications on intelligence matters were at least formally
disguised as ordinary foreign ministry messages. For another thing,
the communication between the Consulate and Tokyo was intercepted only erratically[7] (Farago 1967:227). Additionally, there
were only a few clues to suggest that there were people in the
Consulate who were engaged in espionage and reporting directly
to the Naval General Staff.

In the absence of any solid evidence to indicate the
importance of this source, and in view of the low level of traffic
intercepted as well as the tremendous overload on the American
cryptanalysis establishment, the messages that were after all received
from this variant of Magic were assigned low priority in handling
(Farago 1967:167-68, 232, 278, 333-37; Prange 1981:472-73). This
low priority resulted in long delays in processing and dissemination,
at times exceeding six weeks. Consequently, some of the most
illuminating messages were rendered useless, as they were transmitted in late November and early December 1941 but were only
processed long after the attack on Pearl Harbor had taken place
(SRH-012 1942:188-202).

In passing I might add that in addition to intercepting
cryptographic Japanese diplomatic communication (Magic), the
United States was also tapping the Japanese diplomats' telephones
(as well as other telephone conversations to Japan) and maintaining
some surveillance over their missions in both Washington and

Hawaii (Prange 1981:398–99; 442–43, 447, 477; Wohlstetter 1962:52–54, 61ff.; Dorowart 1983:176). This, however, could be no more useful a source of information than Magic for many of the same reasons mentioned above, and in practice proved a far inferior source for two primary reasons. The Japanese diplomats were not commonly using the telephone for secret conversations with Tokyo, and even when they did they exercised great caution in what they said. Moreover, tapping the Japanese phones created severe legal and security problems, which at least in the case of Hawaii brought about the termination of the eavesdropping on December 2, 1941 (Prange 1981:443).

To comprehend fully the collection situation prior to Pearl Harbor, especially in the critical area of Comint, it is important to observe not what the United States actually possessed in this area but also, and perhaps more importantly, what it did not.

As was already pointed out above, the United States' cryptanalytical success against Japan was largely confined to the diplomatic systems. In the year prior to the Japanese attack on Pearl Harbor, none of the primary cryptographic systems of the Japanese Army and Navy was being systematically recovered by the United States, and not for lack of trying (see below). Taken together with the difficulties in other forms of Comint (e.g., traffic analysis) and the absence of Humint it created a critical gap in intelligence on Japan's intentions and capabilities, especially in the military area. This point is of critical importance for understanding the Pearl Harbor surprise (and, conversely, the Midway success) and will therefore be discussed here at some length.

This intriguing state of Comint on Japan prior to December 7, 1941, was, to a large degree, a product of the general constraints on intelligence and intelligence collection as well as two unique factors having to do with the nature and volume of the Japanese *radio* communication prior to the beginning of the war. With prewar communication needs being inherently less urgent and the bulk of their armed forces still stationed in their permanent bases, the Japanese could rely primarily on rather secure if slower means of communications (e.g., landlines, messengers).

This implied not only that the Japanese military could keep the volume of their radio communication relatively low but also that they could maintain and enforce much tighter communication security measures including, among other things, frequent and orderly changes in and of call signs and cryptographic systems (Safford 1952; Kahn 1967: ch. 1; Farago 1967). The low volume of traffic coupled with the security measures severely restricted the amount of information that could be derived from both cryptanalysis and traffic analysis. The critical importance of this state of affairs can be more fully realized when viewed in its historical context.

Historically, the main source of intelligence on the Japanese Navy was the "Flag Officers Cryptographic System."[8] This was the most important cryptosystem of the Japanese Navy and the one to which it entrusted its most secret communication. It was also, however, the most difficult to crack. The United States was able to break into the system in the mid-1920s and read it almost without interruption until about mid-November 1940 (Kahn 1967:8; Farago 1967:46, 136–37, 268; Rochefort, in PHA 1946 32:369; Safford, in PHA 1946 18:3335–36; Safford 1952). During that period this had been the United State's main source of information on the Japanese Navy (Safford, in PHA 1946 18:3335), and it provided the U.S. Navy with much useful information on the Japanese fleet and its movements (Kahn 1967:8; Farago 1967:268–69; Holmes 1979:46).

In late 1940, however, the Japanese Navy drastically changed the Flag Officers System, introducing a combination of four-character code with transposition superencipherment. A substantial effort to solve the new version of the system was then launched by the most skilled and experienced American and British cryptanalysts but to no avail (Kahn 1967:8, 45; Farago 1967:106–7, 164, 269, 297). The system stoutly resisted all attacks and was never solved. The Japanese themselves discontinued its use in 1942 or 1943, apparently because of its slowness, complexity, and susceptibility to error (Safford 1952:15; Safford, in PHA 1946 18:3335–36), using instead the "Fleet Cryptographic System," also known as the "Operations Code" (JN-25) (see below).

The loss of the Flag Officers system after November 1940 was "catastrophic" in its consequences for the United States (Farago 1967:106–7) as it cost the United States the collection asset that would have been most likely to provide it with warning regarding Japan's intention to attack Pearl Harbor. Farago's view is shared by Captain Laurance Safford, the head of OP-20G (the Communications Security [cryptography and cryptanalysis] Section of the Office of Naval Communications) throughout World War II, and a man who was actively involved with U.S. cryptographic activities since the mid-1920s. Safford has argued that "if we could have solved the Flag Officers System, Admiral Kimmel would probably have known of the Japanese plans, and the Pacific Fleet would not have been surprised on December 7, 1941" (PHA 1946 18:3335–36).

The other major cryptographic system of the Japanese navy was known as the "Operations Code" or JN-25.[9] This was the main fleet's cryptosystem and was very widely used (Safford 1952:14–15, 22; Kahn 1967:8). Introduced on June 1, 1939, the system was comprised of a code with five-digit code numbers with which an additive cypher was employed. American cryptanalysts were quick to define the method of recovery but the process of recovery itself was slow and laborious. Consequently, by November 1941 the system was only spottily read and even that with some delay (Safford, in PHA 1946 18:3335–36; Safford 1952:14–15, 22; Kahn 1967: ch. 1). Moreover, on December 4, 1941 (December 1, according to another version) the superencipherment in the system (though not the codebook) was changed, making it completely unreadable (ibid.). Initial break into the new system was only made by the United States on December 8, 1941 (December 15, according to another version), days *after* the Pearl Harbor attack had been completed, but well ahead of the Midway operation—a point which will be discussed in some detail in the next chapter.

Thus, in the critical days and months of 1941, the United States was having little measurable success in recovering the primary cryptosystems of the Japanese Navy. While several other Japanese naval cryptosystems were being read at the time, those were essentially low-grade systems serving rather specific and narrow functions and therefore of little or no significance as sources of strategic intelligence (Safford 1952:21–22; McCollum 1973:389; Farago 1967:163–64, 318–19; Kahn 1967: ch. 1). The situation with respect to the Japanese Army's cryptographic systems was even worse—none were broken prior to 1943 (Farago 1968:162).

The inability to recover any of the primary cryptographic systems of the Japanese Army and Navy meant that it was virtually impossible for the United States to read the *substance* of their radio communication, thereby creating a serious gap in coverage of the Japanese military. But this shortcoming could have been partly offset had the United States been able to derive much valuable information from "traffic analysis," namely from monitoring and analyzing the volume and pattern of the Japanese radio communication as well as locating the communicating units with the help of direction finders (Prange 1981:664). But unfortunately for the United States, it did not fare much better in this critical area of Comint.

Objective difficulties of topography and unreliability of equipment (particularly HF direction finders) were compounded by elaborate Japanese communication security and deception (McCollum 1973:279–80, 359–61; Farago 1967:267–69, 297 *ff.*; Wohlstetter 1962:32; Prange 1981:353, 362, 424–25, 439–40, 664; Van Der Rhoer 1978:63). The situation was, in fact, so bad that in the six months preceding the Pearl Harbor attack U.S. naval intelligence completely lost track of major elements of the Japanese fleet (especially the aircraft carriers) on twelve occasions ranging in length from 9 to 22 days. In 134 out of 180 days in this period the naval intelligence could not pinpoint with any degree of certainty the location of the carriers (Prange 1981:441; Wohlstetter 1962:41–44).

The only other covert source through which the United States could have systematically obtained advance warning of Japan's intentions was the exchange of information with foreign governments, specifically the British and the Dutch. Indeed the recent books by both Costello (1981) and Toland (1982) tend to attribute to this source warnings that the United States supposedly

obtained prior to Pearl Harbor, the former discussing at some
length warning obtained from Britain (Costello 1981:633–34), the
latter warning from the Dutch (Toland 1982:281–82, 290). While
the nature of these specific warnings as well as others from this
source can only be examined when we consider the warning
picture in its entirety later in this chapter, a few words about the
nature and the scope of this source are in order here. What
follows are, therefore, some observations regarding the cooperation
in intelligence matters between the United States and both Britain
and the Netherlands prior to the Pearl Harbor attack. These
observations are based on a review of the historical data available
to date on the issue.

  First, the evidence suggests that cooperation in matters
of intelligence and exchange of information did indeed take place
between these parties prior to December 7, 1941, but until the
United States' entry into the war they were neither smooth nor
extensive. For until that date, and to a lesser extent even after
it, there was strong resistance on all sides to intimate cooperation
in highly sensitive matters not only out of the desire to protect
sources but also out of respect for each other's neutrality (Hinsley
1979 1:311–14, 2:41–42, 55; Farago 1967:251–59; Haslach 1982).
Second, the information received by the United States from this
source was treated with some caution not only because the original
source of the information was frequently not disclosed (Kahn
1967:486) but also because there was some fear that Britain and
the Netherlands might deliberately slant information they provided
to the United States in order to convince the latter to enter the
war.

  Finally, and probably most importantly, there is strong
evidence to suggest that the British and the Dutch had their share
of problems penetrating the Japanese veil of secrecy, which clearly
affected their own ability to obtain advance warning of Japan's
plans for war with the United States. Thus, for example, very
much like the United States prior to December 7, 1941, both
were apparently unsuccessful in recovering the primary cryptographic systems of the Japanese Navy (PHA 1946 18:3336; Kahn
1967:10; Farago 1967:290). It should also be remembered that both

countries were allocating many of their collection assets to the European theater, at the expense of the Pacific one.

I have thus far reviewed many intelligence sources possessed by the United States prior to the Pearl Harbor attack. If the United States were to obtain *strategic* warning on Japan's intention to launch a war against it and attack Pearl Harbor, it would have had to come from one or more of the sources discussed above. For other collection assets at the disposal of the United States at the time were by their very nature capable of providing no more than last-minute tactical threat indicators even under the best of circumstances (Wohlstetter 1962:13). In this category of sources we include radar, aerial reconnaissance, and aerial photography (Photoint). Even in this area, however, the existing state of affairs was not favorable for the United States. Radar, at the time, was technically deficient, limited in range and performance, and not very reliable. In Hawaii, radar was a recent arrival and was only partially installed; there was a severe shortage of experienced radar operators and it was therefore operated primarily for training purposes and then only for short time spans (ibid.:6–12).

Aerial reconnaissance was similarly limited in scope and range by paucity of planes, fuel, and air crews as well as the higher priority assigned to training missions (ibid.:13). Photoint suffered from many of the same problems as well as some added ones. Air photography and particularly interpretation were still very primitive at the time, and aerial reconnaissance and photography over Japanese territory were prohibited by the political and military leadership until the very last minute prior to the Pearl Harbor attack so as not to provoke the Japanese. Thus, for example, the first reconnaissance mission over the Mandates was only approved by the War Department in late November 1941, and the lone B-24 assigned for the mission did not arrive in Hawaii (from the West Coast) until December 5, 1941 (Prange 1981:461, 63).

Perhaps the most critical problem with these tactical means of collection in Hawaii was that they were so scarce and costly to use that as a practical matter they could only be activated on the basis of an explicit strategic warning. This state of affairs was fully acknowledged by the Navy Court of Inquiry which looked into the Pearl Harbor disaster. In its findings, the Court said with respect to the various plans for tactical collection and defense of the Hawaiian Islands the following:

The effectiveness of these plans depended upon advance knowledge that an attack was to be expected within narrow limits of time and the plans were drawn with this as a premise. It was not possible for the Commander-in-Chief of the Fleet to make Fleet planes permanently available to the Naval Base Defense Officer, because of his own lack of planes, pilots, and crews and because of the demands of the Fleet in connection with Fleet operations at sea. (ibid.:95)

By now I hope to have made it abundantly clear that the United States was indeed poorly equipped, organized, and deployed to collect information regarding Japan's intentions and capabilities in general, and their preparations for attack on Pearl Harbor in particular. In fact, the overall picture is one in which the United States not only lacked *systematic* coverage of the Japanese military, but its sources were actually drying up in the period immediately preceding the Pearl Harbor attack.[10] While the task of reviewing and examining the specific information on Japan's intentions and capabilities obtained by the United States prior to December 7 still lies ahead, the analysis to this point already permits me to make one critical observation. It would seem that under the collection conditions prevailing prior to the Pearl Harbor attack, it would have taken an incredible stroke of luck for the United States to obtain concrete advance warning of Japan's intention to launch the attack.

Finally, I would like to add that a similar assessment of the collection situation prior to Pearl Harbor was previously made by Admiral Arthur McCollum, who at the time headed the Far East Division of the ONI. In his assessment, McCollum emphasized in particular the inherent limitations of Magic, difficulties in breaking the primary Japanese naval cryptographic systems, problems with traffic analysis and direction finding, and above all, the fact that "the sources in Japan were either snowed under, or blanketed, or non-existent" so far as the United States was concerned (McCollum 1973:461). Most other students of the

Pearl Harbor episode have also acknowledged at one point or another some of the limitations and shortcomings of individual intelligence sources, but as I have noted earlier, they show a strikingly different assessment of the overall collection situation. While the views of most of these scholars can be explained away as a product of an indirect and superficial examination of the issue, the same can hardly be said of Wohlstetter's work. After all, Wohlstetter reached a very favorable assessment of the collection situation prior to Pearl Harbor after a comprehensive and sensitive examination of the various collection assets.

Wohlstetter's failure to reach an accurate appraisal of the overall collection situation, despite her awareness of the problems plaguing many of the individual sources (1962:13, 31, 139, 169, 175, 284, 384), therefore strikes me as analytical rather than empirical in nature, largely stemming, as I have suggested earlier, from the application of inadequate criteria for the evaluation of intelligence collection assets. To do justice to Wohlstetter I must add, however, that her failure seems to be only natural (though not less serious) in view of her research method, namely a single case study. Such a method of inquiry necessarily sacrifices generalizability for depth and richness in detail.


Having examined the collection situation prior to the Pearl Harbor attack, we should proceed to analyze the actual warning obtained by the United States from all sources prior to December 7, 1941. Before doing so, a few words of introduction are in order.

The analysis of collection assets cannot, for all its merits, be viewed as anything but an introduction to the main study. For it is on the assessment of the type and quality of warning and other threat indicators actually available to the victim prior to the event that any explanation of surprise ultimately hinges. The Pearl Harbor case is no exception. As I have already suggested, despite all their other differences, practically all the existing explanations of the Pearl Harbor surprise have one common denominator, namely the premise that excellent warning was available to the United States prior to the attack. Roberta Wohl-stetter, for example, has argued that the United States did possess ample warning but failed to recognize it as such, much less act on it, due to background noise as well as a myriad of organizational and bureaucratic factors. Many other scholars share Wohlstetter's principal conviction of the quality of warning, though each tends to emphasize the role of one or another factor in diminishing the warning and impeding its consumption, e.g., deception (Whaley 1973), "groupthink" (Janis 1972), misperceptions (Prange 1981; Millet and Moreland 1976), and organizational behavior and bu-reaucratic politics (Millet and Moreland 1976; Ben Zvi 1976), etc.

I may have already tipped my hand regarding the quality of warning by voicing skepticism concerning the quality of warning that could conceivably have been obtained by the United States through the intelligence sources it possessed at the time. Never-theless, in order to evaluate the validity of the competing expla-nations and establish the validity of my own, I must explore at some length the actual warning situation prior to the Pearl Harbor attack. In doing so I shall follow several general guidelines. For one thing I shall not discuss here every specific relevant report (whether accurate or inaccurate) received by the United States prior to the attack. Such a task is not only practically impossible but also, I would contend, unnecessary and self-defeating. So much has been written, after all, about the individual messages that what is called for is a synthesis, not a boring repetition. I shall, therefore, focus on clusters of reports, summarizing the information provided over time by each of the sources discussed above. This procedure will not only spare the reader much unnecessary detail but will also provide a proper context for weighing the warning, namely the reliability of the source through which it was obtained.

Furthermore, I shall also refrain from examining the noise (irrelevant, inaccurate, and misleading reports) side by side with the signals (accurate and relevant information). Instead, I shall start off with a strong, and clearly unrealistic, assumption that such accurate and relevant information concerning Japan's intentions (signals) as existed was neither coated with nor accom-panied by irrelevant, inaccurate, and/or false information. Then,

I shall attempt to determine what could be learned about Japan's true intentions and capabilities from the signals in their pure form. Consideration of the noise will become necessary only if and when it becomes clear that enough signals were available to warn of the imminent danger and the need arises to explain why the signals failed to carry the day. My procedure essentially approximates a best case assumption regarding the quality of warning, an assumption that is least likely to bear out my hypothesis. Using such an assumption therefore comes close to conducting a crucial experiment. And if my hypothesis proves correct under such circumstances, its plausibility is bound to be considerably enhanced.

Finally, a word about the level of analysis. In the preceding section, I reviewed the collection assets possessed by the United States as a whole (as if it were a unified entity) without disaggregating them into organizations to which they belonged, or theaters in which they were deployed. I intend to adhere to this practice for the remainder of this chapter, and feel justified in doing so for two primary reasons. First, I am not principally interested in determining why the local commanders in Hawaii were surprised on December 7, but rather in explaining why the U.S. government *as a whole* was caught unaware by the Japanese action. Second, I have strong reasons to believe that the government agencies in Washington did possess all the relevant (as well as much irrelevant) information collected through all the sources discussed above, even if none actually had access to all the incoming information. It is worth noting, however, that the commanders in the Pacific and their intelligence staffs, especially in Hawaii, were not equally well informed. They were denied at the time not only much of the information processed in Washington (e.g., Magic), but also some that was collected within their own theater. Some of the implications of this state of affairs will be discussed at the end of this chapter.

Turning now to examine the advance warning of Japan's intentions that was available to the United States prior to the Pearl Harbor attack, I distinguish between the general warnings regarding Japan's intention to launch a war against the United States, and specific warnings concerning their intention to attack

Pearl Harbor. The two types of warnings were obviously related but they did, nonetheless, pertain to sufficiently different bodies of knowledge to justify separate treatment. While an attack on Pearl Harbor could not conceivably occur in the absence of Japan's intention to commence war with the United States, the reverse was by no means true. Japan's initiation of hostilities against the United States without an attack on Pearl Harbor was perfectly plausible if not altogether likely. I shall therefore consider first the general warnings of war, then turn to the specific warnings of an attack on Pearl Harbor.

## Warnings of War

Those who argue that the United States did possess advance "warning" of Japan's intention to commence a war against it (as well as to attack Pearl Harbor) pin their case most frequently on the information provided by Magic. I therefore start my analysis with an examination of the warning provided by this source. Indeed, prior to December 7, 1941, the decrypted Japanese diplomatic communication (Magic), particularly in its most confidential form (Purple), was probably the most prolific and reliable, if not the most revealing, source of information on Japan. Purple, especially in its Tokyo to Washington and Tokyo to Berlin circuits, consistently provided the United States with much useful information on Japan as well as other countries by revealing many of the most intimate and confidential thoughts, meetings, and other actions of the Japanese *diplomats* around the world and their immediate superiors in Tokyo. Leaving aside the light that Magic could and did shed on other important issues, the key question we have to address here is what Magic had to offer in the way of advance warning of Japan's intention to launch a war against the United States.

Throughout 1941 Magic[11] provided the United States with ample information on Japan's strategy for the negotiations between the two countries. Late in the year it revealed their bad faith in conducting the negotiations, their determination to conclude the negotiations by a certain deadline (initially set for November 25, later moved to the 29th), and finally their desire to maintain the appearance of serious negotiations even beyond that deadline despite the realization that the negotiations had reached a deadlock. Perhaps the most ominous sign conveyed by Magic, in the final weeks and days prior to the attack, was Japan's intention to suspend the negotiations, and their *expectation* that their relations with the United States would deteriorate considerably, possibly to the point of a breakdown of diplomatic ties and even an outbreak of hostilities (PHA 1946 12: 154–55, 204). But Magic did not reveal whether Japan's expectation and the concomitant precautionary measures they ordered for such an eventuality were based on their intention to attack the United States or their anticipation of such action by the United States. Even more importantly, Magic failed to provide the United States with any concrete information to the effect that Japan was actually contemplating a war against it.

Until a few hours before the attack Magic did not even suggest a specific time framework within which the severing of relations was likely to occur. Even the last, and probably also the most revealing, Magic message to be intercepted prior to the attack (it was received hours before the attack)—the now famous "fourteen-part message"—indicated no more than that the Japanese were planning a formal suspension of the negotiations with the United States for December 7, 1941 (PHA 1946 12:245).

Lower security variants of Magic and other forms of Sigint, especially traffic analysis, were also the most valuable source of information on the Japanese Navy.[12] Throughout 1941 they portrayed an increasingly ominous picture of the Japanese Navy, making and, in late 1941, completing preparations for massive operations in the Far East. In October and November 1941 Sigint disclosed the intensification of Japanese naval espionage and reconnaissance, the concentration of large elements of the fleet in home ports (known traditionally to precede large-scale operations of their fleet), the tightening of communication security (change of call signs on November 1), and the massive reinforcement of the Japanese Mandated Islands.

By late November and early December 1941, Sigint revealed the further tightening of Japanese communications security (an additional change of call signs on December 1 and modifications of the Fleet Operational Code on December 4); the practice of communications deception; intensive naval activity in the vicinity of the Marshall Islands; the massive movements of troops, equipment, and warships from Chinese and Japanese ports into the South China Sea and Indochina; further intensification of intelligence collection in the Pacific; the completion of the overhaul of ships in Japanese ports, etc. All of the Japanese actions were interpreted, at the time, by U.S. naval intelligence as preparations for imminent large-scale military operations in Southeast Asia, which indeed they were.

Ambassador Grew in Tokyo made a contribution somewhat similar in nature to that of Purple. For while Grew was not privy to Magic and could not derive much relevant information from other sources at his disposal, he was, nonetheless, able to penetrate the Japanese veil of secrecy by virtue of being an extremely skillful reader of Japanese politics and the frame of mind of their leadership. Thus, despite the fact that he possessed no concrete evidence to suggest that Japan was indeed contemplating a war against the United States for late 1941, he warned Washington on November 3, 1941 against "any possible misconception of the capacity of Japan to rush headlong into a suicidal conflict with the United States" (PHA 1946 14:1056) and on November 17 emphasized "the need to guard against sudden Japanese naval or military action in such areas as are not now involved in the Chinese theater of operations" including "the probability of the Japanese exploiting every possible tactical advantage, such as surprise and initiative" (ibid. 27:58).

But for all Grew's skills and foresight, and as accurate and prescient as his warnings may seem in retrospect, we must not forget that at the time he had no hard evidence whatsoever to back his alarming reading of the situation, a fact he had made abundantly clear to his superiors. What Grew sent Washington was analysis and interpretation—not raw information. And in the absence of such information his analysis and interpretation were necessarily general and unsubstantiated (in the sense that they had, at the time, little corroborating evidence).

At the same time the media, both American and Japanese, could offer even less in the way of threat indicators than most of the other sources. For the numerous reasons elaborated above, the quality of the press coverage of Japanese-American relations and the Japanese war preparations had gone rapidly downhill throughout 1941, reaching an extremely low ebb toward the end of the year. Consequently, the contribution of the press to the realization of the prospect of war with Japan was at best marginal and indirect. Lacking any reliable and original information and woefully uninformed and unimaginative in its analysis, all the media could offer in the way of threat indicators was another general indication of the acuteness and importance of the Japanese-American conflict of interests of which the American government was only too well aware.

Other sources of threat indicators frequently discussed in the literature are foreign intelligence services and governments, in particular the British and the Dutch. As I suggested earlier, there is no doubt that the exchange of information on Japan as well as other forms of cooperation in intelligence matters did take place between the United States and both countries prior to December 7, 1941. There is also some evidence to suggest that at the time the United States was also reading secret British communications between London and Washington which contained, among other things, intelligence estimates on the situation in the Far East (Costello 1981:119, 630). The question we therefore have to address is whether the United States did acquire through this channel any advance word regarding Japan's intentions. The answer to this question assumes great significance, since at least two authors claim that the United States obtained through this channel definite "warning" on Japan's plans for attacks on both the British (Costello 1981:630, 633-34) and the Dutch possessions in Southeast Asia (Thorpe 1969:51-54), but it is nonetheless difficult to provide, at least directly. The relevant archives dealing with the exchange of information between the three countries are still largely inaccessible to the general public. Nevertheless, it is possible to check the claims of both Costello and Thorpe and to address the broader issue in a roundabout way—by determining whether either Britain or the Netherlands had themselves managed to acquire any advance word on Japan's plans for war against the United States which they could later pass on to the United States. Fortunately enough, excellent data on this issue is in the public domain.

As for the British intelligence, the most authoritative account of what it knew and estimated during World War II was recently provided by a team of leading British historians headed by Professor F. H. Hinsley of Cambridge University (Hinsley 1979, 1981). This team, which was given complete access to the relevant British archives, has concluded that (1) on issues pertaining to U. S.-Japanese relations the British had "no intelligence of any importance that was not available to the Americans who, indeed, had much that was not available in Whitehall" (Hinsley 1981; 2:76) and (2) the assessment by the British Joint Intelligence Subcommittee (of the Joint Chiefs of Staff) of the situation in the Far East just before the Japanese attack on Pearl Harbor "implicitly excluded the prospect of a direct Japanese attack on U.S. possessions," expected the Japanese to take action in the Far East that would "above all incur the least risk of war with the United States," and calculated only that "if Japan broke off the negotiations [with the United States] she would move against Thailand in early 1942 in order to be ready for an attack on Malaya in the favorable spring whether (ibid. 2:33). Hinsley's team has also determined that prior to the Pearl Harbor attack Britain provided the United States with information on Japan exclusively or almost exclusively in the form of evaluated intelligence (ibid. 2:55).

In view of Hinsley's finding, John Costello's recent claim that on November 26, 1941 Britain provided the United States with "irrefutable proof of an impending attack" which "must have been quite specific, absolutely believable, and from a trusted source" (Costello 1981:633–34) appears totally unfounded. Nor can one find a trace of such warning message in the American archives. Confidence in this conclusion is further reinforced when one realizes that Costello provides no hard evidence to support his thesis that such a warning message was ever sent by Britain, and that he can not really document either the contents of such warning or even its existence. In fact, Costello based his thesis on a rather elaborate series of conjectures and speculations relying on some highly ambiguous circumstantial evidence (ibid.:627–33). Hinsley's account also casts serious doubt on the story of Colonel Bonner Fellers, an American observer in Egypt, who claimed in 1967 to have been told by a British air marshall in Cairo on the morning of December 6, 1941 that "we have a secret signal Japan will strike the U.S. in twenty-four hours" (Toland 1982:296). In any event, even according to his own story, Colonel Fellers did not forward the information to Washington (ibid.).

The British, then, appear to have been in no position to supply the United States with any significant warning on the imminence of war with Japan. What about the Dutch? The available data which is, to be sure, incomplete, suggests that they had been in much the same position. Despite their impressive success in obtaining information regarding Japan's plans to attack territories in the Far East, they apparently had not acquired similar evidence with respect to Japan's intentions regarding the United States (Kahn 1982:39; Farago 1967:290). The data also reveals that prior to the outbreak of hostilities on December 7, 1941, the Dutch had been extremely cautious in their cooperation with the United States on intelligence as well as other operational matters, so as not to infringe on either their or U. S. neutrality (Haslach 1982). Finally, in the public record there is only one account of any warning of Japan's intentions supplied to the United States by the Dutch prior to the Pearl Harbor attack. It is the story of Brigadier General Elliot Thorpe, the U.S. military observer in Java, who claims to have sent Washington several such warnings in early December 1941 on the basis of information he supposedly received from the military commanders of the Netherlands East Indies, and which originated in Dutch cryptanalysis (Thorpe 1969:51–54).

But Thorpe's story does not square with either the record in Washington of the messages received from him during this period or with the testimonies of the key Dutch cryptographer and his Japanese translator who were the original source for his information (Kahn 1982:39-40; Haslach 1982). Even more important in this context is testimony given by the relevant Dutch cryptanalyst about the Dutch state of knowledge prior to December 7, 1941.[13] In his testimony, he noted that he received a solid conviction that a "Japanese armed attack was imminent" on the basis of Japanese code telegrams from all over the world that were intercepted and cracked by his bureau (primarily diplomatic), and then added "that the war would therefore come was obvious to us, but I know for certain that in Japanese telegrams, there was never direct mention of an attack on Pearl Harbor. *Where and when the first Japanese attack would explode was not possible to determine from the telegrams*" (Haslach 1982, emphasis added).

Before we proceed to review the specific signals available to the United States regarding an impending attack on Pearl Harbor, a brief summary of signals discussed in this section seems in order. The overall picture that emerges from the review of these signals can be summarized as follows. Prior to December 7, 1941, the United States possessed ample evidence that its relationship with Japan was highly strained and rapidly deteriorating; there was deadlock and suspension of negotiations, and probably the severing of diplomatic ties was also highly likely. The United States was also well informed that the Japanese were expecting their conflict with the United States to escalate, possibly to the point of open hostilities, and were implementing a series of elaborate precautionary measures to prepare for such a development and cushion its impact once it occurred. Finally, the United States had at its disposal plenty of information to indicate that Japan was actively preparing for massive military operations in the Far East and that the commencement of these operations was imminent and could take place at practically any time after late November 1941.

In the final hours prior to the Japanese attack the United States was also informed that Japan intended to suspend the bilateral negotiations on December 7, 1941. *But the United States did not possess any shred of evidence specifically revealing that Japan was actually going to attack it and that such an attack had been set for a specific time.* As Lyman Kirkpatrick has put it "the United States had no hard intelligence, no conclusive evidence as to what Japan might do . . . the Americans had no concept of the immensity of the disaster ahead" (1969:84–85).

### Specific Indicators of an Attack on Pearl Harbor

Our finding that the United States had not managed to acquire positive evidence of the Japanese intention to launch hostilities clearly addresses one part of the question of what the United States actually knew prior to December 7, 1941. It leaves unanswered, however, the questions of whether the United States did obtain, ahead of time, any information indicating that Pearl Harbor would be subject to an immediate Japanese air attack if and when war between the two countries did break out. It is these questions that I now intend to explore.

The most explicit indication of the Japanese plans to attack Pearl Harbor was also the earliest to arrive, and the only one on the issue to originate in Ambassador Grew in Tokyo. In *January 1941*, during a cocktail party, the Peruvian minister to Tokyo, Ricardo Rivera-Schreiber, informed Edward Crocker, first secretary of the U.S. Embassy in Tokyo, that "he had heard from many sources, including a Japanese one, that the Japanese military forces planned, in the event of trouble with the United States, to attempt a surprise mass attack on Pearl Harbor using all their military facilities." The Peruvian minister added that "although the project seemed fantastic, the fact that he had heard it from many sources prompted him to pass on the information" (PHA 1946 29:2145–46). Crocker hastily relayed the information to Grew, who consulted with his naval attaché and on his advice dispatched the warning in its entirety to Washington. While Grew was very suspicious about the accuracy of the information itself, he had no doubts about his source, and that prompted him to forward the information to Washington. Grew later testified that he had "full confidence" in the Peruvian minister, adding that "I knew him very well, I had known him for years, and I was quite certain that he would not mislead me in anything that he might pass on to me" (ibid. 14:1402).

I might add that in Washington Grew's information was received with even greater skepticism in view of its suspicious origins. As General Miles put it "it was inconceivable that any source in the know business would have communicated that to the Latin American Ambassador" (ibid. 2:819). There was also no corroborating evidence. But despite this assessment of the accuracy of the information in both Tokyo and Washington, it was not taken lightly. Grew's message was passed on without any delay from the State Department to both Army and Navy intelligence, and was brought up in the daily staff conference of the chief of naval operations, which in turn decided to forward it to the commander in chief of the U.S. Pacific Fleet in Hawaii. ONI passed on the information to Hawaii together with its low evaluation of its accuracy, and then proceeded with some detective work to determine the original source of the information. When this investigation revealed that the original source of Rivera-Schreiber's rumor was his Japanese cook, Grew's message was finally discarded and forgotten (Prange 1981:31–35; Wohlstetter 1962:368, 386; Dorowart 1983:179).

Irrespective of the authenticity of Rivera-Schreiber's rumor (and there are still some doubts whether it was authentic in the first place), the important point to observe here is that at the time the warning was not dismissed out of hand despite the lack of corroborating evidence and deeply rooted misperceptions about Japan (Prange 1981:32–35). Instead, it received further treatment and was finally dismissed only after it was determined that it had originated in a source with no conceivable access to the information provided.

Another source for some advance indicators of the Japanese plans regarding Pearl Harbor was Magic. Indications of Japan's interest in Pearl Harbor surfaced in Magic only in the context of one of its inferior (in terms of communication security) circuits, the one between Tokyo and its Consulate in Hawaii. On a couple of occasions after late September 1941, it revealed that the Foreign Ministry (which after the attack turned out to be only a cover for the naval intelligence) was instructing the Consulate to carry out on a routine basis an extensive and systematic surveillance of Pearl Harbor's naval installation, the Pacific Fleet, and the surrounding military installations (SRH-012 1942:142–44). After mid-November 1941, when relations with the United States further deteriorated, this source disclosed that Tokyo ordered the stepping up of surveillance and reporting on these targets (ibid.:158–60).

But while the information obtained through Magic clearly indicated Japan's operational interest in Pearl Harbor as a military target, none of its messages decoded and translated prior to the attack provided any specifics about the type of action, if any, that the Japanese were contemplating against Pearl Harbor or its timing (though some of the messages intercepted before but processed after the attack were much more revealing in this respect). Moreover, there was plenty of other evidence to suggest that Japan was expressing a similar, though possibly somewhat less urgent, interest in other Allied naval installations and ship movements elsewhere in the Pacific (ibid.:144–45, 148–53), and that some of the other information was explicitly requested for the Naval General Staff (ibid.:153).

Additional warning of Japan's operational interest in Pearl Harbor was apparently provided to the United States by the British intelligence in either one or two instances. The first instance concerns a leading British double agent by the name of Dusko Popov (code named Tricycle).[14] Popov revealed in his memoirs (Popov 1974: chs. 11, 13) that in August 1941 he was dispatched to the United States by his German employers to establish a new spy network, and was also ordered to collect information on a variety of issues, very prominent among which were military installations on the island of Oahu, where Pearl Harbor is located. According to Popov's story, he was given by the Germans a detailed questionnaire (which he memorized and immediately destroyed) regarding the military installations in Hawaii, and was asked to make a special trip to Hawaii in order to obtain the answers to the questionnaire. Popov claims that he immediately realized that the purpose of his mission to Hawaii was to collect operational intelligence for Japan in preparation for a torpedo air attack against Pearl Harbor, and that he notified his British operators to that effect. British intelligence then arranged for Popov to meet with FBI agents immediately upon his arrival in New York on August 10, 1941, at which time Popov reproduced for the FBI the detailed questionnaire on Hawaii given to him by the Germans, impressing upon the FBI the significance of the information.

The British faith in Popov, however, was apparently not shared by the FBI, particularly not by its boss J. Edgar Hoover, who personally met with Popov and treated him with great suspicion. While it is still unclear exactly how the information Popov provided regarding Hawaii was handled within the FBI, the records recently declassified by the FBI concerning Popov's affair conclusively reveal that Popov's questionnaire was disseminated by the FBI, at least to ONI, in the fall of 1941 (FBI 1941).[15] In any event, Popov's story is also confirmed by two high-level British intelligence officers, Ewen Montagu and John Masterman. Masterman even reproduced a copy of the questionnaire in the official history of the British double agent operation during World War II (Masterman 1972:79–80); Montagu, in Popov 1974:5–6).

Here I ought to point out, however, that even if we accept Popov's story as perfectly accurate, the reliability of the information he provided regarding Pearl Harbor must necessarily have been questionable. This is the case not only due to the inherent suspicion of double agents (especially ones operated by others), but also because Popov neither possessed a hard copy of the German questionnaire nor did he have any evidence to support his claim (if he indeed made one at the time) that the questionnaire was prepared by the Japanese who were planning to launch a torpedo attack against Pearl Harbor. Finally, even if taken at face value, the questionnaire, very much like the Magic intercepts, *could only indicate Japan's operational interest in Hawaii. It could not reveal any details regarding either decision to attack Pearl Harbor or the intended timing for such an attack.*[16]

Another threat indicator that may have originated in British sources is that supposedly dispatched to Washington by Major Warren Clear. Major Clear, a U.S. Army intelligence officer, was sent to the Far East on a secret intelligence mission in the spring of 1941. During that mission Clear supposedly learned from the high-ranking British officers with whom he had met that "the Japanese were planning to launch attacks against a chain of islands including Guam and Hawaii," information that he claimed to have relayed to Washington (Toland 1982:261). While other documents pertaining to Clear's mission and meetings in the Far East have been found in the archives, there is no trace of Major Clear's report regarding Pearl Harbor, nor is there any other information to corroborate his story. Once again, even if Major Clear's story is accurate (which in itself is at least questionable), his report would have necessarily been general and ambiguous, much more so even than the information obtained from other sources.

It is also possible that Washington received two additional reports on an impending Japanese attack on Pearl Harbor from other foreign sources, especially from the Dutch in the Netherlands East Indies (NEI) and from the Korean underground. The first report was that supposedly sent to Washington by Brigadier General Thorpe in Java, and perhaps also by the Dutch military attaché in Washington (Thorpe 1969:51–54; Toland 1982:281–82, 290, 322n.), on the basis of Dutch cryptanalysis of Japanese radio communication. As I have already pointed out, a very strong case has been made to the effect that the Dutch could not have warned the United States of a Japanese attack against Pearl Harbor or any other American target, for the simple reason that they themselves possessed no such warning. Moreover, the historical records suggest that the threatening information that did originate in Dutch sources in the NEI and was received in

Washington did not mention any threat to American targets in the Far East, only to British and Dutch territories.

The story of the second report is somewhat more complicated. It came from Kilsoo Haan, an agent for the Sino-Korean People's League. According to Haan's story, his friends in the Korean underground in Japan and Hawaii had managed to obtain in the fall of 1941 positive proof that the Japanese were going to attack Pearl Harbor before Christmas (Toland 1982:260). The proof had apparently been provided by a Korean working in the Japanese consulate in Honolulu who "had seen full blueprints of our [U.S.] above-water and underwater naval installations [in Hawaii] spread out on the consul's desk" (ibid.). Haan claims that he made several attempts to communicate the information to high officials of the State Department but that he "always ended up seeing very minor officials who took a very minor view of his warnings" (ibid.:261).

In late October 1941 Kilsoo Haan updated his warning, this time communicating it to Senator Guy Gillette of Iowa. Haan supposedly told Senator Gillette that "he had just discovered the Japanese were definitely planning an invasion for December or January" and that "it called for not only an attack on Pearl Harbor but simultaneous assaults on the Philippines, Midway, Guam, and Wake" (ibid.). Gillette then "alerted the State Department as well as Army and Navy intelligence" (ibid.). Finally, on December 4, 1941, Haan apparently telephoned Maxwell Hamilton of the State Department to inform him that the Korean underground had warned him [Haan] that "the Japanese would attack Pearl Harbor the coming weekend" (ibid.:289). Haan followed a telephone call to Hamilton with a long written report laying out the information on which his warning was based (ibid.).

If Haan's account is fully accurate, then he provided the United States with excellent information which closely approximates the ideal "warning" one would wish to obtain prior to a surprise attack. The fact of the matter is, however, that there is considerable doubt regarding the accuracy of Haan's story. The doubt does not pertain to Haan's claim that he provided the United States with some kind of warning on several occasions in

1941. This part of his story seems to be confirmed by several other oral and written testimonies (ibid.:260–61, 289–90, 311). The doubts have to do with what his reports actually contained, i.e., what he actually said *at the time* rather than what he claims now (with the benefit of hindsight) to have said then. Closer scrutiny of Haan's documents and testimony reveals that contrary to his and John Toland's claim, he did not possess anything even remotely resembling definite or conclusive proof that Japan was going to strike Pearl Harbor on the weekend of December 7. And just as importantly, this examination also suggests that in his communications with the various American personalities, Haan divulged to them (deliberately, or more likely inadvertently) that this was in fact the case.

While Haan may well have had solid evidence to suggest that Japan was intensely interested in Pearl Harbor's military installations, he apparently had nothing of the kind regarding the timing of the Japanese attack on Pearl Harbor. Haan therefore based his warning message on the impending Japanese attack on Pearl Harbor, to the extent that he indeed provided it, on loosely connected, fragmentary, highly ambiguous, and above all, circumstantial evidence. This evidence consisted of no more than Japanese and Italian newspaper articles, a year-old Japanese book, and a good deal of speculation.[17] Finally, whether Haan lacked any solid evidence to back up his warning message, or only projected the impression that this was the case, the result in either case may well have been to invoke strong skepticism toward his information by its recipients, on top of their previously existing suspicion of Haan himself and his cause.

Other than the signals discussed above, the only other indication of an approaching Japanese strike against Pearl Harbor to arrive prior to the event was tactical in nature, and reached only the local authorities in Hawaii. Approximately one hour before the first Japanese planes actually attacked their targets on Oahu, some of these planes were accidentally detected by one local radar station but were not identified as Japanese. Roughly at the same time a few Japanese submarines were spotted and attacked by ships and planes patrolling in "defensive waters" outside Pearl Harbor. Reports of all of these sightings arrived in the command centers only minutes before the attack started, and were being processed and verified when the bombs started falling on Oahu (Wohlstetter 1962:10–18).


We are now able to provide the second half of the answer to the question of the warning and other threat indicators possessed by the United States prior to the Pearl Harbor attack. The United States did manage to obtain a few bits of information, from several sources, suggesting that Japan was actively collecting detailed intelligence of an operational nature on Oahu and especially Pearl Harbor. The nature of the information sought by Japan, as well as the reports by Ambassador Grew and Kilsoo Haan, indicated that Pearl Harbor was a potential, perhaps even likely, target for a Japanese surprise attack in the event of a Japanese-American war. The United States was even informed that Japan had somewhat stepped up the collection of information on Pearl Harbor in late November 1941. But this is as far as the threat indicators went.

Even if we were to assume that prior to the Pearl Harbor attack the U.S. government actually had at its disposal *all* of the threat indicators that various scholars claim it had received, a far-fetched assumption indeed, we would still have to conclude that prior to December 7, 1941, the United States did not possess anything even remotely resembling hard evidence to suggest that Japan was actually set to attack any American target, let alone Pearl Harbor, on December 7, 1941. Nor, for that matter, did the United States have at its disposal any solid information to the effect that Japan was contemplating an air strike against Pearl Harbor as the opening move in a Japanese-American war, if and when such a war occurred. Moreover, what the United States *did* know of the Japanese fleet's capabilities made it appear almost certain that it could not carry out a massive air attack against Pearl Harbor due to the insufficient range of its carrier-based planes as well as the inability of its air-launched torpedoes to function properly in waters as shallow as those of Pearl Harbor

(Wohlstetter 1962:360–61, 369–70; Prange 1981:19–20, 103–6, 159–61, 260, 270, 320–21).

Finally, until approximately one hour before the bombs started falling on Oahu, the United States did not have even one bit of information indicating that *any* Japanese naval or aerial forces were anywhere in the general vicinity of the Hawaiian Islands, let alone within striking distance of Pearl Harbor. And while the United States could not determine with any certainty, on the basis of the information available to it at the time, the location of the First Japanese Air Fleet (the only Japanese force capable of carrying out a major attack against Pearl Harbor), it nonetheless had some good reasons to believe that this carrier force was still in Japanese home waters (Wohlstetter 1962:41–42).

In short, if I were to rank the quality of warning and other threat indicators available to the United States prior to the Pearl Harbor attack on several key dimensions (see chapter 1), I would say that the United States had plenty of information on the identity of enemy (who) and its motivation (why), but its information on the other critical dimensions—*whether* it was going to make a military move against the United States, *where* and *when* the move would take place, and *what* kind of move it had in mind—was appallingly poor, in terms of both quality and quantity.

I must now emphasize that my analysis has thus far dealt with only one rather narrowly defined question, namely how well informed of Japan's intentions the U. S. government was prior to December 7, 1941. The answer I have provided to this question is by no means self-contained. It falls far short of providing a complete explanation of the Pearl Harbor debacle, and in turn also raises three related questions: (1) Why was the United States not better informed? (2) What impact did the numerous organizational, bureaucratic, and individual pathologies (the case of competing explanations of the Pearl Harbor episode) have on the state of knowledge and the final outcome? (3) Did the United States make the best use of the information and capabilities that were after all available to it prior to the Pearl Harbor attack, or put differently—was the appalling state of unpreparedness at Pearl

Harbor inevitable in view of the warning and capabilities that it possessed prior to the attack? It is these three questions that I shall address in the next section. Before I proceed to do so, however, I must first put my answer on the warning question into the proper historical and analytical perspective.

My analysis of the warning issue has thus far examined U.S. information on Japanese intentions and capabilities solely as a function of acquisition of specific intelligence reports, however broadly defined. For my purposes here, I have consciously excluded the "lessons of history" as well as the "logic of the situation" as sources of warning, which is not to deny their importance as a basis for threat perception or their utility as a guide for action. As a matter of fact, a strong case can be made to the effect that much of the perception of threat in Washington in late 1941 did originate in exactly these sources. Specifically, the state of the negotiations with Japan and the historical record of the Japanese as perpetrators of surprise attacks (e.g., Port Arthur 1904) did seem to influence the assessment of the situation by some prominent American policymakers, President Roosevelt in particular.[18]

If I nonetheless decided to exclude these other sources of threat perception from discussion here, it was not for lack of awareness of their importance in generating a threat perception either in general or in the Pearl Harbor case in particular. Rather, I did so because the primary interest of this work is in threat indicators derived from intelligence, based on my conviction that the "logic of the situation" as well as the "lessons of the past" are necessarily amorphous, inconclusive, and highly subjective sources of threat indicators. An even more important justification for focusing strictly on intelligence as a source of threat indicators was the fact that practically all authors who have argued to date that the United States did possess advance warning of the Pearl Harbor attack referred to specific information received by the United States rather than to the "logic of the situation" or "lessons of the past" as its source. In any event, the complex relationship between the various sources of threat perception, as well as between threat perception and response, is explored in some detail in chapter 4.

I would also like to suggest that my findings concerning the quality of warning prior to Pearl Harbor do not seem all that startling when viewed from a historical perspective. After all, testimonies along these lines by some (though by no means all) of the key participants in the Pearl Harbor drama have been with us all along.[19] Thus, for example, Admiral Stark, the chief of naval operations (CNO) at the time of Pearl Harbor, had testified that "we had no definite information or evidence indicating an attack on the United States" (PHA 1946:18:2125). Similar views were also expressed by Arthur McCollum, then head of the Far Eastern Section of ONI, who said that "there was no (what we have come to term now) hard intelligence that Pearl Harbor, as such would be subject to an attack at the outbreak of the war" (1973:395; 1981:81, 85).

This somber assessment of the quality of information available to the United States on Japan's intentions is further supported by the testimony in front of the Joint Congressional Committee investigating the Pearl Harbor disaster by Lieutenant Commander Alvin Kramer who was, prior to the Pearl Harbor attack, the head of the translation and dissemination branch of the Communication Security Section in the Office of Naval Communications (OP-20-GZ). Kramer, who was truly the custodian and distributor of naval cryptanalysis, was asked by Senator Lucas of the Joint Committee, "From all the information you received through Magic, including the much discussed purported winds execute message, was there even received a single word, line, phrase or sentence that would have led you to believe that Pearl Harbor was going to be struck by the Japanese on December 7, 1941," to which he responded, "There never was, sir" (PHA 1946:9:4148).

Since I have reached practically the same conclusions in my independent study, I am inclined to suggest that time has, perhaps, come to accept the statements quoted above at face value rather than treat them as proof of a grand conspiracy.


In this section I will begin to explore some of the implications of my earlier findings regarding the availability of

warning in the context of a broader explanation of the Pearl
Harbor episode as well as the surprise phenomenon in general.
In the process I shall address the three questions formulated
several pages ago. The first issue I would like to tackle is why
the United States was not better informed of what the Japanese
were up to prior to December 7, 1941.

At the outset I wish to point out that my conclusion
that the United States possessed no positive warning on Japan's
intention to attack the United States in general, and Pearl Harbor
in particular, is tantamount to saying that the Pearl Harbor *surprise*
(as distinguished from unpreparedness) was essentially a failure of
*collection*, not of analysis. This novel conclusion, which was also
recently reached by David Kahn on the basis of an independent
investigation of the issue (Kahn 1982:37) is hardly surprising when
one recalls our earlier discussion of the collection situation prior
to December 7, 1941. It still remains to be explained, however,
why the United States was not better equipped to collect information on Japan prior to the outbreak of the war. Here, I can
only offer some brief thoughts on the issue. A more comprehensive
study of this issue is beyond the scope of the present treatment,
and will have to await future research.

As Kahn has correctly observed, the Pearl Harbor
collection failure "was due to long-standing financial, political, and
foreign policy factors in America" (ibid.). To this list of factors I
would add naiveté, morality, and inexperience. In the interwar
period, political considerations (in both foreign and domestic policy)
were clearly important in denying U.S. intelligence the use of
several collection methods that would have had great potential
for revealing Japan's intentions and capabilities. Collection methods, such as espionage and eavesdropping, were ruled out by the
political leadership on the grounds that they were deemed morally
unacceptable in peacetime and their use also entailed some risk
of political embarrassment (Kahn 1967:5, 360; Farago 1967: ch. 5;
Corson 1977: ch. 3; Dorowart 1983: ch. 12). Economic considerations coupled with naiveté and inexperience made matters even
worse, by restricting and constraining collection activities that were
neither politically sensitive nor morally unacceptable. Naiveté and

inexperience obscured the critical need for strategic intelligence in peacetime; in a time of economic depression this was tantamount to denying intelligence the scarce resources it needed to perform its warning duty. The combined impact of all of these factors was to retard, curtail, and even eliminate preexisting collection activities, as well as to prevent, or at least impede, the development of new ones. What little collection activity remained or survived this policy was operating largely ineffectively.

With the growing international tension in the late 1930s, the outbreak of World War II, the increasing involvement of the United States in the defense of Britain and later also the Soviet Union, and especially the deterioration of U.S.-Japanese relations in 1940 and 1941, the prevailing attitude in Washington toward intelligence underwent a significant change. Thus, for example, Henry Stimson, who as Secretary of State in 1929 disbanded the Department's cryptanalytical unit, saying that "gentlemen do not read each other's mail" (Kahn 1967:5, 360), now as Secretary of War supervised the expansion of a similar unit within the War Department. But the change in the attitude of the political leadership toward intelligence was gradual (Corson 1977: ch. 3; Dorowart 1983: ch. 12), and its translation into an improved collection capability consequently slow (Dorowart 1983:177-78). Furthermore, the process of upgrading the collection capability on Japan also involved a significant time lag having to do with the complexity and difficulty inherent in any such process, and suffered from the additional problem of having to assign most resources to the European theater which was assigned the first priority (ibid.:180). It therefore did not proceed very far before December 7, 1941. What was done in this area prior to the outbreak of the war was both too little and too late to permit the effective harvesting of existing sources (e.g., Magic), let alone the development of new ones. It thus failed to prevent the emergence of a critical gap in information on Japan which could be aptly exploited by the Japanese.

Having examined the U.S. collection capability prior to the Pearl Harbor attack, highlighted its failure to forewarn the United States, and discussed what appear to be the underlying causes of that failure, I would now like to integrate these findings into a broader explanation of the Pearl Harbor episode. In particular, I wish to contrast my own explanation of the surprise at Pearl Harbor with competing explanations suggested by Wohlstetter and others.

Recall that earlier I framed my analysis of the threat indicators issue in a way that was least likely to bear out my hypothesis that no solid *warning* was available to the United States prior to the Pearl Harbor attack. I have deliberately assumed that all the signals acquired prior to the event reached Washington in their pure form (i.e., in isolation from background noise) and without delay, and were fully and efficiently disseminated within the U.S. government. Even under this most favorable (indeed unrealistic) assumption, it was not possible to document the existence prior to December 7, 1941 of any hard evidence of Japan's intentions anywhere in the U.S. government. I therefore concluded, with some confidence, that no such warning was ever obtained by the United States. If this is indeed the case there are strong grounds for rejecting all the competing explanations of the Pearl Harbor *surprise* (as distinguished from unpreparedness—see below) which pointed to pathologies in the processing, evaluation, dissemination, and consumption of the available warning as the cause of surprise. Specifically, we can dismiss Wohlstetter's explanation centering on the importance of the background noise in obscuring the signals and causing the surprise (Wohlstetter 1962:387ff.). In view of the paucity of signals, in important respects even their complete absence, the abundance of noise was immaterial.

By rejecting the explanations of the Pearl Harbor surprise of Wohlstetter and others, I do not mean to imply that numerous pathologies in these important areas did not exist at the time—clearly they did. Nor, for that matter, do I intend to suggest that these pathologies did not have any impact on the final outcome, namely unreadiness—they certainly did (see below). Rather, I would contend that the various individual, organizational, and bureaucratic pathologies played no important role in causing the Pearl Harbor surprise. It must, nonetheless, be conceded that it is far from certain that such factors would not have produced surprise even if the United States had been more successful in obtaining early warning of the specific Japanese plans. The nature of the case at hand simply does not permit any valid judgment to be made on this last issue, and I can only address it indirectly through the study of other cases. This task will be attempted in subsequent chapters.

The third and final question we ought to consider here is whether the U.S. government had made the best use of the information that was after all available to it prior to the Pearl Harbor attack. Put differently, the question is whether a Pearl Harbor disaster, at least one of such magnitude, was inevitable in view of the state of knowledge of Japan's intentions and capabilities. The answer to this question is perhaps the most controversial of them all since it is to a large degree a matter of individual judgment, judgment which is necessarily made in retrospect and with at least some benefit of hindsight. Nevertheless, I do hope that an awareness of these problems as well as my framework for analysis (outlined in chapter 1 and employed here) will enable the introduction into the analysis of a sufficient degree of objectivity to make the exercise worthwhile.

The issue of the U.S. government's use of the information at its disposal prior to the Pearl Habor attack can be conveniently disaggregated into three complimentary subquestions: (1) Were the authorities in Washington fully aware of the severity of the situation reflected in the information available to them? (2) If they indeed were so aware, was their alarm adequately translated into orders and actions (if they were not aware, why)? (3) Were the local commanders in Hawaii adequately (though not necessarily fully) informed, through either operational orders or background information, of the degree of alarm in Washington, so that they could have reasonably been expected to take more comprehensive measures than they actually did? Let me address one question at a time.

While I have previously established the fact that the U.S. government possessed no concrete evidence regarding Japan's intentions and was unaware of the location of the First Japanese Air Fleet (i.e., the key aircraft carriers), I have also concluded that in late 1941 ample evidence *was* available to the United States to suggest that relations with Japan were becoming increasingly tense, with further deterioration being possible and even probable. I am fully convinced that in late 1941 the civilian and military authorities in Washington (but only in Washington) were very much aware of the explosive nature of American-Japanese relations, which is not necessarily to say that they were either fully or even properly informed of the developments. It only implies that the reading of the situation by the top civilian and military leaders in Washington was at least as alarming, and perhaps even more so, than could have been expected on the basis of *all* the information available to the U.S. government at the time. As Ben Zvi has correctly pointed out, the prevailing mood in Washington in late November and early December 1941 seemed to reflect the realization that negotiations with Japan were, for all practical purposes, deadlocked and that an outbreak of hostilities with Japan was certain and only a matter of a short time (1976:83–85, 137, 43). There is ample evidence to support Ben Zvi's observation in the statements made and actions taken by the top U.S. policymakers in the two weeks preceding the Pearl Harbor attack; some of this evidence is cited below.

On November 25, 1941, a regularly scheduled session of the War Council took place in Washington. In this session the President brought up the subject of U.S.-Japanese relations and observed that "we [are] to be attacked perhaps [as soon as] next Monday, for the Japanese are notorious for making an attack without warning"[20] (Wohlstetter 1962:239). Secretary of War Stimson, who participated in the meeting and recorded its contents in his diary, noted that the essence of the problem discussed by the War Council was how to maneuver Japan "into the position of firing the first shot without allowing too much danger to ourselves" (ibid.). Admiral Stark (the CNO), who also participated in the War Council meeting, discussed it in a letter he sent the same day to Admiral Kimmel in Hawaii. Stark pointed out that neither the President nor the Secretary of State "would be surprised over a Japanese surprise attack." He added that there were some (apparently referring to the President and Secretary of State) who thought that an attack on the Philippines was likely to occur, and while he personally did "not give it the weight others do" he included that possibility in the letter because "of the strong feeling among some people" (ibid.:255).

An even clearer realization of the certainty, if not imminence, of an armed conflict emerged among the top U.S. leadership on November 26 and 27 following the virtual collapse of the negotiations and the detection of Japanese naval movement in the Far East, particularly off the coast of Formosa (ibid.:243). On November 27 Secretary of State Hull told Secretary of War Stimson of the negotiations with Japan, saying something to the effect that "he had broken the whole matter off" and adding specifically, "I have washed my hands of it and it is now in the hands of you and Knox—the Army and the Navy" (ibid.:258). Even Stanley Hornbeck, Hull's chief adviser on Far Eastern affairs, who was convinced at the time that the Japanese wanted desperately to avoid war with the United States and that war with Japan was not imminent in late November 1941, estimated that there was even a chance that the United States and Japan would be at war before March 1, 1942 (ibid.:265). Finally, upon the receipt of additional information on Japan's military movements, and particularly after being shown the first thirteen parts of the Japanese fourteen-part message, the President remarked "this means war" (ibid.:273).

The alarm of the top U.S. leadership over developments in their relationship with Japan, and their concern for the possibility of an imminent outbreak of hostilities, was not confined to their statements—it was reflected in their actions as well. Successive alert messages sent to the military commanders in the Pacific by both the army and navy in the last week of November clearly manifested great alarm over Japan's intentions. These messages (see SRH-012 1942:15-16) specifically informed the local commanders of the practical termination of the negotiations with

Japan. They explicitly warned that "a surprise aggressive move by [Japan] in any direction including attack on the Philippines and Guam is a possibility" (navy, November 24), that an "aggressive move by Japan is expected within the next few days" (navy, November 27), and that "Japanese future action unpredictable but hostile action possible at any moment" (army, November 27; navy, November 28). The alert message sent by the Navy Department on November 27 was explicitly labeled "a war warning."

The messages sent by Washington to the military commanders in the Pacific not only provided information but also authorized a series of precautionary measures that were previously forbidden for fear of provoking the Japanese, including, for example, the sanctioning of aerial reconnaissance missions over Japan's Mandated Islands (Prange 1981:461–63). The threat perception of the U.S. authorities produced not only military but also diplomatic action, as is clearly evident from the last-minute attempt by President Roosevelt (December 6, 1941) to communicate with Emperor Hirohito in order to prevent the war (ibid.:451–52, 467–68, 477).

It is indeed striking that the U.S. government had reached such an alarming, one may say even prescient, reading of the situation in the absence of specific advance warning of Japan's intentions. The top policymakers in Washington could have hardly made better use of the information available to them, as their reading of the situation was not only compatible with, but frequently actually transcended, the information at hand. This was dramatically evident in the almost universal reaction in Washington on the morning of December 7 to the last part of the fourteen-part Japanese message. Into a message whose substance contained no more than an announcement of the suspension of diplomatic negotiations with the United States at a specific time, the U.S. government read a declaration of war and immediately proceeded to order decisive military action. Thus the CNO, for example, authorized unrestricted air and submarine warfare against Japan on the basis of this message even *before* the Japanese attack actually took place (SRH-012 1942:188; Prange 1981:485–98). All of this demonstrates that prior to December 7, noise, individual misperceptions, bureaucratic politics and organizational pathologies, the "cry wolf" phenomenon, Japanese deception, and the like were all largely insignificnt in shaping the threat perception of the U.S. government in *Washington*. The information at hand as well as the logic of the situation obviously prevailed.[21]

But the prescience and anxiety in Washington, impressive as they may have been, somehow were not translated into military alert in either Hawaii or the Philippines; hence the tragic outcome of the Japanese attacks on December 7. The final question, therefore, is: What happened in the crucial link between Washington and the Pacific theater, and why? The essence of the problem seems to have been the failure to get the military commanders in the Pacific, in the Philippines as well as in Hawaii, to share Washington's assessment of the situation and act accordingly. It was a failure of communication in the broadest sense of the word, one of commission as well as omission, for which both sides (the military chiefs in Washington and the theater commanders in the Pacific) deserve part of the blame. Let us now consider the roots of this problem in both Washington and the Pacific.

Washington's contribution to the communication problem was essentially twofold. On the one hand, the military commanders in Washington failed to provide their theater commanders with explicit and precise orders for action, and on the other hand they deprived these commanders, much more so in Hawaii than in the Philippines, of much useful information essential for making an independent assessment of the situation and interpreting correctly the messages sent from Washington. Both of these problems were particularly acute in the few days preceding the Japanese attack, in which the messages originating in Washington were alarming in tone but rather cryptic in substance. They were uninformative, vague, ambivalent, and even misleading as an operational guide. The only precautionary measures explicitly ordered by Washington as this time were the destruction of codes and papers in the American missions in the various danger spots throughout the Far East, and the protection of personnel, property, and equipment against subversive activity (sabotage, propaganda, espionage, etc.).

Washington's failure to communicate more effectively with its commanders in the Pacific can be attributed, in part, and only in part, to the lack of advance warning of Japan's plans. For however sober its assessment of the situation may have been, in the absence of definite and specific warning to the effect that Japanese *military* action against it (as distinguished from the British and the Dutch) was imminent, the U.S. policymakers could hardly risk ordering or sanctioning vigorous, extensive, and overt precautionary measures in the Far East.[22] Such measures could not only alarm the civilian population but also provoke Japan prematurely. After all, the American military buildup in the Pacific still had a long way to go (even in the Philippines, which was relatively well defended compared to Hawaii) before the United States could comfortably confront the Japanese, and buying time was therefore of the essence.

Ignorance of Japan's intentions affected not only the vigor of Washington's reaction to the emerging threat but its direction as well, and consequently also its efficacy. Since the policymakers in Washington could only speculate about the most likely target in the event of Japan's attack on U.S. possessions, they tended to emphasize, in the messages they sent to the Pacific, the danger to the more obvious targets, namely the Philippines and Guam, thereby at least implicitly minimizing the prospects of an attack on Pearl Harbor. This omission was not lost on the commanders in Hawaii, who believed it was deliberate, which it may well have been—an attack on Pearl Harbor was simply not expected or anticipated in Washington.

Nevertheless, as I have emphasized above, only part of Washington's share of the communication failure can be attributed to the inadequacy of warning. While lack of warning can possibly account for some of the most glaring deficiencies in the messages sent to the Pacific, it cannot by itself explain either the failure to provide the theater commanders with much-needed information available in Washington, or the total absence of oversight over the implementation of the alert measures suggested by Washington. Thus, for example, it is virtually impossible to explain on the basis of the lack of advance warning the army's lack of response to General Short's (the army commander in Hawaii) cable of November 29 where he advised, in reply to the alert message of November 27, that he was taking precautionary measures only against sabotage and local subversion and not against frontal attack (Wohlstetter 1962:67–68). To account for all of these Washington blunders I, like others researching the Pearl Harbor episode, resort to an explanation based on bureaucratic politics, organizational behavior, and the like. I suspect that bureaucratic infighting within the navy, as well as between the navy and the army (ibid.:317–19, 286–89), may well have had a particularly detrimental impact in this context. Still, I wish to reiterate that unlike many other scholars, I believe that these factors were important in shaping the outcome only in this rather narrow and circumscribed context.

When we now turn to analyze the roots of failure that lie in Hawaii itself, we encounter once more a situation where only part of the problem can be explained in terms of the quality of the advance warning. For one thing, ignorance of Japan's intentions was not complete. At least some evidence, however fragmentary and unreliable, existed in both Washington and Hawaii to suggest that Pearl Harbor was a possible target for a Japanese surprise air attack. Moreover, even if the lack of more explicit, specific, and credible warning was enough to secure the Japanese the element of surprise, it was not, by itself, sufficient to assure that Pearl Harbor would be caught completely off-guard and unable to counter their attack. The point here is that intuition, foresight, or simply greater caution are in a sense a "functional equivalent" of conclusive warning. They could have conceivably substituted and partially compensated for lack of advance warning or explicit orders from Washington.

Several senior military officers in Hawaii (both army and navy) indeed displayed this kind of intuition and foresight on several occasions, the latest one being in early 1941. These officers were not only acutely aware of the vulnerability of Pearl

Harbor to a Japanese surprise air attack, but they actually predicted in great detail and with uncanny accuracy the method by which such an operation would be carried out. They even went so far as to demonstrate the feasibility of such a strike and to suggest some countermeasures that could be adopted by the local commanders in Hawaii in order to foil such attack (Prange 1982:93–97; Wohlstetter 1962:22–23). But when these predictions and recommendations were made hardly any evidence was available to suggest that Japan was even actively considering Pearl Harbor as a target, and the resources needed to carry out the countermeasures on a routine basis were very scarce and extremely costly to implement. Consequently, their endeavour, despite endorsement in principle by top navy officials, was relegated to no more than an interesting mental exercise.

By late 1941, when somewhat more explicit warning with respect to Japan's intentions regarding Pearl Harbor had accumulated, little in the way of intuition, foresight, or even prudence was evident in Hawaii. The unavailability of explicit warning, the ambiguity of the directives from Washington, and the absence of foresight and intuition were further exacerbated by the scarcity of resources. No alert measures could be implemented without severely jeopardizing much-needed training and sacrificing long-term readiness, not to mention alarming the civilian population, which was explicitly prohibited by Washington.

The difficult circumstances notwithstanding, in the final analysis I still have a hard time accepting the claim of the top military commanders in Hawaii that the situation as it presented itself to them at the time did not call for any more elaborate precautionary measures than those they actually implemented. In a situation where they were aware of their vulnerability to a Japanese strike, their critical gap in knowledge about the Japanese fleet, and the degree of tension in the American-Japanese relations, at least some reinforcement of the early warning apparatus would have been warranted. I, like some other scholars, attribute the fact that such measures were not taken to a variety of factors, in particular individual misperceptions, group dynamics, organizational and bureaucratic pathologies, and the like. I ought to make it explicit, however, that my conclusions in this context are to a very large degree a matter of judgment. Since I apply different standards of evidence than those commonly used by military boards of inquiry, I must introduce the conventional caveat that my judgment in this respect is necessarily influenced by hindsight, and in this sense at least partially resembles the verdict of a "Monday morning quarterback." It should therefore be treated with some caution.

We have now come a full circle. I started out by trying to determine whether the United States possessed advance warning of the Japanese plans in general, and their intention to attack Pearl Harbor on December 7 in particular. I have established that no conclusive warning on either point was available, essentially making the Pearl Harbor *surprise* an intelligence collection failure. After exploring the roots of this collection failure I integrated the explanation of the Pearl Harbor surprise into a broader explanation of the December 7 debacle in Hawaii.

I determined that despite the unavailability of conclusive warning in either Washington or Hawaii, a remarkably alarming picture of Japanese-American relations did emerge in Washington in the fortnight preceding the attack on Pearl Harbor. I also established that this alarm was somehow not translated into a similar state of alarm (and concomitant precautionary measures) in Hawaii. I traced back the causes of this communication failure, broadly defined, to a variety of factors operating both in Hawaii and Washington including, among other things, operational and political constraints, bureaucratic politics, organizational behavior and, of course, inadequate warning.

Lastly, a word with an outlook to the future. An odd process has been at work since shortly after the attack on Pearl Harbor. The number of warnings received by the United States prior to December 7, 1941, keeps on growing and like a fine wine, so does their quality seem to improve with the passage of time. To a large degree, this process appears to be a product of revisionist historians at work trying to uncover historical evidence to clear one or another of the involved officials, to incriminate President Roosevelt or some other leading public figure and/or support the "conspiracy theory." Since the process is largely independent of declassification of the relevant historical data, it is not likely to end any time soon. The latest example of the genre is the book *And I Was There* (Layton 1985) that came out when this book was already in press. Nevertheless, on the basis of this study I am reasonably confident that conclusive evidence is already available to support my contention that the causes of the Pearl Harbor surprise were essentially structural, having to do with the nature of the American intelligence collection apparatus at the time. I therefore do not expect the incessant search for additional warnings ever to produce the "smoking gun."

# Chapter 3

# Prelude to Midway

"You are supposed to tell us what the Japanese are going to do and I will then decide whether it's good or bad and act accordingly" (Admiral Nimitz to Commander Rochefort *before* the Battle of Midway; Prange 1982:20).

"[Your breakthrough] resulted in as clear a picture as any commander would want to have" (Admiral Numitz to Commander Rochefort *after* the battle of Midway; Potter 1976:101).

Midway was a victory of intelligence, bravely and wisely applied." (Admiral Samuel Elliot Morison; Morison 1949:158)

**Barely six months** had elapsed since the Japanese had successfully attacked the U.S. Pacific Fleet in Pearl Harbor, and they were already preparing for what they hoped would be the decisive naval battle of the Pacific war. Reeling with confidence from an uninterrupted string of victories since December 7, 1941, and enjoying an overwhelming but transitory naval superiority, the Japanese fleet was looking for an opportunity to lure the U.S. Pacific Fleet into a head-on confrontation. The invasion of Midway, a strategically located atoll 1,100 miles west of Pearl Harbor, struck the Japanese as an operation that would create exactly such an opportunity. The Japanese planners envisaged the Pacific Fleet reacting to their invasion of Midway by sailing to its defense, only to discover the bulk of Japan's fleet ready and waiting for them. The Combined Fleet would then be able to take advantage of the element of surprise and bring to bear their substantial local superiority to inflict on the United States a resounding defeat. Such a defeat, the Japanese believed, would finally seal their naval hegemony in the Pacific, isolate Australia, expose the West Coast of the United States to Japanese attacks, and they hoped, also bring the United States to the negotiating table on its knees.

In its planning and early implementation stages, the Japanese Midway campaign bore a great resemblance to their attack on Pearl Harbor. The target (i.e., the U.S. Pacific Fleet) and goals, the critical importance of the element of surprise for the success of the operation, the high stakes for both sides, and even the core of the Japanese forces participating in the operation were all very similar in both instances. And while some differences none-theless existed between the two operations, including the fact that the two countries had already been at war for over six months before the Midway operation took place, the most significant difference between the two cases was in the outcome. An almost total American surprise and overwhelming Japanese military success at Pearl Harbor was replaced by a remarkably accurate American threat perception and a stinging Japanese defeat at Midway.

Thanks to advance knowledge of Japanese plans, re-markable planning and command, and a fair bit of luck, the U.S. Pacific Fleet was able to ambush two of the Japanese task forces taking part in the Midway operation. In the battle that ensued, the Japanese experienced their first major defeat of the Pacific War, losing four aircraft carriers and one heavy cruiser to one aircraft carrier and one destroyer for the United States.[1] Moreover, Japan's defeat also had the effect of checking its expansion in Southeast Asia, while providing the United States with a badly needed breathing spell to rebuild its Pacific Fleet, so badly damaged in the Pearl Harbor attack.

This chapter, however, does not seek to advance an explanation of the American victory in Midway, important and impressive as it may have been. The study of Midway and a comparison to Pearl Harbor (chapter 2) are pursued here as means to an end rather than an ends in themselves. By looking in some depth at an instance of surprise side by side with an abortive surprise situation, and by controlling for their commonalities while contrasting their differences, I hope to generate some new insights into the surprise phenomenon in general.

In view of this goal, I shall not discuss in any detail the actual conduct of the Battle of Midway, which is not only peripheral to our interest here but is also described in great detail elsewhere (see Prange 1982; Morison 1949; and Lord 1967). Indeed, we need to focus on the American intelligence buildup to the battle, the consumption of intelligence estimates warning of the Japanese campaign, and the response to this warning by the operational authorities (primarily Admirals Nimitz and King). These developments created the opportunity that was later skillfully exploited to give the United States what was later called "an incredible victory" (Lord 1967), "the turning point in the Pacific war" (Nimitz) and "the first decisive defeat suffered by the Japanese Navy in 350 years" (King). And they also provide the testing grounds for my hypotheses regarding the origins of both successful and abortive strategic surprise attempts.

This chapter opens with a brief and selective summary of Japan's plans for the Midway campaign, which were carried out almost without a hitch until the confrontation with the U.S. Navy actually took place. It then proceeds to examine the accumulation, in the hands of the U.S. naval intelligence, of raw data regarding Japan's intentions and preparations. I then document the translation of this raw data into coherent intelligence estimates and warning, the consumption of this warning, the response to it, and the obstacles both had to overcome. Finally, I will contrast the intelligence success at Midway with its failure in the Pearl Harbor case, and draw attention to some more general lessons that can be derived from these episodes.

It was in late December 1941 or early January 1942 that the Japanese initiated the planning for what later culminated in the Battle of Midway (Prange 1982:14). The planning originated with Admiral Yamamoto, the commander in chief of the Combined Fleet of the Imperial Japanese Navy and the man who conceived the attack on Pearl Harbor. Yamamoto was dissatisfied with the outcome of the Pearl Harbor operation, despite its otherwise impressive tactical success, since he realized that it fell far short of its intended strategic objectives. The aircraft carriers—the fighting core of the U.S. Pacific Fleet and the primary target of the Japanese attack—had been out at sea during the time of the Pearl Harbor raid and thus escaped unscathed. As a result, the Pacific Fleet, though crippled by the attack, remained a menace to the Japanese "grand design" for Southeast Asia. And American leaders had not reached the level of desperation that would lead them to negotiate a favorable agreement with Japan, as the Japanese had hoped they would if the Pearl Harbor operation succeeded. To make matters worse, time was running out for Japan. The American industrial base, with which Yamamoto was all too familiar, was now mobilized for the war effort and threatened to reverse, before long, the balance of power in the Pacific. Under the circumstances, it was Yamamoto's conviction that Japan could hope to attain its original goals only by quickly launching another bold move in the Pacific, and he was determined to give it a try before it became too late to do so.

Thus, in early 1942, Yamamoto began looking for a head-on confrontation with the Pacific Fleet in which he could bring to bear his overwhelming, but transitory, superiority in ships, planes, experienced crews, armaments, etc. In order to lure the Pacific Fleet into such a confrontation, however, Yamamoto had to overcome a major obstacle. American naval authorities, in both Hawaii and Washington, were fully aware of their weakness in the Pacific and were thus extremely reluctant to commit what little forces they had to a frontal confrontation whose results could prove disastrous for them. Yamamoto therefore had to devise a way of drawing the Americans into such an encounter despite their strong disinclination. And this is where Yamamoto hit upon the idea of using an invasion of Midway as bait for the Pacific Fleet. Midway, he reasoned, was a place the Americans would have to defend and thereby also confront the Japanese fleet.

The plan devised by Admiral Yamamoto and his lieutenants for the Midway campaign (codenamed "Operation MI") called for an operation that would be extremely large and complicated. It required the participation of the lion's share of the Imperial Navy, 145 vessels in all, divided into five major independent forces, some of which were divided again into two or more groups. The forces were to carry out three separate but interrelated actions: occupation of the Western Aleutians, occupation of Midway, and a fleet engagement.[2] The following is a brief description of the plan for each of these actions in the chronological order in which they were supposed to be carried out.

The first action to take place, according to plan, was to be a June 3 attack on the American base in Dutch Harbor by a small Japanese task force headed by Admiral Hosogaya. It was to be followed by an occupation of the islands of Kiska and Adak-Attu in the West Aleutians. This operation (codenamed "Operation AO") had little merit on its own and was primarily designed for diversion purposes, to deflect the attention of the Pacific Fleet from the impending attack on Midway.

The invasion of Midway, the second part of the overall Japanese campaign, was to begin on June 4 with the bombing of Midway by carrier-based planes from Admiral Nagumo's "carrier strike force." The air attack was to be followed on the evening of the next day, June 5, by an occupation of the atoll to be carried out by an "occupation force" supported by Admiral Kondo's Second Fleet. This part of the operation, while of somewhat greater significance than the preceding one, was also seen by the Japanese primarily as a means to an end rather than an end in itself. The attack on and occupation of Midway was to be used first and foremost as a bait to lure the Pacific Fleet into an engagement with the Imperial Navy.

The third and by far the most important part of the operation was supposed to be a major confrontation between the Imperial Navy and the Pacific Fleet under circumstances most favorable to the Japanese. According to plan, the engagement between the forces was to take place only after, and in response to, the Japanese attack on Midway. It was expected to occur as soon as the Pacific Fleet sailed from Pearl Harbor to the rescue of Midway (1,100 miles to its west) and ran into an ambush by two Japanese task forces, Admiral Nagumo's "carrier striking force" and Admiral Yamamoto's "Main Body."

Japan's operational plan also called for additional activities of an auxiliary nature in conjunction with the Midway
operation. These were designed primarily for intelligence gathering
and deception purposes. One such activity was to be a reconnaissance mission over Pearl Harbor by Japanese sea planes (codenamed "Operation K"). This mission was planned for the week
preceding the attack on Midway and was supposed to provide the
Japanese with up-to-date information on the whereabouts of the
Pacific Fleet. Two additional activities in support of the Midway
operation were to be carried out by Japanese submarines. Several
submarines were to launch attacks on Sydney and Madagascar
prior to the Midway operation in order to throw the Americans
off-guard. Other Japanese submarines were expected to sight and
report the movements of the Pacific Fleet, as well as attack it,
once it emerged from Pearl Harbor in response to the Japanese
attack on either Midway or the Aleutians.

What is truly striking about this overall plan for the
Midway operation is not only its great complexity, but also the
tremendous emphasis assigned by the Japanese planners to intelligence collection as well as cover and deception activities. Both
of these features of the plan clearly reflect Japan's realization that
it was about to pursue a high cost, high risk operation, the success
of which depended to no small degree on the attainment of
complete surprise and the possession of accurate up-to-the-minute
intelligence on their adversary. As will become apparent in the
pages that follow, the Japanese failed to meet either of these
necessary requirements, and this failure cost them dearly. It left
them dangerously vulnerable to American counteraction. That this
was the case, however, only became apparent to the Japanese on
June 4. For until that day their preparations for the entire campaign
proceeded rather smoothly and largely according to plan.


I will now proceed to examine the process by which
the United States familiarized itself with the Japanese plans and
reacted to them. This will be done in three stages. I will look at
the sources of information on the Imperial Navy's war plan

possessed by the United States at the time, review the information actually derived from these sources and then, in the next section, examine the consumption of this intelligence by the operational authorities.

## Sources of Information

In chapter 2 I examined in some detail the sources of information on Japan that were at the disposal of the United States prior to the Pearl Harbor attack. I paid particularly close attention to collection assets with the potential for systematic detection of Japanese naval plans, only to determine that prior to December 7, 1941 these were either very poor or completely nonexistent. Much of what was said there about the collection conditions prevailing prior to the attack on Pearl Harbor also holds true for the period between December 7, 1941 and June 1, 1942. There is, however, one major exception. While most American sources of information on the Japanese Navy (such as Magic) had been drying up in the days prior to Pearl Harbor and continued to do so in the days that followed (McCollum 1973:461), one cluster of sources of critical importance—Comint, and especially cryptanalysis—did spring into life after the beginning of the war. And it was this source that provided the United States with a truly comprehensive and highly accurate warning of the Midway operation.

While the outbreak of the American-Japanese war had a highly adverse impact on most other sources of information on Japan, it had exactly the opposite effect on Comint.[3] The commencement of hostilities accelerated considerably the pace of operations and other events and led to the geographical dispersal of many units of the Japanese Combined Fleet. These developments, in turn, forced the Imperial Navy to resort to much more intensive and extensive use of radio communications. They also made tight communications security much more difficult to maintain. As a result, Comint in all its forms (direction finding, traffic analysis, and cryptanalysis) had all the potential for becoming a most important and prolific source of information on the Combined Fleet. It was up to the Allies, however, to realize this potential, and they indeed proved able to do so.

The major breakthrough in the field of communications intelligence that proved critical for the American success at Midway occurred in the area of cryptanalysis, and more specifically in the recovery of the main cryptographic system of the Japanese Navy.[4] Recall that this system, known as the Operations Code or JN-25, was the most widely distributed and extensively used of the Japanese naval cryptosystems, and the one in which about half the messages were transmitted (see chapter 2 as well as Kahn 1967:562 and Lewin 1982:301–3). Messages encrypted in the system were spottily read by the United States prior to December 4, 1941, when the Japanese changed the encipherment in the system and it became completely unreadable. However, since the change in the system was confined to the cipher keys and did not include the extensive codebooks as well, the problem the American cryptanalysts had to overcome was by no means insurmountable. Com 16, the U.S. Navy's communication intelligence (CI) unit in Corregidor (Philippines), managed to break into the new cipher keys within two weeks of the change (Kahn 1967:563; Safford 1952:15). By Christmas 1941 messages sent in the system were once more being read by the Americans, but these readings were tantalizingly poor (Kahn 1967:563). Much obviously remained to be done in order to transform the Operations Code into a source of strategic warning.

A truly concerted effort was then mounted by the U.S. Navy's cryptanalytical establishment to complete the recovery of the Operations Code system. The participants in this effort, besides Com 16 ("Cast") in the Philippines,[5] were OP-20G ("Negat")—the CI unit in the Navy headquarters in Washington—and Com 14 ("Hypo")—Com 16's sister unit in Pearl Harbor. The three units cooperated very closely both among themselves and with the British cryptanalysts in Singapore (Lewin 1982:85–87), exchanging messages, recovered groups, etc. (Kahn 1967:564). Gradual progress in reading the text of the messages sent in this cryptographic system was consequently made, and by early May of 1942 approximately one third of the code's lexicon had been recovered. This progress made it possible to read 90 percent of an ordinary cryptogram, because the recovered groups were those most commonly used (ibid.:567). At that point in time, however, it still was not possible to read the information on the timing of future operations contained in the cryptograms, since it was transmitted in an additional cipher used in conjunction with the Operations Code. This additional time-date cipher was especially hard to crack since it was not commonly used, but by May 24 or thereabouts it was also successfully recovered.

With the growing success in the recovery of the Operations Code system in the spring of 1942, and with traffic analysis and direction finding to supplement it, U.S. intelligence coverage of the Japanese Navy had reached a high point during the *buildup* for the Midway campaign. But this situation did not last through the battle itself, for on May 28 the Japanese had finally introduced a long-planned change in the cipher used in the Operations Code systems.[6] This change made the system completely unreadable to the Americans for quite a few months. In consequence, the U.S. Navy was effectively deprived of its primary source of information on its Japanese adversary for the duration of the Battle of Midway and the entire week preceding it.

The loss of the Operations Code was an obvious American setback, since it meant that henceforth the movements and plans of the Combined Fleet could only be derived from much inferior sources, i.e., traffic analysis, tactical reconnaissance by planes and submarines, and certain peripheral low-grade cryptosystems which the United States was still able to recover (Holmes 1979:98; Prange 1982:131, 137). Nevertheless, the adverse consequences of this development were not nearly as severe as they would have been had the change in the cryptosystem occurred when originally planned. For by the time it happened (May 28, 1942) *the most intimate details of the Japanese Midway campaign had already been revealed to the United States* by Japanese messages sent in the old (and therefore readable) version of the Operations Code cipher.

Now that we are familiar with the principal American sources of information on the Imperial Japanese Navy during the spring of 1942, we may proceed to examine the information the United States had actually derived from them at the time regarding the Japanese plans for the Midway operation. This we shall do in two stages. First, I will review *chronologically* the accumulation of information on the Japanese plans in the hands of the American communications intelligence units. Then, I shall examine the difficulties these units, and particularly the one in Pearl Harbor (Com 14) encountered and overcame in the process of transforming this raw data into a most detailed, reliable, coherent, and categorical warning to the operational authorities.

My discussion in both this and the next section draws rather heavily on a recently declassified history of the role of radio intelligence in the American-Japanese naval war, 1941–42 (SRH-012 1942). This document, produced in September 1942 by the U.S. Navy's communications intelligence establishment, provides what is by far the most comprehensive and authoritative review of the intelligence background to the Battle of Midway, and therefore serves as the basis for my discussion here. But the account provided by this document is rather dry and impersonal, and at times also cryptic on certain aspects of the intelligence production that are of great interest to us here. To highlight and elaborate on those relevant points that receive little or no attention in this primary document I will, therefore, tap other primary sources as well as some secondary (but independent) sources.

### The Intelligence Buildup to Midway: A Chronological Review

Some indications of what later turned out to be Japan's plans for the Midway operation had surfaced in intercepted Japanese messages as early as March 9, 1942. At the time, however, there was little more in the messages than the suggestion that another Japanese naval operation of an uncertain nature was in the offing for sometime in the future, although Com 16 did then speculate that the operation might be directed against the Aleutian Islands. In the two months or so that followed, there was little concrete information in the messages or in any other source to shed additional light on this forthcoming operation. Signs of a new Japanese campaign in progress did not reemerge until late April (during the final stages of preparations for the Battle of the Coral Sea), and the importance of this campaign did not manifest itself until May 2, when an intercepted message revealed the existence of a striking force. From that day onward, however, the information on the forthcoming operation accumulated rather rapidly.

Decoded messages of May 5-6 disclosed that the Japanese were planning operations that would require extensive refueling at sea, and that arrangements for large replacements of air personnel were being made. Further assurance of planned action was given when a lengthy order, outlining the program for a conference of all Japanese Air Commanders, came to light. The list of subjects to be discussed at the meeting obviously indicated reconnaissance and attack methods *for a very important movement*. Additional messages of May 8-11 indicated that operations were to commence about May 21 when aircraft carriers accompanied by destroyers were to move into the Saipan-Guam area. A message of May 12 revealed the shipping of military equipment, bombs, and shells to Truk for the requirements of the new campaign.

It was an intercepted message of May 13, however, that first mentioned one definite objective for the impending Japanese operation[7]—the occupation of an area denoted by the symbol "MI." Within a few days U. S. cryptanalysts were able to identify "MI" as Midway, thanks, in part, to additional decoded messages that contained requests for charts of the Hawaii area (a detailed discussion of this identification process will follow). In the interim, other May 13 intercepts revealed much important data on the organization of Japanese forces, their plans, and methods of attack. They also indicated that the date for departure from Saipan of some units participating in the operation was changed to some time in June. In the eyes of the American radio intelligence analysts, these and other messages revealing great Japanese activity in supplying bombs and food, plus the presence of numerous destroyer units in the area, were signs that the Japanese might be preparing a striking force *to the south or toward Hawaii.* By May 15, *three weeks before the Battle of Midway,* these analysts were able to conclude from the information at hand that the Japanese were making very detailed plans for the occupation of Midway and its further use as a base for subsequent operations.

Important details of the Japanese carriers' part in the project were then divulged in a May 16 message, which stated that planes of the First Air Fleet were going to make attacks from a point 50 miles northwest of Midway, from N-2 to N-day. More decrypted Japanese messages (May 16–18) which contained requests for air mail delivery of necessary charts, urgent demands for the ammunition destined for Midway, and movements of several units from Yokosuka, only piled up evidence that a tremendous campaign was underway. The goals of the operation were then clarified by an important May 18 message which mentioned *the Aleutians as well as Midway* as an objective of the impending operation. The same dispatch also disclosed the position to be taken by the Japanese submarines before the attack on Midway as "150 miles to the east (?) of Oahu."

By May 20, the American cryptanalysts had been able to piece together large parts of Japan's operational plan for the Midway operation. Nevertheless, some aspects of the operation still remained unclear, incomplete, or uncertain. But intercepts of May 20–27 resolved all ambiguity and uncertainty. They provided a most comprehensive, explicit, and detailed blueprint of the Japanese plan, disclosed last-minute changes, and revealed the completion of the preparations for its implementation. By far the most important of these final intercepts was a May 20 intercept of Admiral Yamamoto's operational order for the Midway operation. This order, which detailed *the complete Japanese order of battle for the assault on Midway and the Aleutians,* was intercepted in its entirety and by May 25 was approximately 90 percent recovered (Holmes 1979:89; Kahn 1967:567).

Another particularly important message intercepted on May 20 gave a list of letter symbols to be used as designators for certain places and areas. This message, coupled with several others that were intercepted in the following few days, enabled the U.S. cryptanalysts to identify with confidence the locale for many of Japan's planned operations which were otherwise mentioned in the messages only by their designator value. Other intercepts of the same day disclosed that the Occupation Force was to have its own independent aviation arm when Midway was taken, and reflected Japan's supreme air of confidence that Midway was already theirs.

Additional intercepted messages of the May 20 to 27 period shed light on other aspects of the impending operation. Thus, for example, messages on May 21 provided some new insights into *the second phase of the campaign*. They explicitly revealed that the capture of Midway was to be only the first step in the plans. That this was indeed the case also became apparent from the number of Special Landing Troops that were being added to the Occupation Force. May 21 messages also provided another strong indication of the *imminence of the operation* when they disclosed that elaborate training was being ordered by the Japanese for all of the Midway units.

On May 22, a decrypted messsage provided the United States with the call signs of Japanese forces that were to take part in the Midway operation, thereby enabling further identification of these forces. Intercepts of the following day disclosed that an important conference of the Japanese naval staff members was taking place at the time to discuss the coming operation. They also revealed further reinforcement of the Japanese naval units in the Saipan area and, even more important, that seven supply ships were assigned for *the third phase of the Combined Fleet's campaign*. Then, on May 24, messages disclosed that plane and pilot reinforcements were sent to the aircraft carriers *Akagi*, *Hiruyu*, *Kaga*, *Soryu*, and another unidentified carrier. They also divulged that airfields were being made ready and huge supplies of fuel were being stored at Wake, that the Occupation Force had received orders to bring with it as large a quantity of air-base equipment as possible, and that another convoy of supplies had arrived at Saipan. During the day, an intimation was also received that the Japanese were soon to change their code.

Intercepted messages on May 25 unveiled detailed orders for the Occupation Forces, and revealed that reserve pilots were being brought in for the Striking Force. They also disclosed that another destroyer group was added to the Second Fleet which was to attack Midway. The schedules and locations of Japanese convoys, en route to seize Midway, were next discovered (May 26), and more call signs for the operation areas were found in deciphered Japanese dispatches. It was also revealed that additional units were attached to the Midway forces and that an urgent request went out from Saipan for seaplane replacements by *June 3*. The significance of this date was not lost on U.S. Navy CI units.

Finally, a very important May 27 message indicated that the Occupation Forces were to rendezvous at 27° North, 170° East, and another dispatch ordered machinery and American engineers captured at Wake to be sent to construct an air base at Midway. Then, from May 28 through the whole Battle of Midway, very little information could be gathered from Japanese messages, because the long-expected change in the Japanese cipher had finally taken place.

For intelligence to prove effective in its threat identification and warning function it is insufficient that pertinent information on the adversary be collected in time. It is also necessary that the collected information be evaluated and integrated, however informally, into a more or less coherent intelligence picture, and disseminated promptly and accurately to policymakers. However, in the processing of the raw data, by collection agencies as well as intelligence analysts and managers, some threat indicators may be magnified and reinforced while others are attenuated and dismissed. Furthermore, choices are being made at

this stage of the process not only with respect to the substance
of the intelligence but also with respect to the style and method
of its dissemination, i.e., when and how policymakers will be
presented with threat indicators. All of these choices, in turn,
shape to no small degree the way policymakers finally react to
the information they receive (see chapter 4). Thus, if we wish to
understand the origins of success, as well as the roots of failure,
in perceiving a strategic threat, we should examine both the kind
of threat indicators collected by intelligence services and the exact
nature of the processing and dissemination of this information to
the policymakers.

In the preceding pages I have already satisfied the first
of the above requirements by documenting the *raw intelligence*
buildup to the Battle of Midway. I have demonstrated that the
American CI units had been able to gather excellent raw data on
the Japanese plans and preparations for the Midway campaign.
Some of this raw data, primarily deciphered and translated intercepts, was disseminated in its raw form (although with some
background comments) directly to the operational authorities in
both Washington and Hawaii. The operational authorities were
also the recipients of daily intelligence summaries prepared by CI
units. But as could be expected, most of the raw data was forwarded
*solely* to naval intelligence personnel,[8] and in any event, it was
with them that the principal responsibility for the assessment of
this information rested.

It was the official duty of the intelligence officers on
the staff of both CinCPac and the CNO (though not ONI)[9] to
piece together these messages, as well as relevant information
obtained from other sources, into a coherent intelligence picture
of Japan's intentions and capabilities—one that would serve as the
basis for the operational authorities' assessment of the enemy's
probable courses of action (Lewin 1982:295n). Thus, in order to
satisfy the second of the above requirements and determine what
threat indicators were made available to the authorities prior to
Midway, I now proceed to examine the processing of the raw
data by the intelligence advisers to Admiral Nimitz (CinCPac) in
Hawaii and Admiral King (CNO) in Washington.

It is difficult to determine exactly when in the spring of 1942 U.S. naval intelligence first began to suspect an impending Japanese attack in the general direction of Midway, but the earliest manifestation of such a suspicion that I have been able to discover dates back to mid-April 1942. At that time, Commander Joseph Rochefort (head of Com 14), in response to a request from Admiral King for a long-range estimate of Japan's intentions, provided a four-part estimate. This estimate stated, among other things, that some indicators foreshadowed a major Japanese operation in the Pacific, one that could not as yet be pinpointed with respect to either date or place (Lewin 1982:91; Lord 1967:19; Holmes 1979:85; Potter 1976:78). It was nonetheless believed that there was a *strong possibility* that the operation would occur in the Central Pacific (Holmes 1979:85). It was not until the end of the first week of May, however, that the Hawaiian Islands and more specifically Midway *explicitly* surfaced in the intelligence estimates as a *possible* target for the forthcoming Japanese operation.

When the first explicit identification of Midway as a *possible* target for the operation emerged, it was based on no more than a rather elaborate series of inferences and shrewd guesses. These had to do with the context in and frequency with which what was believed to be the Japanese "area designator" for Midway ("AF") appeared in the Japanese radio traffic. And as was painfully evident at the time to all concerned, the identification of Midway as the possible Japanese target was problematic in at least two respects. Both the conclusion that "AF" was going to be the target for the operation and the identification of "AF" as Midway were *initially* based on no more than circumstantial and frag-mentary evidence (Lewin 1982:107-8; Potter 1976:79; Holmes 1979:88-89). But the early inferences regarding the identity of the target, coupled with the awareness of the fragility of the evidence on which it was based and the importance of the issue at stake, nevertheless facilitated and prompted efforts to uncover positive confirmation of both critical inferences and gather additional details on the forthcoming campaign (Lewin 1982:101, 106-8; Holmes 1979:89-91). And these efforts were indeed to bear fruit.

By May 15, naval intelligence at Pearl Harbor was able to conclude with somewhat greater certainty that the Japanese might well be pursuing three separate but possibly simultaneous offensives (Command Summary 1942:471, 482; Potter 1976:79). One such offensive was identified as a cruisers and carriers operation against the Aleutians, probably Dutch Harbor. The other offensive was described as a major landing attack against Midway, for which it was believed *that the main Japanese striking force would be employed.* The latter was also thought to include a raid on Oahu. The operation was expected to take place during the first part of June. In retrospect this estimate seems truly impressive in both its uncanny accuracy and the fact that it was made *three weeks* before the actual confrontation was to take place. The only (and rather minor) inaccurcy in this estimate had to do with the raid on Oahu. What was believed to have been a plan for an air raid on Oahu (the "K Operation") turned out to have been merely a plan for an aerial reconnaissance mission there (see below).

As for the estimates prepared by naval intelligence in Washington, these initially reflected a somewhat different opinion regarding Japan's intentions, largely as a result of late receipt of certain key intercepted messages (*Command Summary* 1942:489-90; Buell 1980:200-1). With the arrival of these delayed messages, OP-20G essentially accepted Com 14's identification of "AF" as Midway, and the difference in estimates was quickly resolved. By May 17, the Washington estimates were therefore portraying a picture that was very similar to that earlier drawn for Pearl Harbor. They concluded that Japan's attempt to capture Midway and Unalaska (in the Eastern Aleutians) would occur on May 30 or shortly thereafter. The May 17 estimate suggested that the Midway attack "may possibly be preceded by shipborne air raid on Oahu" (*Command Summary* 1942:490) and that Japan's intentions included an "effort to destroy a substantial portion of the Pacific Fleet" (ibid.). The estimate also contained a listing of Japanese naval forces believed to be designated to participate in both parts of the operation, an assessment that the Japanese might be planning for a landing in Beaver Inlet (in the Aleutians), and an expectation that the portion of the First Japanese Fleet not directly involved in the attack on Midway would assume a supporting position west of Midway. Again, this was a remarkably accurate estimate regarding the overall picture, with only minor inaccuracies concerning details of the Japanese plan.

Estimates in both Washington and Pearl Harbor were updated on May 21, and again were in general agreement with each other. The estimates now reflected certainty with respect to the identification of "AF" as Midway and contained a remarkably complete picture of the Japanese plan for the attack on Midway and the Aleutians. According to the Pearl Harbor estimate:

The Combined Fleet was to be divided into (a) a Northern Force, (b) a First Carrier Striking Force, and (c) a Midway Invasion Force. The Northern Force included a Second Carrier Striking Force which was to open the attack with a diversionary raid on the American base at Dutch Harbor in the Aleutians. Transports of the Northern Force would then land troops on the western Aleutians Islands of Attu, Kiska, and Adak. The First Carrier Striking Force, coming down from the northwest, would launch the main attack with an air raid on Midway. Meanwhile, the Midway Invasion Force, from Guam and Saipan, would be approaching Midway from the southwest. It would be met at sea and escorted the last 650 miles by the Japanese Second Fleet, including part of the Battleship Division 3. (Potter 1976:31)

The May 21 estimate included many additional details regarding the composition of each of the Japanese forces. Of particular importance in this context was the determination that only the four veteran Japanese aircraft carriers Akagi, Kaga, Hiryu, and Soryu would participate in the First Carrier Strike Force, while the two newest and largest Japanese carriers assigned to this force—Shokaku and Zuikaku—would not be able to take part in the forthcoming campaign (ibid.). Thus, the only critical element still missing in the May 21 estimate was the exact timing of the impending operation. While it was estimated that the Aleutian-Midway attack would occur in early June, no precise time for it could as yet be given.

The final round of naval intelligence estimates of Japan's plans for the operation was prepared on May 25 and 26.

These estimates did not significantly differ from their predecessors other than in the much greater detail about the forthcoming campaign that they contained. Many of the additional details included in this late estimate were derived from the Operation Order issued by Admiral Yamamoto on May 20, which was almost completely deciphered by May 25 (Kahn 1967:568–70). Significantly enough, the estimate was also able to forecast, thanks to the success in recovery of the time-date cipher, that the Japanese operation against the Aleutians would begin on June 3, and that against Midway on June 4. Based on methodic calculations of winds, currents, and weather, a careful study of charts, and a complete review of the evidence, Lieutenant Commander Layton, the Fleet Intelligence Officer, was even able to predict with amazing accuracy the details of the Japanese carrier attack on Midway on the morning of June 4. He informed Nimitz that the Japanese carriers' planes would "come in from the northwest on bearing 325 degrees and they will be sighted at about 175 miles from Midway, and the time will be about 0600 Midway time" (Potter 1976:83).[10]

Thus, more than a week prior to the commencement of the confrontation the American intelligence picture was by and large complete. It was comprehensive, timely, and remarkably accurate. The only significant element missing from it, one that would not be discovered until several months later, was the participation in the operation of another task force (the "Main Body") under the direct command of Admiral Yamamoto himself, comprised of Battleship Divisions 1 and 2 of the First Fleet. As this force was stationed in the Japanese Inland Sea for quite some time prior to the operation, it was not necessary to transmit orders to it by way of long-range radio, and none could therefore be intercepted by the American CI units.

I have thus far been able to demonstrate that ample indicators of the Japanese threat were present in the raw intelligence data, and that these indicators were picked up by naval intelligence and transformed rather flawlessly into a comprehensive and timely intelligence warning. What remains to be explained, therefore, is how the operational authorities actually consumed the warning presented to them. In addressing this issue, I will be focusing primarily on *two critical aspects* of the consumption of warning: first, the emergence, prior to Midway, of a perception of threat among naval policymakers regarding Japan's intentions, and second, the presence of diverse impediments and obstacles to the consumption of warning by policymakers. The latter is of particular concern here since it touches upon one of *my primary hypotheses in this study*, namely that warning originating in a reliable source can overcome even severe barriers to receptivity (see chapter 1). Confidence in the validity of this hypothesis would be greatly enhanced should it be demonstrated, upon close scrutiny, that a remarkably accurate threat perception had emerged among the American policymakers prior to Midway *despite the presence* of what we would otherwise be inclined to think of as severe, perhaps insurmountable, barriers to receptivity.

A perception of Japan's threat to Midway had begun to surface among the naval policymakers sometime in late April 1942.[11] Its initial emergence had as much to do with threat indicators based on intuition and the "logic of the situation" as perceived by Admiral Nimitz as with the intelligence warning. Warned by Com 14 that a new Japanese offensive in the Pacific was in the making, and cognizant of the geostrategic location of Midway and its importance for the Japanese "grand design in the Pacific," Nimitz began to examine the defense requirements of Midway. He considered the danger to Midway to be both real and serious enough to warrant a personal visit there, which he conducted on May 2, to examine its defense problems (Potter 1976:78). During the visit, Nimitz made a decision to reinforce Midway against a possible amphibious attack by Japan. Then, shortly after his return from Midway, Nimitz was apparently informed of the evidence that had accumulated in the preceding days pointing to an incipient Japanese buildup for the forthcoming operation. This led him to conclude that the Japanese now had sufficient force in the Central Pacific "to raid in the Central and North Pacific areas" (Costello 1981:271).

The next important development occurred on or about May 8.[12] Lieutenant Commander Edwin Layton, Nimitz's Fleet Intelligence Officer, briefed Nimitz on the alarming yet fragmentary and inconclusive evidence pointing to "AF" (Midway) as the primary target of the forthcoming Japanese campaign. Nimitz's reaction was guarded. He neither accepted the estimate nor fully endorsed it. After quizzing Layton closely on the basis for the identification of "AF" as Midway, Nimitz ordered that the highest priority be assigned to a positive identification of "AF" (Lord 1967:22; Potter 1976:72; Lewin 1982:108; Prange 1982:20). Furthermore, upon the urging of Layton and in view of his own preoccupation at the time with another pressing matter (the conduct of the Battle of the Coral Sea), Nimitz sent Captain L. D. McCormick—his war plans officer—to *review the raw data* on which the intelligence estimate was based (Lord 1967:22). McCormick came away fully convinced of the validity of Rochefort and Layton's estimate, a feeling he apparently managed to pass on to Nimitz (ibid.).

Nimitz' growing confidence in the reliability of the source of his information on Japan's intentions, coupled with the accumulation of additional and more conclusive evidence, led him, around the middle of May, to *accept in principle* the updated intelligence estimate. However, since he was not as yet fully convinced of the accuracy of the estimate, his acceptance was still *tentative* (Potter 1976:79–80). Moreover, when the estimate came under attack from several circles, Nimitz assigned another member of his staff—Captain James Steele—the task of reassessing the findings of the fleet intelligence organization. Specifically, Steele was instructed by Nimitz to play the role of a *devil's advocate*, challenging "every bit of information put forward by Layton and Rochefort and their assistants" (Potter 1976:80; Prange 1982:47; Lord 1967:25).

The appointment of Captain Steele notwithstanding, by *mid-May* Nimitz had accepted, for all practical purposes, the intelligence estimates. He "assumed for purposes of planning that the Japanese would attack Midway and that this blow would be preceded by a secondary strike against the Aleutians" (Potter

1976:79), and proceeded to take diverse actions to meet these impending developments. He tightened his control over the available American forces in the Pacific, ordered further reinforcement of Midway by air and sea units, and instructed (and later expedited) the assembly of his fleet units in Pearl Harbor. Furthermore, to counter the anticipated Japanese diversionary attack against the Aleutians, Nimitz dispatched to that area a token task force under the command of Admiral Theobald. All of these actions had either the explicit or tacit approval of Admiral King, who by May 17 had also come to accept the main thrust of the intelligence estimates (Command Summary 1942:489–90, 502; Potter 1976:80–82; Lord 1967:23–26; King and Whitehill 1952:379; Buell 1980:200–01).

By May 17, therefore, Nimitz and King had committed most of their Pacific force to the Hawaii-Midway line and the rest to the Aleutians. Once made, this commitment became irrevocable. There was no way these forces could later be significantly redeployed in time for an impending Japanese operation against a different target. That Nimitz and King made this commitment while fully aware of its implications is, perhaps, the best proof that they had indeed endorsed the key conclusion of the intelligence estimate pointing to the Midway-Hawaii area, rather than the South, North, or East Pacific, as the locale of the main Japanese attack (King and Whitehill 1952:379). Nevertheless, it must be realized that neither Nimitz nor King had at that time fully endorsed the other major conclusion of the intelligence estimate, which suggested that Midway, and not Pearl Harbor, would be the primary Japanese target in the forthcoming operation. King and Nimitz, however, apparently had somewhat different reasons for not endorsing that conclusion.

In the case of Nimitz, he apparently merely intended to defer his decision on this aspect of the estimate, for two primary reasons. On the one hand, a decision on where within the Hawaiian region to deploy his fleet (and therefore also whether or not to accept the estimate on this issue) did not have to be made for another week to ten days. On the other hand, Nimitz apparently reasoned that the evidence available at that time to support the conclusion of the estimate regarding the primary Japanese target

(Midway) was not, as yet, fully conclusive, and that there was every reason to expect better evidence on the issue to surface within a few days.[13]

Admiral King's calculus in refraining from endorsing the Midway part of the estimate, however, appears to have been somewhat different. He realized that the evidence on this critical issue was inconclusive, and apparently did not know of the possibility of verifying the identification of "AF"; he wished, therefore, that Nimitz would "play it safe." He wanted Nimitz to defend Hawaii and avoid the risk of a head-on-confrontation with the Japanese navy, which could cost the Americans dearly at a time when they could ill afford it (Buell 1980:200-1; Command Summary 1942:490). Nimitz, however, held his own. He would wait for evidence to accumulate until the last possible moment before finally making up his mind either way, and in the meantime would "base his plans on the assumption that the intelligence estimates are correct" (Potter 1976:83).

In the days that followed, Nimitz continued to review the incoming information on the Japanese preparations for the Midway campaign (Command Summary 1942:502, 538). But it was not until May 24 that he concluded that a final decision on the intelligence estimate (and the ensuing fleet deployment) would have to be made in a day or so. Before making this critical decision, however, Nimitz wanted to be as confident as possible of the validity of the intelligence estimates. He therefore summoned Rochefort to a personal interview with him and his planners the following day (May 25), ordered Layton "to make a careful review of all the data he had from radio intelligence and other sources of information and to derive as precise a forecast of the coming attack as possible," and instructed his plotting officers to "check the supposed Yamamoto plan against all other sources of military intelligence" (Potter 1976:82-83).

The complete review of the situation on May 25 brought Nimitz up to date on the latest in the intelligence estimates, which by now were much more detailed and conclusive. It also made it clear to him that he should not expect much additional information on the Japanese advance, as intercepted messages revealed that the Japanese were about to change their code system (SRH-012 1942:309). And perhaps most importantly, the review also provided Nimitz with intimate *firsthand* acquaintance with the source of his information, thereby enhancing his confidence in the reliability of the source and the information it supplied. Thus, *after some debate with the skeptics in his headquarters* (see below) Nimitz *accepted the intelligence estimate in its entirety*, and proceeded to act on the basis of its conclusions (Command Summary 1942:506–21). In the days that followed, Nimitz relied most heavily on that intelligence in the briefings and orders he issued to subordinate commanders (e.g., regarding the desirable timing and location for deployment of the Pacific Fleet), and even allowed the intelligence to guide him in the conduct of his personal routine. In fact, Nimitz was so confident of his reading of the situation based on the intelligence estimates that he was not even thrown off by contradictory (and misleading) tactical reports of reconnaissance planes which he received during the early phases of the campaign. Nimitz (correctly) ammended these reports to fit the intelligence estimates and counseled his Task Forces commanders to act likewise (Potter 1976:93).

In the preceding pages I demonstrated that Nimitz's (and to a somewhat lesser extent King's) acceptance of the intelligence estimates, while essentially complete, was neither blind nor automatic. Here I wish to go one step further and prove that this acceptance came about *despite the presence of numerous factors that could have led Nimitz and King astray.* What follows below is a review of all of these factors.

### Japanese Cover and Deception

Japan's goals for the Midway operation were most ambitious, and as a result called for an extremely complex and highly risky operation, the success of which clearly hinged on the attainment of complete surprise. To that end, the Combined Fleet had envisaged an array of cover and deception measures that would first conceal its intentions and preparations for the Midway operation, and then deceive the Americans about its real target. As it turned out, these practices, once implemented, proved too lax and incomplete to prevent the Americans from detecting their preparations and uncovering their true intentions early in the game. Yet if this was the final result, it was not for lack of trying on the Japanese side, but rather despite their sustained efforts in this area.

To *deceive* the Americans regarding the primary target(s) of their forthcoming operation(s) in the Pacific, the Combined Fleet carried out, in May and early June, a series of diversionary raids across the Pacific, and practiced communications deception (Prange 1982:357; Morison 1949:78). To *cover* its preparations for the Midway campaign and other operations, the Combined Fleet implemented a series of communications security measures. It curtailed, whenever possible, the use of long-range radio communications, made extensive use of codes and ciphers in its communications, and ultimately also imposed a strict radio silence on the forces participating in the Midway campaign (Prange 1982:71). These measures were to be complemented by a major change in the Operations Code cryptographic system, scheduled to go into effect on April 1. Logistical and operational difficulties, however, forced two delays in the introduction of the change in this system, and it was finally implemented only on May 28.

## Suspicion of Japanese Deception

While Japanese deception itself was largely ineffective in throwing the U.S. Navy off track, American suspicion of Japanese deception, particularly communications deception, did actually come rather close to achieving that result. Fear that the information obtained by the CI units amounted to no more than a Japanese ruse—misleading information deliberately planted by the Japanese for American consumption—was quite widespread among American naval planners and flag officers (Command Summary 1942:510, 545; Prange 1982:47, 73; Lord 1967:27–28; Morison 1949:80). In fact this fear permeated virtually the entire discussion of the intelligence estimates, and it further intensified in the second part of May when the gradually improving intelligence elicited from many the reaction that it was simply "too good to be true" (Potter 1967:83; Command Summary 1942:510, 545). Concern on these grounds was even expressed by Chief of Staff George C. Marshall, who was particularly intrigued by an intercepted message of May 20 in which the Japanese Fourteenth Air Corps requested its mail to be forwarded to "AF" (Midway) (SRH-012 1942:292). This seemed to Marshall and others "a little bit too thick," and disturbed them greatly (PHA 1946 3:1158), although, by itself, it was insufficient to lead Marshall to dismiss the intelligence estimates of Japan's intentions.

That the Japanese would indeed be practicing communications deception was by no means inconceivable. After all, they had done so before, most notably prior to the Pearl Harbor attack, and with what could have appeared to them as great success. It was, therefore, neither impossible nor even unlikely that they would again practice such deception prior to major naval operations. Furthermore, not only prior experience with the Japanese, but also the quality of the intelligence prior to Midway, as well as the apparent presence of serious flaws in Japan's plans as portrayed by this intelligence, were perfectly valid grounds for exploring the possibility of misinformation.

Thus, it is not surprising that even Admiral Nimitz himself had at one point early in the game entertained the thought that the information he was receiving might be a ruse (Prange 1982:37–38). Upon learning more about the source of the information he was receiving (see below), however, Nimitz came to trust it and defend its reliability in front of his skeptical officers (ibid.; Potter 1976:82–83). This was indeed the most striking feature of the suspicion of Japanese deception prior to Midway. Most if not all of those who suspected a Japanese ruse, in both Washington and Pearl Harbor, were inexperienced in intelligence matters, and only marginally familiar with the source or the process by which the information presented to them was derived.

We must remember that the exact nature of the source supplying the critical information on the Japanese plans for the

Midway campaign, i.e., cryptanalysis, and more specifically, recovery of the primary cryptographic system of the Japanese navy, was a closely guarded secret. So secret, in fact, that Nimitz did not share it even with the American admirals commanding the task forces that would take part in the operation (Kahn 1967:571; Potter 1976:82; Holmes 1979:86; Lord 1967:35; Lewin 1982:105n; Command Summary 1942:543). These admirals, and most of the other select group officers who enjoyed access to the intelligence estimates, were unfamiliar with the true source of information and were inclined, even encouraged, to believe that it was either traffic analysis or perhaps Humint—two types of sources that are much more susceptible to misinformation than cryptanalysis in general, and recovery of high-quality ultra-sensitive cryptographic systems in particular.[14] It is therefore hardly surprising to discover that in at least one instance during the Midway operation this compartmentation practice actually backfired and led to dismissal of warning.

The case in point, and the one that perhaps best illustrates the influence that acquaintance with (and consequently also trust of) a source of information can have on fear of deception and acceptance of warning concerns Rear Admiral Robert Theobald. Recall that in mid-May Nimitz dispatched Theobald, in command of a small task force, to the Aleutians in anticipation of the Japanese diversionary raid against this area on June 3. Later, on May 28, Nimitz notified Theobald that his intelligence indicated that the Japanese intended only to raid Dutch Harbor whereas Attu, Adak, and Kiska were the Aleutian Islands they actually intended to invade (Potter 1976:88; Lewin 1982:100). Nimitz did not, however, provide Theobald with a clue to the nature of the source for this information or, for that matter, with any other explicit measure of its reliability. Theobald was thus left in a situation in which he had a very poor basis for assessing the validity of the information provided by Nimitz.

Operating under the impression that the information supplied to him by Nimitz had originated in traffic analysis, and reasoning that nobody "would bother to occupy such worthless bits of land" as the western Aleutians, Theobald concluded that the information "was a ruse planted by the Japanese." Since he believed that the purpose of the ruse was "to draw him westward so that they could get behind him for landing at Dutch Harbor or perhaps in Alaska" (Potter 1976:88; also Prange 1982:155–56; Kahn 1967:571; Lewin 1982:100), Theobald decided (on his own), to deploy his force 400 miles south of Kodiak, where it proved practically useless in countering the Japanese attack.


### Conflicting Estimates and Military Doctrine

The obstacles to acceptance of the naval intelligence estimates were by no means confined to fear of Japanese deception or the practice thereof. Particularly prominent among the other obstacles then present were conflicting estimates and military doctrine.

Unlike the naval intelligence estimates, which by mid-May were remarkably accurate, detailed, and prescient, army intelligence estimates of the period were lacking in all of these qualities. In late April and throughout May, the army estimates were rather general and inconclusive, pointing to a general danger of Japanese strikes against Hawaii, Alaska, Australia and, most important, the West Coast of the United States, especially San Francisco and San Diego (Costello 1981:272–73; Lord 1967:21, 24; Prange 1982:37–38, 47, 66, 96). One major reason for this striking deficiency in army estimates seems to have been the poor data base available to army intelligence at the time. It was apparently deprived of raw naval intercepts, and denied the background necessary for a correct assessment of the sanitized and diluted estimates and other data which it nonetheless managed to obtain from the navy[15] (Lord 1967:24). As a result of this handicap, army intelligence resorted to the more *conservative doctrinal approach* in assessing the enemy's courses of action, an approach emphasizing enemy *capabilities* rather than probable intentions and, even with respect to the latter, assuming a worst-case scenario.

The emphasis on Japan's capabilities in army intelligence estimates resulted in great confusion and a high level of anxiety among army commanders in Washington, the West Coast,

Alaska, Hawaii, and Australia. For Japan's capabilities at the time were such that it could effectively operate in virtually every part of the Pacific. And the data then available to these army commanders (from sources other than the Operations Code) was sufficiently ambiguous to permit practically any speculation regarding the likely Japanese target(s). Consequently, army commanders, including Chief of Staff Marshall, Secretary of War Stimson, General Douglas McArthur (in Australia), General Emmons (in Hawaii), and General Arnold (on the West Coast), all expected Japanese attacks in their respective theaters in April, May, and early June 1942, and repeatedly attempted to impress their points of view on navy commanders (Prange 1982:27, 46–47, 66, 96, 139–40, 159, 365; Holmes 1979:91; Lord 1967:21, 24, 27; Costello 1981:272–74).

The army's attempts to influence the navy's reading of the situation did not meet with any measurable success. Although the army's warning—that military doctrine, past experience, and prudence all called for the use of capabilities rather than intentions as the basis for threat assessment—did strike a responsive chord in the navy, it ultimately did not dissuade the navy from acting on the basis of probable intentions.[16] Top navy commanders were simply too confident of their source of information on Japan's intentions, and too constrained in terms of the resources available to them, to be either willing or able to accept the army's recommendations and act on their implications.

## Credibility of Intelligence

To gain acceptance, intelligence estimates of Japan's intention to launch the Midway operation had to overcome not only diverse objections pertaining to their substance, but also more general skepticism regarding the value and validity of the intelligence product. The lingering skepticism toward intelligence in general, and intelligence estimates in particular, was not insignificant prior to December 7, 1941. But the surprise attack on Pearl Harbor, which was widely perceived to be an intelligence failure, did much to discredit the intelligence product and personnel even further, particularly since it was widely believed that the failure occurred despite the possession of an excellent source of information on the opponent, i.e., Magic (Lewin 1982:90,, 93, 105; Van Der Rhoer 1978:50, 66; Prange 1982:19–20; Buell 1980:174; Dorowart 1983:184–93).

While some quantitative and qualitative improvements were made in American intelligence in the period immediately following the Pearl Harbor attack, prior to Midway these hardly manifested themselves in a way that would significantly alter the prevailing attitudes toward intelligence.[17] The reputation and image of intelligence would experience a significant face-lift once it could prove, as it did in the Midway instance, its remarkable potential. But for it to be able to do so, it needed not only to generate excellent estimates but also to have them accepted and acted upon by policymakers. This was the crux of the "catch 22" situation which naval intelligence faced on the eve of Midway, a situation that was exacerbated by the disturbing elements of the warning itself that were noted above. These merely reinforced the concern and skepticism that consumers of the intelligence on Japan's intentions already felt toward intelligence estimates. And the task intelligence was facing in selling its product was further complicated by tight compartmentation that prevented it from revealing to most of its consumers—though not to the top-level civilian and military leaders—the true identity of the source of its information on the Japanese plans.

With such a long series of severe barriers and obstacles to the consumption of intelligence, one has to wonder how intelligence was able nonetheless to produce prior to Midway a remarkably accurate threat perception among U.S. naval policymakers. A conclusive answer to this question lies beyond the reach of this work since it requires assertions of causality that my study cannot really sustain. What my in-depth study of the Midway episode and comparison of Midway to other historical cases (Pearl Harbor in particular) nonetheless permit me to do is to offer a highly *plausible* explanation of this intelligence success—one that is not only consistent with available evidence and knowledge but is better than alternative explanations. In the preceding pages I have offered some scattered thoughts on the issue. Here I seek to incorporate them into a more comprehensive explanation.

The factors I judge to be primarily responsible for the intelligence success at Midway can be summarized as having to do with either the characteristics of the warning itself or the features of its consumers and consumption process. As far as the nature of the warning itself is concerned, it is quite evident that the *remarkable detail, scope, and conclusiveness of the warning*,[18] *as well as the impeccable credentials of its source*, were important in enhancing its appeal and persuasiveness. But had these been the only important factors, the same warning should have produced an identical, or at least very similar, perception of threat among different consumers, which clearly was not the case. We must, therefore, look for the other pieces of the puzzle elsewhere, and I believe that these can be found in characteristics of the consumers of warning and in features of the consumption process.

One factor that strikes me as particularly important in determining the influence of the warning on the policymakers' threat perception is the degree, not to say intimacy, of their acquaintance with the source from which the threat indicators originated. It is my belief that the evolution of Nimitz' threat perception over time, and the difference between his threat perception and those of King, Theobald, Marshall, Stimson, and other senior officials, can largely be explained by the difference in their exposure to, and degree of familiarity with, the intelligence source(s) and methods. And while the limitations of my research strategy deny me the capability to establish any causal link such as I believe exists between source awareness and warning acceptance, it does nonetheless permit me to offer the following analysis which does lend some support to my belief.

The available data clearly suggests, for at least some of the key American participants, a *strong correlation* between the degree of their familiarity with the source of information (and the process by which it was produced) and the level of their confidence in the intelligence warning. I have already noted the rejection of

warning by Admiral Theobald who was unfamiliar with its source
and suspected it to be an inferior and unreliable one. Conversely,
the warning was accepted without reservation by the two other
task force commanders operating under Nimitz in the Midway
campaign—Admirals Fletcher and Spruance. And while Fletcher
and Spruance, like Theobald, were also kept in the dark with
respect to the exact source of warning, they, unlike Theobald,
were at least provided by Nimitz and his intelligence officer with
a strong indication of the credibility of and confidence in that
warning (Prange 1982:101-2).

Furthermore, it is also evident in the data at hand
that the growth of Admiral Nimitz's confidence in the credibility
and authenticity of the warning closely corresponded with the
increase in his familiarity with the source and the method by
which it was produced. A similar observation can even be made
with respect to Admiral King, except that in the latter's case
neither his confidence in the warning nor his acquaintance with
its source went as far as they did in the case of Nimitz. Certainly
King was well acquainted with the source of the warning. But he
was less intimately familiar with certain aspects of the warning
production process, especially those pertaining to the identification
of "AF." Thus, it is hardly surprising that while King accepted
the warning in principle, he did not fully endorse the identification
of "AF" as Midway.

While the correlation between familiarity with and
trust in the warning can be established with some confidence for
the top *naval officers*, the paucity of relevant data does not permit
similar observations regarding the other senior policymakers, especially Marshall and Stimson. With respect to the latter, all that
can be established with confidence on the basis of the fragmentary
data available is that General Marshall had received some raw
intercepts and that he was fully aware that they had originated
in cryptanalysis (PHA 1946 3:1158). Yet it would seem that Marshall
was under the impression that the source for the intercepts and
consequently also the basis for the warning was Magic rather than
the Operations Code (Lewin 1982:9-12).

In any event, it is highly unlikely that in the Midway case either Marshall or Stimson, let alone lower level army commanders, possessed intimate knowledge of the relevant sources and methods, if only because these were strictly under the navy's control. And if this was indeed the case, then the correlation between confidence in the warning and familiarity with its origins would also be found to exist for Marshall and Stimson. They had some general knowledge of the source for the warning, and accepted its general theme—that a large-scale Japanese naval operation in the Pacific was in the making for early June. But they lacked (I suspect) more intimate knowledge of the process by which the (controversial) details of the warning were derived, and indeed refused to accept that part of the warning, i.e., the identification of the method and locale for the forthcoming Japanese operation.

Here a word is in order regarding the features of the advisory process and the way in which they fit into our explanation. In my judgment, Nimitz's advisory process, and especially the various procedures he instituted for examining and reexamining the intelligence product (e.g., playing the devil's advocate), played a critical role in strengthening his confidence in the warning, much beyond what would have been possible otherwise. And it was this high level of confidence, I submit, that largely made the difference between endorsement and dismissal of the warning. I would further suggest that the absence of any similar advisory practice and/or process elsewhere in the system could help explain the greater level of skepticism toward the warning by other high-level officers, civilian as well as military.

Finally, we also have to consider the impact of personality traits on consumption of warning. This is, perhaps, the most difficult part of the task, since it calls for separating the impact of personality traits from the effects of other, less idiosyncratic factors (the synergistic effect). My conclusions in this area must therefore be treated with great caution.

As I have already made clear, unlike several other scholars, I do not attribute *overwhelming* importance to personality traits in determining receptivity to warning. I believe that the evidence supplied thus far does, by and large, support this conviction. Still, I do find in the Midway case, evidence to suggest once more (see chapter 4) that the beliefs of policymakers can actually serve to sensitize them to warning. The case in point concerns Admiral Nimitz and his premonitions regarding a possible Japanese invasion of Midway. Recall in this context that Nimitz made a visit to Midway to review its defense situation on May 2, well before any hard evidence had emerged to suggest a concrete Japanese threat to the atoll. An even earlier expression of his concern for the defense of Midway in the event of a major Japanese attack was provided in the last week of April. In a conference with Admiral King that took place in San Francisco between April 25 and 27, Nimitz explicitly raised the possibility of a Japanese attack on Midway "by a force composed of two or more carriers with accompanying fleet units." He also expressed his opinion that such an attack "could be beaten off only by United States Fleet forces" (King and Whitehill 1952:377).

The above discussion suggests that Admiral Nimitz was highly sensitive and receptive to warning concerning a possible Japanese attack against Midway, possibly more so than any other senior American policymaker of the time. But that discussion does not reveal what were the sources of his extra sensitivity. And while Nimitz's personality traits could conceivably be the source for such sensitivity, in my examination of the available data I have not been able to identify any unique personality traits to account for his sensitivity. It is, therefore, my judgment that a more plausible explanation of Nimitz's extraordinary sensitivity could be provided by *nonpersonality factors*, especially his institutional role as commander in chief of the U.S. Pacific Fleet.


Having concluded the analysis of the various aspects of warning and threat perception in the Midway episode, I will return to my point of departure and seek to explain the sharp contrast in outcome, as far as threat perception is concerned, between Midway and Pearl Harbor.

The quality of warning that was available to the United States prior to the two Japanese surprise attempts strikes me as the most critical variable accounting for their sharply different outcomes. As I have established in both this and the preceding chapter, the warning available to the U.S. policymakers prior to Midway was comprehensive, conclusive, and extremely accurate, and also originated in a highly reliable source, while this was not the case for important aspects of the warning preceding the Pearl Harbor attack, i.e., that Pearl Harbor itself would be attacked (versus merely that the Japanese were initiating war and about to attack elsewhere). But while I believe that the evidence supplied thus far provides strong support for my assessment of the quality of warning in both cases, I realize that this evidence is not, in itself, sufficient to sustain my contention regarding the critical role of the quality of warning in determining the outcome (whether surprise or threat perception). What does supply the missing support for my contention is the great similarity between Pearl Harbor and Midway in so many important respects (other than outcome, of course). It is this similarity of the important dimensions of the two cases that creates what functionally approximates a controlled experiment, and rules out many of the competing explanations for the difference in outcome between the two instances.

Still, at least one additional important difference between Pearl Harbor and Midway does nonetheless exist. The former surprise attempt occurred in the course of war initiation while the latter took place when war was already under way. It is this difference that gives rise to the most serious challenge to my explanation. The logic underlying this challenge is that the outbreak of open hostilities between the United States and Japan, as well as the Pearl Harbor experience itself, substantially altered the nature of the threat perception problem faced prior to Midway. Specifically, the argument is that the threat perception problem after the Pearl Harbor attack was sufficiently different, and, in essence, also considerably easier, than that prior to Pearl Harbor, so much so as to make a comparison of these two cases meaningless if not altogether misleading.

If the above argument is essentially valid, then I cannot use the contrast in outcome between Pearl Harbor and Midway as evidence to support my proposition regarding the role of warning in shaping outcomes. For in such a case other variables could be said to have played an equal or greater role in causing surprise at Pearl Harbor and threat perception at Midway. I do not believe that this is a central aspect of the explanation. While I do not wish to deny in any way that the commencement of the American-Japanese war, as well as the Pearl Harbor experience, did not have many important consequences, they did not *fundamentally* alter the nature of the threat perception problem after Pearl Harbor, and certainly did not make it any easier to overcome. Put differently, I still believe that the comparison between Pearl Harbor and Midway is both valid and useful for my purposes here, and will attempt to demonstrate this below.

Those who argue that the nature of the threat perception problem had significantly changed between Pearl Harbor and Midway—most prominently Richard Betts (1982a)[19]—build their case on one or more of the following complementary claims: (1) the strategic conditions and the political context in wartime are entirely different from those in peacetime and there are not political, psychological, or strategic incentives to disbelieve threatening intelligence; (2) after the Pearl Harbor attack the identity of the adversary and his hostile intentions was no longer in question, thereby easing the warning and threat perception problems; (3) after Pearl Harbor greater concentration of effort was possible to determine Japan's intentions thanks to both the crystallization of the problem and the larger allocation of resources for the purpose; (4) the personal involvement of the top political and military leadership in the assessment of the foreign threat *declined* significantly between Pearl Harbor and Midway, thereby largely removing the adverse impact of politics and politicians on the assessment of warning on Midway; (5) a learning process had been at work between the two instances, making warning and threat perception easier after Pearl Harbor than they had been before. Let me now address each of these claims.

With regard to the first assertion, recall my point that while it is true (it is, in fact, a truism) that strategic conditions in peace and wartime are different, this, by itself, provides insufficient grounds to assert in the abstract that the incentives for accepting threatening intelligence (i.e., warning) are also entirely different because in wartime there are no disincentives for accepting the warning (see chapter 4). First, the above assertion assumes that in peacetime there are only disincentives for accepting warning. But as I argue and demonstrate throughout this study, there also are strong *incentives* for taking peacetime warning seriously. Second, if one extends to wartime the same logic applied by Betts to the unearthing of disincentives for believing warning in peacetime, one is bound to discover that very similar disincentives for accepting warning also exist in wartime.

To realize that in wartime there are also disincentives for accepting warning one only needs to look at the Midway case. The serious deficiencies in American military capabilities (and the resulting constraints on the ability to respond to warning), as well as the political commitment to a policy of "Europe first" and the costs of deviating from it, are just two of the factors that should be (at least according to Betts' logic) considered to have been strong disincentives for accepting warning of a major Japanese naval offensive in the Pacific in general, and against Midway in particular. The upshot of this discussion is, therefore, that the first objection to my comparison of Midway and Pearl Harbor is not well founded. It is based on a distorted view of the disincentives for accepting warning both in peacetime and in wartime, and suggests differences between peacetime and wartime that are not really there.

As for the second claim, the fact is that the outbreak of open hostilities between the United States and Japan did not make the warning and threat perception problems existing prior to Midway *significantly* different and fundamentally easier than those existing prior to Pearl Harbor. My point here is that the only dimensions of warning and threat perception that the beginning of the war could have conceivably resolved with complete certainty, namely *who* is the enemy, *whether* and *why* he is likely to act, were already known to the United States with virtual certainty *before* December 7, 1941. The key questions that had to be answered prior to Pearl Harbor, namely *where, when*, and *how* the Japanese were going to act, remained the same prior to Midway. The Japanese had numerous courses of action open to them prior to Midway, and the task of determining *what* they were intent on doing, *where, how*, and *when* they would do it, was again the crux of the problem.

With respect to the third claim, there is no doubt that the beginning of the war did enable a greater concentration of American effort in the intelligence and warning functions. But this increase in the resources allocated to intelligence (manpower, equipment, etc.) was not significant enough by the time of Midway to ease substantially the difficulty of determining Japan's intentions, for several principal reasons. First, the gradual increase in resources allocated to intelligence and warning had begun long before the attack on Pearl Harbor. It had its origins in 1940 and was further accelerated in the summer of 1941 (see chapter 2). Second, while the expansion process did gain additional momentum after December 7, 1941, as a result of the long time lag involved in training new personnel, the development of new sources, and the manufacture of equipment, the increase in resources was not immediately translated into a corresponding increase in intelligence capabilities in the Pacific. Thus, America's deliberate efforts to increase intelligence capabilities[20] had met with only very limited success by May 1942.[21] Third, most of America's war-related efforts in the period immediately following the U. S. entry into the war, in intelligence as in other areas, were directed at the European theater rather than, and frequently at the expense of, the Pacific theater (Costello 1981:273; Prange 1982:159; Buell 1980:chs. 14, 15; Dorowart 1983:180). Finally, the entry into the war had produced not only growth in the resources allocated to intelligence but also a corresponding expansion of the missions assigned to it and the difficulties encountered in fulfilling them.[22]

The fourth of the above claims is possibly the most interesting of them all. It asserts, in effect, two things: first, that the involvement of the political leadership in assessing the threat prior to December 7 was essentially detrimental; and second, that this involvement largely dissipated prior to Midway, thereby improving the military commanders' receptivity to warning. Both of these assertions, I would argue, are largely unfounded. In regard to the first, recall that I have already demonstrated that prior to Pearl Harbor the top political leadership in Washington was, by and large, much more alarmed over developments in the relationship with Japan than was the top military leadership. It actually tried, albeit with little success, to impress its alarming threat perception upon the military commanders rather than retard their receptivity to threat indicators.

Furthermore, in sharp contrast to the fourth assertion, there is also ample evidence to indicate that the political leadership, including the President, was actively involved, in the spring of 1941, in the assessment of Japan's intentions and the planning of defensive measures and naval operations in the Pacific.[23] While the involvement of the political leadership in matters relating to Japan and the Pacific may well have been more superficial and less sustained than that prior to Pearl Harbor, in part due to the preoccupation with the war in Europe, it was, in all likelihood, much less conducive to the perception of a threat to Midway. For the primary concern of the American political leadership in this context during April and May 1942 was the war in Europe (especially the survival of the Soviet Union) and the security of the West Coast. Overruling strong opposition from the navy as well as General MacArthur in Australia, the political leadership, the President included, as well as the Joint Chiefs, endorsed the position of General Marshall that the defeat of Germany should take precedence over the defeat of Japan. The political leadership, in fact, exerted pressure on the military commanders to concentrate on the war in Europe and the defense of the West Coast of the United States, at the expense of Australia and the Pacific theater.[24] The empirical evidence therefore cuts against both of the assertions presented above.

Finally let us deal with the fifth claim, which suggests that the Japanese attack on Pearl Harbor had served as an important learning exercise, making warning and threat perception signifi-

cantly easier thereafter. Here it is important to distinguish between
the intelligence-related lessons that were initially drawn from the
Pearl Harbor experience and those that were derived later after
a much longer reflection on the experience of World War II.
The latter clearly bolstered the conviction that strategic intelligence
is both potent and necessary, and ultimately led to the establishment of the first American civilian peacetime intelligence organization—the CIA. But the lessons initially drawn from the Pearl
Harbor experience, and the ones that were still prevalent on the
eve of Midway, were sharply different. The immediate impact of
the Pearl Harbor debacle was to shatter confidence in intelligence
and discredit intelligence organizations and products. Under these
circumstances, the receptivity of policymakers at all levels to
intelligence warning was lower than before, contrary to what the
above claim would have us believe.

   The upshot of the above discussion is, I believe, that
the problems of warning and threat perception in Midway and
Pearl Harbor were rather similar and comparable. By implication,
my findings regarding both issues are both valid and generalizable.
I thus feel confident in suggesting that the difference in the
intermediate outcome between Pearl Harbor (surprise) and Midway
(threat perception) can best be accounted for by the qualitative
difference in the warning preceding two instances. The importance
of this finding certainly transcends the specific insights it provides
into the events at Pearl Harbor and Midway.[25] It also clearly has
some implications for explanations of the surprise phenomenon
in general. These broader implications, as well as other theoretical
and methodological insights than can be derived from the "structured focused comparison" between Pearl Harbor and Midway,
will be discussed at some length in the concluding chapter.

# Chapter 4

# On Warning,
# Threat Perception,
# and Response

**A recurrent theme** in the preceding chapters has been the importance of the relationship between warning and response. Indeed, one cannot hope to provide adquate historical explanations of instances of surprise and/or unpreparedness, let alone develop a policy-related theory of both phenomena, without resorting to careful analysis of the relationship between warning and response. Thus far, however, I have devoted to the topic no more than a few passing remarks. In this chapter I shall, therefore, try to deal with it in a more systematic and comprehensive fashion.

By now conventional wisdom has it that warning and response are two closely related phenomena. To quote Alexander George, "the problem of warning should not be separated from the problem of how to respond to available warning" (1979a:14). Nevertheless, the nature of the relationship between warning and response is not widely understood, and it is certainly more complex than is implied in the above statement. Warning and response, despite their close relationship, are not linked to each other either directly or inextricably. For one thing, warning is only one determinant of threat perception and likewise response is just one type of action. For another thing, the relationship between warning and threat perception, as well as between threat perception and action (response), is a rather complex one, in the sense that warning is neither necessary nor sufficient to produce response. Thus, warning (as defined in the study) may fail to produce accurate threat perception and accurate threat perception may still not result in adquate response.[1] As Peter Calvacoressi has suggested, "intelligence is one thing and making use of it is another. Fore-warned is not always forearmed" (1981:79). Similarly, action (re-sponse) is sometimes initiated as a precautionary measure in the absence of warning.

In view of the complexity of the relationship between warning and response, it is prudent to treat both phenomena initially as if they were part of analytically discrete processes, one of threat perception, the other of action consideration and im-plementation. Only then, once the unique features of each phe-nomenon have been studied, does it make sense to introduce into the analysis the dynamic-interactive dimension of their relationship as well. This procedure simplifies the discussion and enables one to capture the full complexity of the relationship between warning and response which, in turn, makes possible an attempt to integrate them in a meaningful way into a policy-related theory. I shall therefore pursue this course in the pages that follow.

An alarming perception of a possible emerging threat is what motivates policymakers to consider (though not, by itself, to initiate) response. It therefore seems prudent to start my dis-cussion by exploring the origins of threat perception.

## On Warning and Threat Perception

One is tempted to suggest that the key factor shaping policymakers' perception of threat is the quality of warning they receive—warning defined as information pointing to an acute or potentially acute foreign threat which is obtained and processed by intelligence agencies. This suggestion is, obviously, not without merit. Intel-ligence (of which warning is a subset) clearly carries some weight with policymakers, particularly in matters of high stakes such as those under discussion here. The empirical evidence nonetheless suggests that warning is not the only important factor shaping policymakers' threat perception. How else can we explain the fact that warning, on occasion, fails to produce an alarming threat perception and, conversely, alarming threat perception does at times emerge when warning (as defined here) is absent? The question we have to address in this section is, therefore, twofold: what determines the fate of warning in the hands of policymakers, and what other sources, aside from warning, have the capacity to produce an alarming threat perception among a nation's top leadership. I deal with both parts of the question below.

My research suggests that the initial reaction of policymakers to warning largely depends on three factors: (a) certain features of the warning itself; (b) possession of other pertinent information on the issue at hand; and (c) political and personality traits of policymakers. Let us consider each of these factors.

### Features of the Warning

The transparency of the national interest and the high stakes involved, for both the policymakers and their country, make it highly probable that any information designated by intelligence as warning will get to the attention of the top leadership. Once in possession of such warning, however, policymakers can react to it in a variety of ways. They may accept it in full or in part, downgrade it, or dismiss it altogether. What their reaction will be in each case is determined to no small degree by the specific features of the warning presented to them, in particular its quality and form.

As far as the quality of warning is concerned, it may vary greatly from one case to another depending on the limitations of the data and the judgment of the intelligence authorities in the specific circumstances. Warning may thus be more or less ambiguous, explicit, detailed, categorical and, above all, convincing. Furthermore, warning might reach policymakers in the form of intelligence estimates rather than "current intelligence" (Kent 1969:16-17; Hughes 1976). And estimates may or may not be unanimous (as far as endorsement by all intelligence agencies is concerned), adding additional ambiguity to the warning.

It is quite self-evident that warning that is explicit, categorical, and the like is also more likely to carry the day with policymakers than warning that is inferior in one or more of these respects. Laboratory studies of perception indeed confirm the importance of the strength and clarity of the stimulus in shaping perception (De Rivera 1968:53ff.). Even warning that ranks fairly low on most or all of these dimensions (and can, therefore, be ignored or dismissed without causing much anxiety), cannot be rejected by policymakers without leaving behind some residual awareness, if only a lack of certainty that there is no threat at all. Thus, at the minimum, warning will raise the awareness of policymakers to the possiblility (even if not the probability) that certain ominous developments will take place. And as Klaus Knorr correctly points out, "once the possibility of threat is recognized, whatever the probability attached to it, true surprise is excluded" (1982:14). An example drawn from the context of the Cuban missile crisis will illustrate this point.

On September 19, 1961, approximately one month before the United States first learned of the presence of Soviet ballistic missiles in Cuba, the United States Intelligence Board (USIB) approved without dissent an intelligence estimate on the Soviet arms buildup in Cuba. This estimate concluded, in effect, that the Soviets would not introduce offensive missiles into Cuba (Hilsman 1967:172). U.S. intelligence apparently had no hard evidence pointing in that direction, and conversely there were rather forceful arguments to suggest that the Soviets would not pursue such a risky course (ibid.). Nevertheless, the intelligence estimate hedged "by noting that medium or intermediate range missiles in Cuba would significantly increase the Soviet capacity to strike at America's heartland and go far toward altering the balance of power between East and West." The estimate therefore "urged the intelligence community to maintain a continuous alert" (ibid.).

And so, despite the widespread belief in Washington that the Soviet Union would not risk deploying offensive missiles in Cuba, both the intelligence community and national policy-makers were made very much aware of the possibility that it might, nevertheless, occur. They became, consequently, more sensitive to any information pointing in that direction (ibid.:170, 174–76, 187–88). So much so, in fact, that in September President Kennedy went to extraordinary lengths "to ensure against leaks if intelligence ever did come in on offensive weapons and thus permit time to devise a policy for dealing with the problem." He "ordered special security arrangements, which included a special code word, Psalm, that ensured that all those who would need to know would get intelligence on offensive weapons, *but that no one else would get it*" (ibid.:187, emphasis added).

## Other Relevant Information

Even in circumstances where intelligence does issue warning of an impending strategic threat, that warning is only one type of information policymakers are likely to possess when they come to assess the situation and determine whether it indeed poses a major threat. Policymakers usually have at their disposal several additional sources of relevant information. One such source is the media, which most policymakers monitor rather closely. Another source is the intelligence establishment itself, which disseminates to policymakers other intelligence products as well (including raw data), some of them in large quantities. But the political leadership usually possesses certain additional sources of information, which are partially or wholly unavailable and inaccessible to the intelligence agencies issuing the warning. The latter include, among other things, assessments by experts other than those in the intelligence community, and, above all, confidential diplomatic communications with foreign governments and, on occasion, the leadership of the principal antagonist posing the threat about which intelligence may have been warning.

Finally, it is important to point out that an alarming threat perception could also emerge on the basis of policymakers' interpretation of the amorphous "lessons of the past" and the "logic of the situation" rather than, or in conjunction with, any specific information they receive. I have already noted the importance of the "logic of the situation" in causing alarm over Japanese intentions among U.S. policymakers prior to Pearl Harbor. Raymond Cohen provides additional evidence for the importance of this basis for threat perception. In his six historical case studies he observed that geographical proximity to the adversary coupled with "an atmosphere of tension and mistrust in the ongoing relations" with it made for sensitivity to threatening signals and extreme pessimism in their interpretation (Cohen 1978:96-97). As a result the action of the opponent was viewed as a stepping over of a "boundary" on a conceptual dimension or an infringement of the rules of the game, thereby triggering a very alarming threat perception (ibid.:100–01).

But information other than institutional intelligence warning obtained by policymakers can not only be an independent source of threat indicators producing an alarming threat perception (in the absence of warning), but also a background against which warning is evaluated when it is available. It might support and amplify warning or conversely contradict, confuse, and weaken it. Consequently, it is entirely possible that the rejection of warning by policymakers (even if it turns out, in retrospect, to have been a blunder) will be caused not by cognitive pathologies or misplaced political predilections, but rather by rational and sensible considerations. The example that follows underlines this point.

When President Sadat of Egypt publicly announced in early November 1977 his willingness to travel to Jerusalem, suspicion of his ulterior motives was running high among most of the Israeli leadership (Weizman 1981:24–29; Handel 1981:324ff.). But while most of the policymakers were just doubtful about whether Sadat's willingness to visit Jerusalem was genuine, and skeptical about whether such a trip was intended for more than propaganda purposes, Israeli intelligence was truly concerned. The Egyptians were known by Israel to contemplate another war with Israel toward the end of 1977, and were also conducting at the time a large-scale military maneuver which they could use once more as cover for war preparations (Weizman 1981:24–29; *Maariv* 1977). It was, therefore, feared that a visit by Sadat to Jerusalem would deceive the Israelis and distract their attention from the Egyptian war preparations. The Israeli chief of the general staff at the time, Lieutenant General Mordechai Gur, was, in fact, so alarmed over the possibility that he resorted to the unprecedented move of awarding an interview to a leading Israeli newspaper in which he warned the government and public of Sadat's deception and war aims (*Yediot Ahronot* 1977).

The Israeli government, however, dismissed out of hand the various warnings of Sadat's "true" intentions. The minister of defense publicly reprimanded the chief of the general staff, and the prime minister issued Sadat a formal invitation to visit Jerusalem. The available evidence suggests that Menachem Begin and his foreign minister, Moshe Dayan, were able to dismiss the warning because they were quite familiar with the background to Sadat's public move. They had been negotiating and communicating with him, both directly and indirectly, since the summer of 1977 (Dayan 1981:ch. 3; Handel 1981:303–4, 346–47).

But policymakers ought to question the validity not only of any intelligence, warning included, but also of information they obtain through other sources. Otherwise, they might easily succumb to the temptation to use these other sources to dismiss unwelcome warning even when there are not valid grounds for doing so. The performance of the British prime minister on the eve of the Falkland Islands crisis (March 1982) seems to be a case in point.

The evidence currently available in the public domain[2] strongly suggests that British intelligence explicitly warned its government on July 1981, well ahead of the Argentinian invasion of the Falkland Islands (April 2, 1982), of the distinct possibility of such action and the circumstances under which it was likely to occur. The intelligence assessment of Argentina's likely courses of action, circulated on July 9, 1981, stated in its concluding paragraph that "if Argentina concluded that there was no hope of a peaceful transfer of sovereignty, there would be a high risk of its resorting to more forcible measures against British interests, and that it *might act swiftly and without warning*." The intelligence estimate further suggested that "in such circumstances military action against British shipping or *a full scale invasion of the Falkland Islands could not be discounted*" (FCR 1983:27, emphasis added).

Following the latest round of negotiations between Britain and Argentina over the fate of the Falklands, in February of 1982, British intelligence, as well as several other sources, including some public ones, supplied the British policymakers with ample evidence of the growing irritation in Buenos Aires over the state of the negotiations. They also suggested that the Argentinian anger toward Britain was mounting, and in March even indicated that the Argentinian military was making preparations for what could possibly be an invasion of the Islands (ibid.:40–47). Yet, until the very last moment, neither British intelligence nor any other sources could unravel the fact that a decision to invade the Falklands had in fact been made by the Junta (ibid.:55ff.), apparently because no such decision was actually made until very shortly before the operation got underway (ibid.:73,84).

In any event, while Prime Minister Thatcher was clearly intrigued by the warning and other threat indicators reaching her (ibid.:45), that was not the case with Lord Carrington, then the British foreign minister. Following the lead of some of his lieutenants responsible for dealing with Falkland Islands matters, Carrington consistently downplayed the Argentinian threat to the Islands (ibid.:80–82; *Times* 1982b). And the prime minister effectively decided to accept the judgment of her experienced and trusted foreign minister on the matter.[3] As a result, the warning and other threat indicators were largely discounted until it was too late to launch an effective military response to the impending Argentinian action. Thus, if this account of the events is indeed accurate, and the published official report of Lord Franks' Committee (1982) does lend it much credence, then the Falkland Islands crisis provides an excellent example of a case where warning, albeit inconclusive, is dismissed when it contradicts other (and more welcome) information and advice available to the principal policymaker.

*Political and Personality Traits of the Policymakers*

The attitude of policymakers toward incoming warning is not entirely information-driven. To an important degree it is also determined by the personality of the policymakers themselves, which combines features of both "ordinary" human beings and "political animals."[4] Being "ordinary" human beings, policymakers manifest common biases in information processing. Their assessment of warning is, therefore, likely to be colored by their general beliefs, perceptions, desires, expectations, and preferences (George 1979a:17, 1980:14–20, Ch. 3; De Rivera 1968:53ff.; Jervis 1976: part 2). These, then, can serve as "filters that screen, channel, or block the executive's receptivity to information and advice from others" (George 1980:47). Moreover, like other human beings, policymakers are also susceptible to other cognitive impediments such as framing and anchoring (Tversky and Kahneman 1974, 1981), consistency seeking (George 1980:61–65), stress avoidance (ibid.:50–53; Janis and Mann 1977:57–58, 107–33), etc. And as "political animals," policymakers may well introduce additional biases into their processing of information, biases having to do with their political outlook, policy commitments, organizational affiliation, etc. (Jervis 1976:128–30; Janis and Mann 1977:74–79; George 1981: ch. 5).

But contrary to the prevailing view, personality traits of policymakers do not necessarily predispose them to dismiss or downgrade warning and other threat indicators. There is a strong case to be made to the effect that the personality variables are as likely to improve their receptivity to warning as they are to retard it. After all, some personality features may actually sensitize policymakers to ominous developments and amplify the warning and other threat indicators they receive. While examples of such instances are hardly ever presented in the surprise literature, whereas examples of the opposite phenomenon abound, this should not be interpreted as evidence for a causal relationship between cognitive rigidity and surprise. To quote Steve Chan, "what appear as reasonable cause-effect relationships in a small sample may turn out to be fortuitous correlations. . . . While the extant literature suggests that cognitive rigidity is a major cause for warning failures, this variable in fact does not discriminate very well between successful and unsuccessful outcomes" (1979:174).

There is ample empirical evidence to support the proposition that policymakers' personalities do, at least in some cases, sensitize them to threat indicators. Raymond Cohen, for example, has recently found in six historical cases that he studied that policymakers' negative images of the opponent and their mistrust of his behavior actually served to heighten their sensitivity to threat signals (1978:97). And Steve Chan points out that those who had some anticipation of surprise events like Pearl Harbor, Korea, and Cuba, "such as Ambassador Grew, Ambassador Muccio, and Senator Keating, did not appear to be more open-minded or less committed to their beliefs about the enemy's intention that their less clairvoyant colleagues" (1979:174). Similarly, Chan questions whether Churchill, who is frequently credited by historians with demonstrating remarkable foresight, had in fact more valid or less rigid beliefs than Chamberlain, for example (ibid.). The following example will underline this point.

Winston Churchill first predicted a German attack on the Soviet Union as early as June 1940, and repeated it on numerous occasions thereafter. When he first made the prediction, more than a year before the attack was actually going to take place, it amounted to little more than uncanny political speculation. As F. H. Hinsley points out, "it ran ahead of German's preparations—ahead indeed of Hitler's first instructions that attack should be prepared" (1979 1:429). Moreover, when Churchill first made his views on the subject known, the possibility of a German attack on the Soviet Union "had not been advanced in [any] intelligence paper reaching the Cabinet or the Chiefs of Staff" (ibid.:431). If anything, British intelligence was strongly inclined to believe that Germany would not attack the Soviet Union before it invaded Britain (ibid.). Churchill, however, held to his views and British intelligence finally came to share them, but only two to three weeks before the attack actually took place (ibid.:476–77).

In any event, it is interesting to note Hinsley's conclusion that because political speculations in Britain (by Churchill and others) about the possibility of a German attack on the Soviet

Union first emerged "before there could possibly be any foundations for them in intelligence, it strengthened the disbelief with which the intelligence bodies later greeted such geniune pointers as they received to Germany's intention" (ibid.:429).[5] It is equally plausible, however, that the concerns and premonitions of policymakers may actually sensitize statesmen and their intelligence advisors to the possibility of an ominous development. As I have suggested earlier, the views of American policymakers on their relationship with Japan prior to the Pearl Harbor attack (see chapter 2), and of Nimitz prior to the Midway operation (see chapter 3) seem to be cases in point.

The main concern of this section has been with the origins of threat perception. My principal interest in intelligence and surprise has necessarily led me to focus my attention on the relationship between warning originating in intelligence and threat perception. I have, therefore, dealt primarily with the factors that determine policymakers' attitudes toward incoming warning. Nevertheless, as I have suggested earlier and wish to reiterate now, an alarming threat perception can emerge independently of intelligence warning. In this sense other sources of information as well as premonitions, perceptions, and the foresight of policymakers are the "functional equivalents" of warning (as defined here). And since it is the perception of threat that triggers the consideration of response, it is its accuracy rather than its origins that is truly consequential. In considering the impact of threat perception on the efficacy of response later in this chapter I shall, therefore, deal with the accuracy of the perception of threat rather than its origin.

In the following pages I will begin to bridge the gap between threat perception and action (response). Initially, I shall consider the impact of the capacity and willingness to respond on policymakers' receptivity to threat indicators (warning included). Then, I will proceed to determine under what circumstances an alarming threat perception will actually produce an effective response. Finally, I will complete the discussion of threat perception and action by first introducing into the analysis the dynamic-interactive dimension of the threat perception-response relationship and looking at its practical implications.

## The Impact of Capacity
## and Willingness to Respond

The question I wish to address here is to what extent policymakers' willingness and capacity to respond affects their receptivity to threat indicators (warning being one such indicator). As for the willingness part of the question, Alexander George has argued that there is sometimes "a subtle feedback from a policymaker's anticipation of the response he might have to make to warning that affects his receptivity to warning" (George and Smoke 1974:574). His point is that "it is difficult to accept warning as valid without doing anything about it," and that taking "available warning seriously always carries the *penalty* of deciding what to do about it"—penalty, since it "may require policymakers to make new decisions of a difficult or unpalatable nature" (ibid., emphasis added). According to George, policymakers avoid this dilemma by becoming less receptive to warning (1980:74–75). While this calls attention to a truly important phenomenon, it does so in an incomplete manner. Let me elaborate on this point.

As I have already suggested, the emergence of threat perception (acceptance of warning) presupposes a basic *willingness*, if not eagerness, to consider response. To quote Robert Jervis, "when people are prepared to act on what they learn they do not shun undesired news" (1976:375). George is therefore correct insofar as he suggests that policymakers' unwillingness to take action (respond) will impede their receptivity to threat indicators. But to argue, as George does, that perception of threat may entail a cost for policymakers (having to make unpalatable choices) is insufficient grounds to assert that policymakers will indeed be unwilling to recognize a threat when they are warned of one.

After all, there is another half to the equation as well. Failure to respond to warning also entails a considerable risk (political and personal as well as national) when the threat materializes, and adequate response to warning can provide the policymaker and his country with tremendous rewards. Both create an incentive (consisting of a carrot as well as a stick) to recognize threat when it emerges, an incentive which, in all likelihood, far exceeds the (short-lived) disincentive.[6]

Thus, even to the extent that the cost/benefit ratio is indeed an important variable in determining receptivity to stimuli (as George argues on the basis of De Rivera's findings), it is far from certain that its impact is actually to inhibit rather than improve policymakers' willingness to perceive threat. I would not deny that some leaders may have a rather myopic view of the costs and benefits of threat recognition, a view that necessarily attaches much greater value to the immediate costs of taking warning seriously than to the mere risks of the longer term penalties for failing to do so. Such leaders would obviously be more inclined to shun bad news than others. But I would, nonetheless, contend that overall, the penalty of having to consider response (i.e., policy change) in the event that threat is recognized is not a significant factor in impeding receptivity to strategic (and only strategic) threat indicators, causing strategic surprise (for my definition of strategic surprise see chapter 1).

The point here is that the area of warning indicators of strategic threats combines rather unique features which make it less susceptible to such pathologies than most other areas of policymaking.[7] It is a circumscribed and narrowly defined area, the national interest in it is relatively transparent and noncontroversial, the stakes are very high, and the penalties and rewards for responding to threat indicators or failing to do so appear almost instantaneously (i.e., there is a short maturation time of the threat). In other issue areas that lack some or all of these characteristics I would, however, expect the unwillingness of policymakers to incur the penalties of having to reconsider earlier decisions and alter policy to be much more pronounced.

The second part of my original question concerns the influence of the *capacity* (as distinguished from willingness) to respond, or at least policymakers' perceptions of that capacity, on their receptivity to warning and other threat indicators. Robert Jervis has provided an impressive review of the existing literature on the issue. He suggests that the available evidence provides support for the proposition that the "predisposition to perceive a threat varies with the person's beliefs about his ability to take effective counteraction if he perceives danger," although "many anomalies, confusions, and contradictions remain" (1976:374). Jervis' other principal finding in this area can be summarized as follows: "The shutting out of undesired information is most apt to occur when there are no incentives for accuracy." If a "person can do nothing to avert a danger, there is no payoff, from either psychological or rational perspective, in detecting it . . . and he might as well gain the passing satisfaction of avoiding unpleasant thoughts" (ibid.:376).

It is important to observe, however, that Jervis' conclusion to the effect that the inability to respond creates a "defensive" attitude toward danger and reduces the receptivity to threat indicators pertains only to the extreme case in which the target feels *totally* helpless (hopeless). According to Jervis, a less extreme situation, where there are only some constraints on or difficulties in initiating response, could very possibly have the opposite effect. It could enhance rather than retard the receptivity to warning, creating a "vigilant" attitude toward threat indicators which will increase the capacity to respond effectively to an impending danger (ibid.:374-75). I suspect the cases in which at least some response is possible to be the most common (as well as most interesting) ones, and therefore expect a sense of vulnerability commonly to play the role of sensitizing policymakers to threat indicators. This proposition should hold particularly true for strategic threats, cases where the stakes for both the policymaker and the state are so high that a sense of total invulnerability is highly unlikely. I find some support for this proposition in Raymond Cohen's aforementioned study, where he discovered that in five out of six cases examined, a sense of vulnerability indeed served to enhance policymakers sensitivity to threatening signals (1978:98).

Still, to suggest, as I just did, that a sense of vulnerability is not likely to be a common obstacle to strategic threat perception is not to deny it any role in determining the type of action one would initiate in response to a perception of strategic threat. Since the sense of vulnerability is a continuous variable, it is not only possible but even probable that its exact value in each particular case will influence the selection of response. I shall, therefore, elaborate on this issue below when I discuss the relationship between threat perception and response.

## Threat Perception and Response

Response, as I have repeatedly suggested, is a highly complex phenomenon involving many intricate stages. What we frequently see as a single observable outcome (e.g., unpreparedness or lack of effective response) can be, in fact, the product of strikingly different causal paths only some of which have their origins in surprise (see figure 1). Therefore, in order to improve our understanding of the response process, whether as a first step toward making policy prescriptions or as an end in itself, we must attempt to delineate all of these paths, a task that is obviously difficult and problematic but nonetheless well worth the effort. Recall that my method of dealing with this task is to examine the response process in stages, first looking strictly at the threat perception part of the process, then looking strictly at the action initiation and implementation part of it, and only finally combining the two. Having explored the evolution of threat perception in the preceding section, I now proceed to deal with the action initiation and implementation process. I find it useful to do so by way of illuminating the various barriers that must be overcome for a decision on response to be made and successfully implemented.

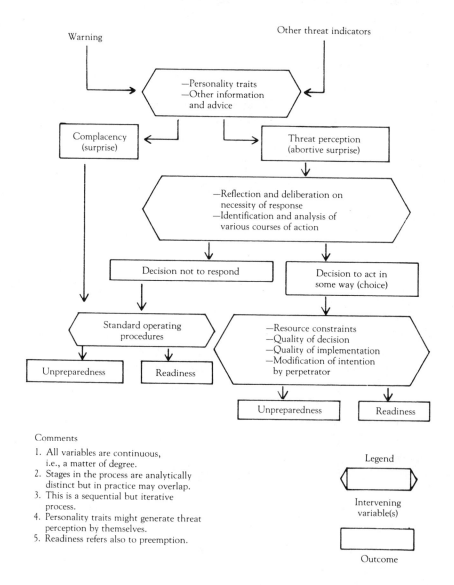

Warning

Other threat indicators

—Personality traits
—Other information
and advice

Complacency
(surprise)

Threat perception
(abortive surprise)

—Reflection and deliberation on
necessity of response
—Identification and analysis of
various courses of action

Decision not to respond

Decision to act in
some way (choice)

Standard operating
procedures

—Resource constraints
—Quality of decision
—Quality of implementation
—Modification of intention
by perpetrator

Unpreparedness

Readiness

Unpreparedness

Readiness

Comments

1. All variables are continuous,
i.e., a matter of degree.
2. Stages in the process are analytically
distinct but in practice may overlap.
3. This is a sequential but iterative
process.
4. Personality traits might generate threat
perception by themselves.
5. Readiness refers also to preemption.

Legend

Intervening
variable(s)

Outcome

Figure 1: Threat Indicators and Action (Response)
—A Flow Chart

Suppose that an intended surprise target does manage to obtain "ideal" warning (i.e., warning that is detailed, comprehensive, timely, categorical, and reliable) and that this warning indeed provides an alarming and remarkably prescient threat perception among the top policymakers of that country. Does this *guarantee* that effective response will follow? The answer to this question is obviously negative, but its theoretical and practical importance requires that I dwell on it at some length.

Threat perception, as I have suggested above, indeed reflects a willingness, at least in principle, to respond to threat. But perception of threat and willingness to respond do not automatically translate into action. A decision has to be made whether, how, and when to respond. This decision, implicit and unconscious as it may be, is essentially a matter of judgment by the political leadership—judgment with respect to the necessity, feasibility, practicality, desirability, and timing of both response in general and specific types of action in particular. The existence of this intervening stage (variable) between threat perception and response means that threat perception will not result in any observable action in the following three cases: when (1) no response is believed to be feasible; (2) a decision is made not to respond (or no decision is made to respond); and (3) a decision to respond is made but not carried out. It is also possible to conceive of a fourth scenario in which some action (response) is initiated but is either not intended to counter the threat as such, or proves ineffective in doing so. These, then, seem four logically exhaustive and mutually exclusive dichotomous scenarios[8] conforming to a single observable outcome—unpreparedness.[9]

In practice, however, these four scenarios are neither mutually exclusive nor dichotomous. In any given situation, they may apply to a greater or lesser degree, and elements of several or all of them may be present simultaneously. Thus, a historical instance of "unpreparedness" is typically a result of a situation in which not only the standard operating procedures are inadequate to counter the threat, but also some types of response are impossible, others are ruled out for one reason or another, still others are approved and not carried out, and finally those that are implemented prove ineffective for a variety of reasons. Nevertheless, for the purposes of the present analysis, it would be useful to look at each of these scenarios as an "ideal type." Only some of the historical examples will reflect the greater complexity of reality.

According to the first scenario, a response is regarded as not feasible. This state of affairs may be the result of either unavailability of resources to mount a response before a threat materializes or, and less likely, the lack of authority to initiate any kind of response. Both of these are, to an extent, a function of the timing of the threat recognition. It might be reached at such a late or otherwise inopportune point in time that the initiation of response is virtually impossible. Thus, for example, General MacArthur has argued that even if the United States had managed to obtain a 72-hour advance warning of the North Korean intention to invade the South, it would have made very little difference; getting any sizable body of U.S. troops from Japan to Korea was a matter of three weeks (MacArthur Hearings 1951, part 1:239–40).

The British apparently faced a similar situation with respect to the Falkland Islands crisis in March 1983, described in the British Ministry of Defense contingency plans as the "26-day gap" (*Sunday Times* 1983:17). For a sizable British naval force to reach the Islands in time for the Argentinian invasion it would have had to leave the British Isles early in March 1982. But the British government possessed no definite word on the imminence of the Argentinian invasion until March 31, 1982, only three days before the invasion was to take place (FCR 1983:73).

The second scenario involves a situation in which while response options are available, a decision is made not to respond. For our purposes here a conscious or unconscious decision not to decide about response (when both decision and response are feasible) is tantamount to deciding not to respond. In both cases the decision not to initiate a response can be guided by one or more of three principal considerations. Response might be deemed by policymakers to be impractical (in contrast to the earlier scenario where it simply was not feasible), undesirable, or unnecessary.

Policymakers are likely to rule out response as impractical when they believe that the existing time and resource constraints permit only the implementation of measures that are not cost-effective. Specifically, they might consider the only measure feasible under the circumstances prohibitively expensive in terms of their direct costs of application, e.g., in loss of human lives, destruction, etc. More interesting, however, and I would submit also more common, are the somewhat similar cases where a decision is made not to respond on the grounds that any such action would be undesirable. In these cases, cost-effective options for countering the danger at hand are thought to exist, but the political leadership still finds some or all of them unacceptable on other grounds. Moral and political considerations (both foreign and domestic) seem particularly important in this context, frequently leading policymakers to rule out response altogether, or at least forego some courses of action that would otherwise seem particularly attractive, e.g., military preemption. The decision of the Israeli cabinet on October 6, 1973 not to launch a preemptive air strike against Syria and Egypt is a case in point.

On the morning of October 6, 1973, the Israeli policymakers were virtually certain that the Arabs would launch a massive attack against Israel later in the day (Agranat Commission 1975:23-24; Meir 1975:426-27). The Israeli leadership was also fully aware of the fact that the military reserves were not as yet mobilized (though not perfectly cognizant of the implications of this fact), and highly confident of the capacity of the Israeli air force to launch a massive preemptive strike against both Syria and Egypt before the attack began. And yet, they decided not to go ahead with the preemptive strike. The evidence strongly suggests that they did so on the logic, heavily reinforced by Henry Kissinger, that the political price Israel would have to pay for the military preemption would be intolerable (Nakdimon 1982:112, 114-15, 125, 132-33, 164; Bartov 1978:9-24; Dayan 1976:575-78; Agranat Commission 1975:24; Schiff 1974:38-44; Meir 1975:426-27.

A similar decision was made by the Executive Committee (ExCom) of the American National Security Council during the Cuban Missile Crisis. Deliberating on a response to the Soviet deployment of ballistic missiles in Cuba, ExCom initially seriously considered the option of launching a disarming air strike against the missiles before they become operational (Kennedy 1969:9). Other drawbacks of this option notwithstanding, it was not ruled out—according to one plausible interpretation which may or may not be correct—until Robert Kennedy raised strong objections to it. He argued persuasivley that launching such a strike would be tantamaount to perpetrating "Pearl Harbor in reverse." He apparently convinced some other members of ExCom, and finally also the president, that such action "could not be undertaken by the United States if we were to maintain our moral position at home and around the globe" (Kennedy 1969:16–17; Allison 1971:69, 123–24, 132–33, 203).

Interestingly enough, President Roosevelt felt much the same way on the eve of Pearl Harbor. Recall that on December 6, 1941 he reacted to the thirteenth part of the Japanese fourteen part message by saying "this means war" (quoted in Prange 1981:475). He then went ahead to discuss with his advisor Harry Hopkins the deployment of the Japanese forces. Hopkins volunteered "that since war was undoubtedly going to come at the convenience of the Japanese it was too bad we could not strike the first blow and prevent any sort of surprise." Roosevelt agreed and is quoted as saying, "No, we can't do that, we are a democracy and peaceful people" (ibid.).

Another theoretically interesting case where response might be considered undesirable has to do with a situation in which the target believes that the perpetrator's action, if carried out, will actually work to his—the target's—advantage. Under such circumstances, policymakers will have a strong incentive not to initiate any response, especially not an overt one, irrespective of how cost-effective it promises to be, for fear of tipping off the perpetrator and leading him to reconsider, modify, or cancel his original plans. A somewhat similar case where response could be deemed undesirable touches upon a problem unique to warning derived from intelligence. When threat perception originates in warning, and warning in a much-coveted and highly sensitive intelligence source, there is a strong incentive to refrain from any action that might expose the source or detract from its capacity to provide useful, even critical, information in the future. This, however, imposes rather severe constraints on the type of response that could otherwise be made to the threat, and presents policymakers with a painful dilemma, namely to risk exposing the source (by initiating action), or to sacrifice other core values by not taking action. An example from the World War II context will illustrate the point.

According to several historical accounts, Winston Churchill possessed advance warning of Germany's intention to launch a massive bombing raid against the city of Coventry, codenamed "Operation Moonlight Sonata," on the night of November 14/15, 1940. Churchill, according to these accounts, then made the painful decision not to evacuate the city's inhabitants for fear of exposing his source of information—the German Air Force's Enigma (Ultra)—the Allies' most important and sensitive source of information on Germany. Churchill, the story goes on, did nonetheless take the less risky action of alerting the RAF and the jamming units, as well as Coventry's fire, ambulance, police, and air wardens, but these measures proved largely ineffective. And when the German air raid on Coventry materialized, it inflicted heavy casualties (554 dead, 865 seriously wounded) and mass destruction (Winterbotham 1974:60–61).

The accuracy of some parts of this story has recently been called into doubt by several new and apparently more reliable studies by Hinsley (1979 1:316–18), Jones (1978:147–52), Lewin (1980:100–2), and others. These new accounts suggest that Churchill was spared the painful dilemma because British intelligence was unable to identify with any certainty ahead of time the target for the German air raid of November 14. But as Hinsley himself points out, similar, though perhaps less painful, dilemmas were faced by the British on numerous other occasions throughout World War II, and quite a few were indeed resolved in favor of protecting the intelligence source (e.g., in attacking the supply convoys to Rommel during the North African campaign; see Hinsley 1981 vol. 2, ch. 21). The message of the story therefore remains valid even if the story itself is not fully accurate. Policymakers are willing to go to great lengths to protect valuable sensitive intelligence sources for future use, even when considerable immediate cost and sacrifice is involved.

In passing I might add that response is, perhaps, most commonly dismissed as undesirable on the grounds that it might turn into a "self-fulfilling prophecy," causing war to occur where it could have otherwise been averted. How much weight policymakers attach to this consideration, however, varies from one case to another depending, to no small degree, on their confidence in the inevitability of the danger and the accuracy of the threat indicators. I shall therefore dwell on this case at some length in the next section.

I have already discussed cases where threat perception does not trigger response because the latter actually is, or is at least believed to be, unfeasible (first scenario), impractical, or undesirable (second scenario). But a decision not to respond is also possible when policymakers are convinced that it is unnecessary to take action to counter an impending threat. The point here is that a decision to initiate response to a threat is not made strictly on the basis of threat perception (defined as recognition of the adversary's hostile intentions). It is also shaped by an assessment, however implicit and unconscious, of the implications of the adversary's action for one's values, an assessment that necessarily takes into consideration one's assets, capabilities, vulnerabilities, etc. This "net assessment" of sorts may well lead even policymakers who are fully cognizant of their adversary's intentions to conclude that no special or additional measures are required under the circumstances. They may simply be under the impression that existing policies, standard operating procedures, a state of readiness, and the like will suffice to handle the evolving threat. Let me illustrate the point by drawing once more on the example of the Yom Kippur War.

Until the outbreak of the Yom Kippur War it was widely believed in Israel, including by most of the political and military leaders, that the *regular* army would be able to hold out against a massive Arab attack long enough to facilitate orderly mobilization of reserves, a process normally requiring 48–72 hours.

Bearing this in mind and knowing that the regular Israeli army had been on maximum alert since the preceding day, the top Israeli leaders were not overly alarmed to learn on the morning of October 6 that a full-scale Arab attack was expected to take place later in the day, long before the mobilization of reserves could be completed. They reasoned that despite the lack of sufficient warning to mobilize the reserves, the military situation did not call for a politically costly decision to launch a preemptive air strike against the Arabs and therefore decided not to go ahead with the planned air strike. As it turned out, the Israeli policymakers were not entirely wrong. The regular Israeli army did manage to hold out until the reserves were mobilized. But this was only possible thanks to a quicker mobilization of reserves than had been previously anticipated, and at a very high cost, particularly in terms of human casualties. The high casualty figures subsequently led some of the policymakers to lament their earlier decision (Nakdimon 1982:114–15).

A very similar case, involving "simple" misunderstanding but resulting in no less severe consequences, can also be noted with respect to the Pearl Harbor episode. At least some of the top naval authorities in Washington were convinced, or at least claim to have been convinced, that the Pacific Fleet had left the harbor and sailed to sea after the first alert message from Washington was received in Hawaii in late November 1941. They therefore reasoned that the fleet was no longer vulnerable to a Japanese surprise attack, and decided not to send any additional messages to alert the Pacific Fleet (Prange 1981:408–9). Similar confusion also existed between the army commanders in Washington and General Short in Hawaii.

What the two cases vividly illustrate is, therefore, that in shaping response to strategic threat, a policymaker's notions regarding his own side could well be as important as his perceptions regarding the other side. As such the cases draw our attention to an important potential barrier to the translation of an alarming threat perception into a decision to respond. But as can be seen below,[10] the Yom Kippur case has another important insight to offer. It also demonstrates that even when policymakers do perceive a threat and believe some response to be feasible, practical, de-sirable, and necessary, and make a decision along these lines, unpreparedness may still be the final outcome. For one thing, the decision on the countermeasures to be taken might not be sound in the first place. For another thing, the implementation of these measures might be deficient. And finally, it is even possible that an excellent decision that is flawlessly implemented will prove partially or totally ineffective because the perpetrator had modified in the interim his original behavior and plans.

In conclusion, I wish to remind the reader that my primary purpose here has been to demonstrate the independence of threat perception and response. I sought to do so by examining variations in the nature and efficacy of response as a function of developments exclusively within the decision making and imple-mentation processes. My principal focus has therefore been on the obstacles standing in the way of effective response. It must be realized, however, that I did not intend, nor does my analysis permit it, to draw any valid conclusions regarding the likelihood that response will prove (in) effective. For one thing, I have only looked at the obstacles effective response must overcome. For another thing, the empirical evidence on the issue is far from conclusive, partially as a result of limitations of the data. I shall, nonetheless, offer some thoughts on this last issue in my final chapter.

I have thus far looked at warning and response in isolation from each other, holding one constant while manipulating the other. This practice was adopted deliberately to highlight the features that are unique to each process. But this practice will no longer do. Making further progress in understanding both phe-nomena and formulating a policy-related theory requires that I bring the analysis closer to reality. This, in turn, calls for integrating the concepts of warning and response in a unified framework for analysis, a framework that also incorporates the dynamic-interactive dimension of their relationship. It is to this task that I now turn.

### Warning and Response:
### Some Practical Considerations

Introducing into my discussion of warning and response a dynamic-interactive dimension essentially means exploring the ways in which variations in the warning process affect the efficacy of response to threat. Thus, while I have previously assumed that warning would be ideal in terms of its quality (i.e., scope, specificity, certainty, reliability, timeliness, etc.) and capacity to dominate policymakers' threat perception, I will now relax this unrealistic assumption and consider the possibility that warning will be deficient in one or more of these respects. I will evaluate the impact of such deficiencies on the capacity to mount an effective response, and look into possible solutions for rectifying and/or offsetting these deficiencies.

It is widely believed that the quality of warning generally improves only as the time of the confrontation draws near, to the point that warning does not become either definite or complete, if it ever does, until shortly before the threat materializes. Insofar that this is indeed the case (an issue I shall address in the final chapter), states must be able to carry out one or more of the following strategies: (1) initiate at least some response on the basis of partial and/or ambiguous warning; (2) mount a "decisive" response (preemptive and/or preventive) on the basis of a very short warning; or (3) tolerate some disaster—withstand the initial impact of a surprise move—and still mount a decisive response. I shall first examine each of these strategies separately, then discuss the possibility of lumping them together. The evaluation of the strategies will be made on the basis of their impact on the likelihood of military confrontation, the cost of military confrontation if it occurs, and the cost in peacetime.

#### Strategy 1

Initiating response on the basis of partial or uncertain warning has two rather obvious but nonetheless important advantages. It diminishes the likelihood of being caught by surprise (reduces the cost of confrontation if it occurs), and it does not require a considerable investment in peacetime (routine) readiness. Both advantages, however, come at a very significant cost. Sensitizing intelligence to alert policymakers to the possibility of a strategic threat even when they are unsure about its existence,[11] let alone its details, and urging policymakers to act on the basis of such warning, which is what this strategy is all about, necessarily increases the likelihood of false alarms.[12] To use the terminology of communication theory and an analogy to radar, attempts to minimize type 1 errors (no warning sounded when it should have been) by raising sensitivity necessarily increase the probability that type 2 errors (warning sounded when it should not have been) will occur[13] (see figure 2).

The risk of more false alarms should not be taken lightly as their consequences may be dire indeed. Yet what kind of consequences follow from false alarms depends on the nature of the reaction to them by the policymakers and the type of response they eventually trigger. Thus, it is possible that false alarms will result in a significant waste of resources when they provoke unnecessary action. They may also erode somewhat the receptivity to future warning through what is known as the "cry wolf syndrome." But by far the worst possible consequence of false alarms is that they will significantly increase the likelihood that a military confrontation will take place. They can do so in two principal ways. First, like every other warning of impending threat (but obviously with even less justification), false warnings can create a strong incentive to preempt, especially when there is a substantial premium on the first strike or when the alerted leaders are nurturing excuses for initiating war themselves. Second, even when the target opts for a reaction to the false warning that is defensive in nature, it is still possible that his reaction will be misinterpreted by the opponent as offensive, and lead the latter to hostile action that he did not have in mind originally.

But while the strategy of acting on the basis of uncertain warning can have undesirable consequences and be highly destabilizing, just like the "launch on warning" strategy in the

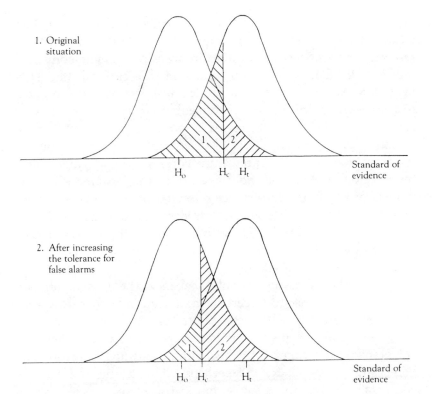

1. Original situation

$H_o$    $H_c$  $H_t$

Standard of evidence

2. After increasing the tolerance for false alarms

$H_o$  $H_c$      $H_t$

Standard of evidence

All other things being equal, the effect of lowering the standard required for issuing warning (shifting the $H_c$ to the left) is to reduce the likelihood of surprise (type 1 error) but raise the probability of false alarm (type 2 error).

Legend:

$H_o$: hypothesis that no threat exists
$H_t$: hypothesis that a threat does exist
$H_c$: criterion (standard of evidence required) for choosing $H_t$ over $H_o$.

Shaded areas depict probability of ⟋⟋⟋ surprise

⟍⟍⟍ false alarm.

Comment: The relative positions of $H_o$, $H_t$, and $H_c$ have been selected only for illustrative purposes and are not intended to reflect the actual probabilities of either type of error.

Figure 2: The Trade-Off Between Surprise and False Alarm

nuclear context,[14] this need not necessarily be the case. Policy-makers may be very much aware of the danger inherent in responding to uncertain warning in ways that might convert it into a "self-fulfilling prophecy" and lead to accidental war. They may, as a result, exercise great caution in selecting their response to such warning. In fact, fear of accidental war seems very prevalent among policymakers and acts as a powerful restraint on their response to uncertain threat. I have already pointed out the importance of fear of a premature confrontation in moderating the reaction of American policymakers to the Japanese threat on the eve of the Pearl Harbor attack (see chapter 2). There is some evidence to suggest that similar considerations also guided Joseph Stalin and Moshe Dayan in reacting, respectively, to warnings of an impending German invasion of the Soviet Union (1941) and an Arab attack on Israel (1973).

The awareness of policymakers of the dangers inherent in excessive response to uncertain threat can indeed redress some of the most serious deficiencies of strategy 1. This is so because there are several types of limited response that can diminish vulnerability to strategic threats without making confrontation significantly more likely, and perhaps even making it less likely. Alexander George, for example, has identified six possible uses of inconclusive warning (1979a: 21-22) that at least in the abstract seem to meet these criteria. The possible uses according to George are:

1. To step up the information search.
2. To alert forces in order to reduce their vulnerability and improve their readiness.
3. To reinforce deterrence by signaling a more credible commitment.
4. To take measures that will reduce one's political/ diplomatic costs from the emergent crisis in the domestic or international arena.
5. To conduct a decision rehearsal, i.e., rehearse the decision problem one would be confronted with if the warning of crisis proved to be justified.

6. To review one's commitment to a weak ally who would become the target should the crisis emerge.

Further consideration of all of these possible uses of inconclusive warning is beyond the scope of this work. Nevertheless, given the primary interest of this work in intelligence and its uses for crisis avoidance and management, I shall briefly illustrate below the importance as well as potential inherent in utilizing inconclusive warning to step up information search in general, and intelligence collection in particular.

By November 8, 1950, after the Chinese Communist forces had crossed the Yalu and subjected U.S. and South Korean forces to tactical combat, U.S. intelligence was able to detect a significant Chinese military presence in North Korea. Yet it was still doubtful whether the Chinese would actually directly commit these forces to large-scale military operations against U.S. forces in Korea (NIE 2 1950). By November 14, however, enough intriguing, albeit inconclusive, information regarding the Chinese involvement in Korea had accumulated in Washington to stir considerable alarm over their intentions. Meeting on that day, the National Security Council took note of these developments and concluded that "it was of the utmost importance that the real intentions of the Chinese Communists be ascertained as soon as possible." As a matter of urgency it therefore recommended to the president, among other things, that he "intensify covert action to determine Chinese Communist intentions" as well as use other available channels to "ascertain Chinese Communist intentions" (NSC 81/2 1950).

At least the NSC (National Security Council) recommendations with respect to the intensification of clandestine collection seem to have been implemented with great speed and efficiency. By November 24, two days before the Chinese attack took place, the CIA was able to update its earlier estimate of China's intentions in Korea. Drawing on additional information obtained in the interim from sensitive sources in the People's Republic of China, some apparently with access even to the Party leadership, the CIA reached a most alarming (and in retrospect remarkably accurate and prescient if somewhat incomplete) reading of China's intentions and capabilities (NIE 2/1 1950). Interestingly enough, this CIA estimate even seems to have carried the day with the top leadership in Washington, as Secretary of State Dean Acheson later testified (MacArthur Hearings 1951, part 3, p. 1834), though the policymakers somehow failed to translate this threat perception into any concrete action.[15]


### Strategy 2

The second strategy seeks to compensate for belated warning (threat perception) by developing a capability to mount, on very short notice, a "decisive" preventive and/or preemptive response. This could be done, for example, by making arrangements for the rapid mobilization of reserves (e.g., the militia system in Israel and Switzerland), pre-positioning arms, munitions, and supplies in strategic locations, and developing a massive air-lift capability (e.g., POMCUS—pre-positioned American war material in Western Europe, the American Rapid Deployment Force), etc.[16]

The greatest attraction of this strategy is that it makes it possible and practical to exercise flexibility in response to threat by delaying irrevocable or fully provocative action until warning of higher reliability and certainty becomes available. By making it possible to delay the determination of whether the threat is real or imagined until much closer to the event, this strategy reduces the probability of both surprise and false alarms (see figure 3). Thus, while the actual contribution of strategy 2 may still vary depending on the specific circumstances and manner in which it is applied, at least in the abstract it seems a stabilizing strategy, insofar as it diminishes the prospects of accidental confrontation and also reduces the likelihood of a deliberate confrontation by reinforcing the deterrence posture.

It is in its actual implementation that strategy 2 might acquire some destabilizing elements as well. Some types of advance preparation to minimize response time are prone to mishaps which in turn might trigger a chain reaction. Other such preparations enhance not only defensive but also offensive capability, thereby

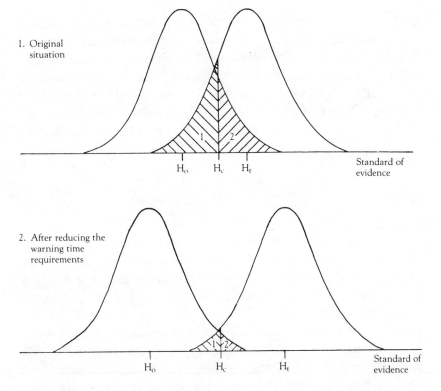

1. Original situation

$H_o$  $H_c$  $H_t$     Standard of evidence

2. After reducing the warning time requirements

$H_o$  $H_c$  $H_t$     Standard of evidence

All other things being equal, the effect of reducing the warning time required is to move $H_t$ and $H_o$ apart, thereby also diminishing the probability of both kinds of errors, type 1 (surprise) and type 2 (false alarm). Put differently, the difference between real threat and a false alarm becomes clearer the closer it gets to the event.

Legend:

$H_o$: hypothesis that no threat exists
$H_t$: hypothesis that a threat does exist
$H_c$: criterion (standard of evidence required) for choosing $H_t$ over $H_o$.

Shaded areas depict probability of     surprise

     false alarm

Comment: The relative positions of $H_o$, $H_t$, and $H_c$ have only been selected for illustrative purposes and are not intended to reflect the actual probabilities of either type of error.

Figure 3: The Impact of Changes in Warning Time Requirements on the Probability of Type 1 and 2 Errors

creating for both sides an incentive to preempt at the first sign of trouble (e.g., the development of a railway infrastructure in Europe prior to World War I; civil defense in the nuclear age). But by far the most serious drawback of this strategy is its cost in peacetime. Maintaining a viable response capability of the kind required by this strategy necessitates a massive initial investment as well as sustained expenditure for maintenance, modernization, training, etc.

### Strategy 3

As defined earlier, the essence of strategy 3 is to develop the capacity to "tolerate" the opponent's initiation of hostilities and still be able to mount a decisive response (i.e., war fighting/war winning capability).[17] But as Israel found out on October 6, 1973, even strategies 1 and 2 *combined* can be insufficient for preventing a costly and painful setback from taking place.[18] When for one reason or another a country does not resort to or fails to implement the two other strategies, it is on the existence of strategy 3 that survival, independence, sovereignty, or welfare may ultimately depend. The capacity to withstand a painful initial setback and still respond decisively, which is what strategy 3 is all about, plays an even more important role in enhancing deterrence and preventing accidental and deliberate war than any of the other strategies. After all, it completely removes the burden of warning from intelligence and enables the target to defer his response until the threat actually materializes.[19] The importance of this strategy is particularly evident in the nuclear era when a "second strike" capability ("assured destruction") obviates the need for a much more destabilizing type 1 strategy such as "launch of warning." The strategy nonetheless entails significant costs in peacetime, to ensure survivability of the capacity to response after an initial setback, and even more considerable ones in the event that confrontation does occur.

Several important conclusions clearly emerge from the above discussion. All three principal strategies to compensate for uncertainty of warning have considerable merit, but none is without serious drawbacks as well. Furthermore, none of the strategies is adequate by itself, and it is a challenge to find the right mix of several or all of these strategies. The ideal solution is, therefore, one based on selecting and mixing some elements of each strategy in a way that is commensurate with one's capabilities, priorities, and the unique circumstances of the case. This, in turn, implies that the exact mix of elements chosen may well vary from one strategic problem to another, as well as between and within countries over time, which indeed it does. Thus, for example, a mix of strategies, which is desirable for a small and highly vulnerable country like Israel, is clearly not optimal for a large and relatively invulnerable country like the United States. What is, nonetheless, common to all countries is the practical problems they face in adopting any of these strategies. When attempting to implement them, they have to devote much attention to detail to make sure that the overall objective of the strategy is not subverted or compromised in the process of implementation.

At this point I ought to make clear also what all three strategies to compensate for uncertain warning do not and cannot do. They do not minimize the uncertainty of warning, and they do not help in any way to produce an accurate threat perception. As such they leave much to be desired. Because it is costly and risky to compensate for uncertainty, a strong incentive exists to reduce it, however marginally. Similarly, because the accuracy and timing of a perception of threat can significantly affect the success of any response initiated to counter it, there is a premium for improving both. The need therefore arises to find ways to supplement, if one can not completely substitute for, the strategies for uncertainty. Two complimentary approaches for redressing these problems are commonly advocated. Let us consider them.

## The "Intelligence" Solution

The first approach for enhancing the capacity to respond effectively, and reducing the reliance on strategies that are inherently costly and risky, is one that seeks to minimize uncertainty by making efforts to produce satisfactory warning sooner (see figure 4). Efforts along these lines usually proceed in several complementary directions. One is typically the upgrading of intelligence collection, especially of certain types of collection that are most likely to produce early warning, namely Sigint and Humint. Intensification of collection is said to result in a better intelligence product (Gazit 1979:54–55) although it does have some inherent limitations (see chapter 1) and undesirable side effects, primarily the inundating of intelligence services with enormous quantities of information to process. At least some of these side effects can, however, be offset by assigning more manpower to the task of screening the information, automating the process and, most important, by intensifying collection in a rather selective and focused manner. Emphasis on collection therefore seems a promising way to reduce the uncertainty, though only modestly so.

Efforts to improve intelligence's capacity to warn policymakers on time can be, and are in practice, directed also at a subsequent stage of the intelligence production process, namely *evaluation*. Traditional efforts in this area have largely been confined to tinkering with the organizational structure and budget, the recruitment and training of the analysts, the management of the process, etc. More recently, however, rather significant efforts have also been made to improve the ability of intelligence agencies—at the level of both the individual analyst and the organization as a whole—to identify and warn of impending strategic threats. These efforts currently proceed in two directions. One is the incorporation into the evaluation process of quantitative methods (Heuer 1981a; Singer and Wallace 1979; Hopkins 1980; Jodice 1982) based on recent developments in the fields of social science and computer technology. The other direction, which has received considerable attention in recent years, is the development and

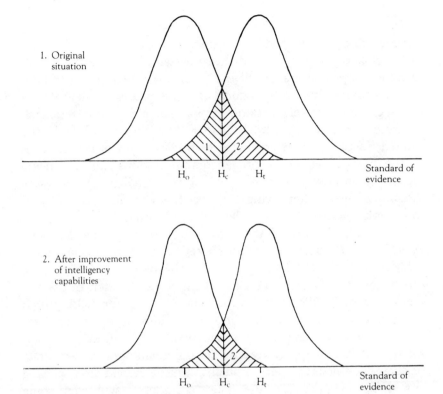

1. Original
   situation

$H_o$     $H_c$     $H_t$      Standard of evidence

2. After improvement
   of intelligency
   capabilities

$H_o$     $H_c$     $H_t$      Standard of evidence

All other things being equal, the effect of improving one's intelligence capabilities (enchancing the capacity to detect threat indicators) is to decrease the width of the probability distribution (i.e., to lower the standard deviation), thereby reducing the likelihood of both type 1 (surprise) and type 2 (false alarm) errors.

Legend:

$H_o$: hypothesis that no threat exists
$H_t$: hypothesis that a threat does exist
$H_c$: criterion (standard of evidence required) for choosing $H_t$ over $H_o$.

Shaded areas depict probability of      surprise

     false alarm

Comment: The relative positions of $H_o$, $H_t$, and $H_c$ have only been selected for illustrative purposes and are not intended to reflect the actual probabilities of either type of error.

Figure 4: The Impact of Improvements in Intelligence Capabilities on the Probability of Type 1 and 2 Errors

adoption of analytical techniques and organizational arrangements designed to overcome and/or compensate for common pathologies in information processing and threat assessment. Here the idea is to raise analysts' awareness of the problems inherent in the evaluation process, and to introduce into the process review procedures, dissent channels, periodic reappraisal, and postmortem analyses, etc. (*Jerusalem Post* 1982; Lauder 1985; Shmuel 1985). In the United States, modern computer technology and other advances in the area of secure real-time communications are also being tapped to improve the final stage of the intelligance process— *dissemination*—by improving the speed, scope and reliability of information transmission (Belden 1977; Gravely 1982).

Evaluation of the actual contribution made by post-World War II efforts to improve intelligence warning capacity is a highly complicated job, even under the best of circumstances, due to the exceptional complexity of the subject matter. But severe limitations on public access to the data necessary for making such an assessment make matters far worse. Thus, it is virtually impossible for an outsider to assess independently, and in any meaningful and valid way, the recent developments and current state of affairs in this area. Here, I shall therefore refrain from passing any direct judgment on the issue, although I will offer some thoughts on related issues, primarily on the basis of deductive reasoning, in the concluding chapter.

## The "Consumption" Problem

The second complementary approach to the response problem is one that aims at a smoother, faster, and more reliable translation of intelligence warning, as well as other information and advice, into threat perception. The critical problem that has to be overcome in this area is policymakers' difficulties in absorbing and reacting to information pertaining to a strategic threat. Eliminating the problem is virtually impossible, since its roots lie in the general weaknesses and limitations of individuals and small groups as processors of information and makers of choice (see chapter 1). Nevertheless, the task of *diminishing* the problems in this area is by no means hopeless.

The identification and diagnosis of the pathologies and impediments inherent in threat perception and decision making has raised the consciousness of these problems among students as well as practitioners of defense and foreign policy. It has also made it possible to search for ways of redressing these problems. Consequently, some progress has been made in the development and even implementation of formulas for improving threat perception and policymaking (see George 1980:chs. 7–12; Janis:1972 ch. 11) through modification of the advisory process (e.g., through the introduction of multiple advocacy, devil's advocates, and dissent channels).[20] Much more obviously remains to be done in this area. But the unique features of the subject matter (high stakes, transparency of the national interest, etc.) have inspired some confidence in the belief, which I share, that the development and implementation of discriminatory (and therefore more effective) practices for dealing with strategic threats are humanly possible and politically feasible. In any event, the stakes are so high that concentrated efforts in this area are widely believed to be worthwhile.


Finally, a brief conclusion. In this chapter I have explored various features of the warning and response process. I have examined, in particular, the problems inherent in the process as well as common approaches for dealing with them. Here and there reference was made to the actual application and implementation of some of these strategies and solutions. Specific and detailed policy prescriptions in this area, however, lie outside the scope of this work. Nevertheless, in closing I do wish to offer one general observation regarding the utility of remedies to warning and response problems, an observation drawing on an analogy to a chain. The strength of a chain is equivalent to the strength of its weakest link. When significant weakness exists in all or most of the links, improvements in only some of them, as drastic as they may be, will not result in any significant difference in the strength of the chain as a whole. Improvements are required across the board. By the same logic, to make a practical difference, problems in every stage of the warning and response process need to be addressed. In this sense the various solutions and strategies discussed ought to be considered complementary and their utility interdependent.

# Chapter 5

# Strategic Surprise
# in Perspective

**The primary purpose** of this study has been to try to improve the understanding of strategic surprises and related phenomena such as threat perception and response to threat. It was with this goal in mind that the existing literature on these issues was reviewed, its weaknesses delineated, and a new methodological approach to the study of these phenomena proposed (chapter 1). Some empirical evidence in the form of two historical case studies (chapters 2 and 3) as well as illustrations drawn from other historical instances (chapter 4) was then brought to bear on my principal hypotheses. Finally, chapter 4 sought to integrate aspects of warning and surprise into a broader theoretical framework of detection, perception, and reaction to strategic foreign threats. Here, I wish to go one step further, and extract from my case studies some broader insights into the strategic surprise phenomenon in general, and the study of surprise in particular. Thus, I shall first briefly present my prinicipal methodological and theoretical findings, and then proceed to discuss their generalizability beyond the temporal and spatial domain from which they were derived.

Perhaps the best place to start this discussion is with the methodological findings, for these are applicable, in principle, to any study of surprise, and therefore transcend in importance the limited theoretical insights that could be derived from my modest effort here. Possibly the most important methodological lesson this study can offer is that which pertains to the procedure for assessing the quality of warning. As I have pointed out (see chaper 1), an evaluation of the quality of warning and other threat indicators that one possesses regarding his adversary's impending moves is a necessry first step for any explantion of strategic surprise. It is precisely for this reason that it ought to be made with rigor, precision, and above all, much attention to detail. My study of Pearl Harbor has clearly demonstrated that unless all of this is done (and previous studies of the episode have indeed failed in this regard), one is likely to reach misleading conclusions regarding the causes of surprise.

What my study further suggests is that the warning available to an intended surprise target should be assessed on each of the five dimensions of surprise (who, why, what, where, and when) (George 1979a:14-16), but also that the quality of warning with respect to each of these dimensions ought to be ranked, at least implicitly, on several qualitative scales (i.e., how timely, cat-egorical, comprehensive, and reliable it is). In this context the study also indicates that it is most useful to distinguish between warning, which I define as "information obtained and processed by intelligence agencies pointing to an acute or potential foreign threat" and other threat indicators (see chapter 4). This distinction, not clearly or consistently made by earlier writers, plays an im-portant role in the present study.

A related insight concerns the importance of primary sources for the study of strategic surprise. Primary sources are obviously invaluable for any kind of historical research. But my experience here, primarily, but not solely, with the Pearl Harbor episode, suggests that the need to consult primary sources is especially acute where the assessment of warning is concerned. Secondary sources, it would seem, frequently provide such a fragmentary and distorted picture of the issue that relying on them as one's principal source of data commonly leads to erroneous conclusions.

Both of the case studies, as well as some of the illustrations in chapter 4, also point to the need to adopt a more sensitive and discriminating approach to other aspects of the surprise phenomenon. As I have explained and illustrated in chapter 4, it is crucial that we learn to distinguish between the empirically related but analytically separate phenomena of threat perception (surprise), decision to act (respond), actual action (response), and the final outcome (i.e., readiness or unpreparedness). In particular we ought to refrain from the currently prevalent practice of using either unpreparedness or absence of warning as the only operational indictors for the occurrence of surprise.

Finally, a word on research strategy. Two lessons on this matter can be derived from this study. The first concerns the serious limitations of single ("disciplined-configurative") case studies for building theory on strategic surprises. These problems, which have already been recognized for case studies in general (George 1979b, 1982; Eckstein 1975:92ff.), become particularly apparent when one replicates any single case study of surprise using a comparative perspective. This practice, which I have followed in the analysis of Pearl Harbor, exposes the weaknesses of the single case study approach and, by contrast, illustrates the advantages inherent in a "structured, focused comparison," even when only a small number of cases can be studied.[1] The second lesson has to do with the utility and importance of comparing cases with great similarities in many of the independent variables and sufficient variation on the dependent one.[2] As the comparison between Pearl Harbor and Midway vividly demonstrates, the potential inherent in the comparative approach to the study of surprise could be greatly enhanced if we contrast abortive surprise attempts with successful ones.

I now wish to turn to the theoretical findings. Before I do so, however, I would remind the reader that the primary theoretical goal of this study has been to further our understanding of the surprise phenomenon on such issues as its cause(s), frequency of occurrence, inevitability, etc. Recall that earlier studies have observed many instances of surprise and identified numerous obstacles that stand in the way of both accurate threat perception and adequate response. I sought to refine and expand on these findings, first by introducing a heretofore neglected explanation of surprise—one based on the type and quality of institutionalized warning available to a surprise target—then by determining under what conditions such warning is likely to be available, overcome barriers to receptivity, produce a prescient threat perception, and lead to effective response. Toward this end I postulated and set out to test empirically three interrelated statements:

1. The intelligence services of an intended surprise target are able, at least on occasion, to acquire and produce timely comprehensive, reliable, and extremely accurate warning.

2. The unique features of the problematic situation faced by the target (especially the incentive structure) make it likely that intelligence warning possessing many or all of the above qualities would succeed in producing a perception of threat among the target's policymakers even in the presence of severe and diverse barriers to receptivity.

3. The various human and organizational pathologies and other barriers to threat perception are most likely to determine the outcome (i.e., surprise) primarily when there are serious deficiencies in the warning and other threat indicators available to the policymakers.

Overall, the findings in our case studies are highly consistent with my explanation of surprise in general, and the three hypotheses in particular. This consistency clearly enhances the relevance and utility of my theoretical framework. Yet the intrinsic limitations of my research strategy are rather pronounced, and require that the findings themselves, if regarded as generalizations, be treated with caution. Thus, the conclusions that follow are necessarily provisional in nature, subject to assessment and revision in future research.

In regard to the first hypothesis, the Midway case demonstrates rather conclusively that excellent warning is (or at least was) not merely possible in principle but also turned out to be empirically achievable. This is not to say that such high-quality warning is either common or easy to acquire—a separate issue which I shall address below—but rather that such warning is, in principle as well as sometimes in practice, attainable. While this finding may seem to many to be intuitively correct, perhaps even trivial, it nonetheless runs counter to the common wisdom in the literature (e.g., Betts 1980; Wohlstetter 1962, 1965; Handel 1980). And in any event, the existence of such warning has not heretofore been documented in any study of surprise. As for the practical importance of this proposition, it lies first and foremost in the fact that it sets a standard of quality against which the available warning (and other threat indicators) in any given case can be compared. Such a standard is required to facilitate more accurate assessment of warning, which currently is frequently imprecise and biased (see below), and by implication is also necessary to provide the basis for a more valid and/or more comprehensive explanation of surprise.

My second hypothesis again derives much support from the Midway case. The study of that case vividly demonstrates (and some of the cases discussed in chapter 4 additionally illustrate) that excellent strategic warning,[3] while not automatically accepted by policymakers, can nonetheless carry sufficient weight to overcome numerous and diverse organizational pathologies and other barriers to receptivity, and dominate policymakers' threat perception. In this context, the study also confirms the critical importance that the type and assessed reliability of a source[4] of information plays in determining the weight assigned to the information it provides.[5] The study does, nonetheless, suggest that some reformulation of my original hypothesis is required, namely that information derived from a reliable source is likely to have considerable impact *only when its consumers are truly familiar with the identity and reliability of the source*, at least in general terms. As both Midway and other historical cases demonstrate (Betts 1982b:94; Hinsley 1979:1:138–39), warning that has all of the desired features (including the reliable source) fails to shape policymakers' perceptions when the latter are deprived, for one reason or another (usually "sources and methods" protection), of knowledge of the source or deceived about its true identity.

When we turn to discuss the empirical findings regarding the third hypothesis, a serious problem is encountered.

To suggest with some confidence that excellent warning can prevent surprise (as I did above), it is sufficient to demonstrate that such was the case in at least one prominent historical instance. But to confirm the third hypothesis as well, that surprise commonly occurs exactly when high-quality warning and other explicit threat indicators are not available, requires supporting evidence from a large number of cases, whereas here only one instance of surprise has been explored in some depth. My empirical findings regarding the generalizability of the third hypothesis—despite its seeming face validity—are, therefore, provisional. Nevertheless, my reexamination of Pearl Harbor, an instance of surprise that is widely believed to have been preceded by excellent warning, does illustrate in a rather compelling way that it is a common practice for scholars in the field to overrate the quality of warning and other threat indicators that were available in the cases they study. Thus, even if this study cannot, by itself, establish inadequate warning as a leading cause of surprise, it is sufficient to draw attention to a heretofore little regarded causal pattern leading to surprise, one based on inadequate warning. Since this hypothesis itself has considerable face validity, the support for it provided in the present study could be dismissed as making only a marginal contribution to the theory of strategic surprise were it not for the common practice in the field to dismiss explanations of surprise based on deficiency in warning, and advocate instead more "exciting" explanations—those based on information processing pathologies or barriers of one kind or another (see chapter 1).

In addition to the support the case studies provide for my original hypotheses, they also offer—together with the analysis presented in chapter 4—some insights into the relationship between the target's perception of threat and its reaction (response) to it. Particularly important among these insights is my finding that perception of a foreign threat among a country's top policymakers seems to emerge, on occasion, from threat indicators other than warning, i.e. independently of intelligence warning, and at times even in contradiction to intelligence estimates. The significance of this finding lies in the fact that threat perception of this nature can and does trigger consideration and initiation of response, very much as does threat perception that emerges on the basis of institutional warning. To date, this possibility has received little attention in the literature and needs to be further explored.

A related insight developed in the present study has to do with problems associated with acting on the basis of threat perception. My study suggests that the obstacles encountered in perceiving a strategic foreign threat (whatever its source) are exacerbated and probably also dwarfed by the difficulties a target may experience in attempting to devise and implement an effective reaction (response) to such a threat. This appears to be the case insofar as reaction/response is sensitive to all of the problems of threat perception as well as many additional ones. Thus, unlike most other studies in the field which tend to emphasize perception of threat as the critical link in translating warning into an effective reaction (response), my study indicates that the problems a target experiences in deciding whether and how to respond may well contribute more to being caught unprepared than do the problems of arriving at a valid perception of threat. Thus, I expect efforts to improve one's warning capabilities and receptivity to intelligence indicators to meet with only partial success unless they are accompanied by corresponding improvements in the capacity to react. My conclusion on this matter is, therefore, rather similar to that reached by some previous writers, namely that the problem of reaction (response) to threat requires no less attention than is currently devoted to the problems of warning and threat perception (George and Smoke 1974:ch. 20; George 1979a:14, 20-24).

Finally, I wish to use this study to throw some light on one additional issue of considerable importance, namely the likelihood that excellent warning will be available to the intended target of a strategic surprise attack. Before I can address this issue, however, a caveat is in order. The insights derived from this study up to this point have largely pertained to matters of principle. As such they could be established with some confidence on the basis of empirical evidence drawn even from a single case study. The same, however, does not hold true for the hypotheses I now wish to offer; since they deal with frequency distributions and probability they can be asserted with confidence only on the basis of research based on a number of cases that constitute a representative sample of the universe of cases. Since my study does not meet this requirement—and, indeed, it would be difficult to meet, since much of the relevant data on the warning issue for other cases of surprise is unavailable in the public domain—such hypotheses cannot be easily subjected to empirical testing. Nonetheless, some thoughts on the issue can be offered primarily on the basis of deductive reasoning. The reader must be aware, however, that these observations are tentative and provisional, and their validity is subject to reassessment in future studies.

My effort to determine how likely it is that excellent warning would be available to an intended target of a strategic surprise attempt centers on two complementary questions. First, how likely was such warning during the well-researched and documented period of World War II from which my case studies were drawn? And second, can one generalize from the World War II experience to the present and near future? What follows below is an attempt to address both of these questions.

With respect to the World War II experience, there were repeated instances in which excellent strategic warning was available to intended targets of surprise. And while it is not possible to provide a confident estimate of the proportion of cases in which such warning was acutally available, fairly reliable historical accounts of British, American, and German experience[6] suggest that this was so in a substantial number of cases. The possibility remains, however, that developments since that time, in intelligence and other related areas, have made such strategic warning less (or more) likely in today's world. The key question we have to address here is, therefore, whether we can validly generalize from the World War II experience to the present and near future. I believe that the answer to this question is essentially affirmative, and shall try to explain why below.

Even among the scholars who believe, as I do, that World War II was a period in which intelligence did succeed in obtaining excellent strategic warning on many occasions, there are those who maintain that since that time intelligence capabilities in this area have declined significantly. Those who subscribe to this view usually support it by making one or more of the following claims: (1) World War II is a misleading point of reference—an exception that only proves the rule—since in earlier periods intelligence had rarely been successful in acquiring such warning; (2) the task intelligence faces in attempting to acquire strategic warning has become significantly more complicated and problematic since World War II, as a result of certain political and technological developments in the environment in which intelligence operates; and (3) improvements in intelligence's capacity to acquire strategic warning before, during, and after World War II have since been outpaced and outdone by improvements in security measures designed to deny foreign intelligence access to strategic threat indicators. Walter Lacqueur echoed all of the above claims recently when he wrote that in World War II "signal intelligence *was* of decisive importance for the first time and perhaps the last time in the history of strategy. Given the technical improvements in coding that have been made since then a repeat performance seems unlikely" (1981:19). Let us consider each of these claims.

In regard to the first claim I would submit that the intelligence successes of World War II, impressive as they may have been, did not constitute a radical departure with the past in anything but the unprecedented amount of publicity and documentation they received. While radio communication was used much more extensively in World War II than ever before, and as a result Comint became a more important and prolific source of intelligence, remarkable intelligence successes in detecting and warning of acute foreign threats, through Comint as well as other sources, had long preceded World War II. The recovery of the "Zimmerman telegram" during World War I is just one particularly well-known case in point.[7] Thus, if past experience is indicative at all of present conditions it is likely that intelligence successes will outlive World War II and occur in the present and future as well.

The second argument against using the World War II experience as a guide for current conditions is based on the claim that fundamental changes have occurred since that time in the environment in which intelligence operates which alter and essentially complicate its warning task beyond comparison. There is no doubt that profound changes have indeed taken place since World War II in the intelligence environment. Numerous significant political changes have dramatically increased the number and type of potential foreign threats that intelligence must monitor, while diverse technological innovations have indeed accelerated significantly the pace of events, diminishing the time available for intelligence collection and assessment. But as extensive and profound as these changes may have been, it is far from clear that they have fundamentally altered the previous balance between the perpetrator's capacity to launch surprise moves and the target's capacity to detect (and react to) them.

To argue with some confidence that the balance has been fundamentally altered, or, conversely, to refute such a claim, would require an extensive comparison and assessment of both past and present international systems and intelligence capabilities—a comparison that has not been rigorously made before and that lies outside the scope of this work. I can, however, point out that the adverse political and technological changes noted above have not occurred in isolation: other developments that have also taken place during same time period, such as in raw intelligence capabilities, social science research, telecommunications and information processing, etc., could have conceivably compensated for at least some of the adverse developments noted above.

The third claim, which suggests the current superiority of defensive over offensive technology in intelligence collection, has even less evidence to support it than the two preceding claims. Again, the suggestion that significant improvements in security measures and counterintelligence have been made since World War II does have some validity. But these improvements could not have gone very far in solving the basic vulnerability of one's secrets to foreign intelligence due to severe objective limitations on the capacity to hide and conceal large-scale, complicated, and often controversial plans, decisions, and actions. Furthermore, improvements in raw defensive intelligence capabilities have also met with similar upgrading of the offensive ones. The introduction of all-weather reconnaissance satellites and electronic surveillance and fast and secure communication gear for spies are just a few salient examples.[8] Related improvements have also been made in the capacity of intelligence to collect, transmit, process, and securely disseminate huge quantities of information in extremely short time periods.

In fact, it is quite strongly believed by at least some experts in the field that post-World War II developments in intelligence sources and methods have actually *outpaced* the defensive countermeasures in certain areas, with the net result being an increase in the capacity of intelligence to detect and provide timely warning of some types of acute foreign threats. These experts point out that the multiplication of collection sources and methods has had an especially profound impact on intelligence capabilities. The diversification, complementarity, and multiplication of collection assets has made it possible not only to increase the scope of intelligence coverage but to refine its focus as well, thanks largely to the synergism between multiple complementary collection systems. It has also made it difficult to deceive the intended target and conceal from him one's intentions and capabilities through manipulation of his intelligence sensors.[9] Today, in comparison to World War II, there simply are many more sensors, and they are also much more sensitive, reliable, and fast.

To illustrate some of the points made above with respect to the current balance between offense and defense in intelligence it is, perhaps, useful to examine one specific aspect of the third claim made by Lacqueur, namely that modern codes are much more secure than the ones available during World War II.[10] This claim is truly puzzling for several reasons. To begin with, cryptography and cryptanalysis are shrouded everywhere in an unparalleled cloak of secrecy that makes it virtually impossible to determine how successful cryptanalysis is at any point in time, and the present is no exception. Recall that it was only very recently that we found out about the magnitude and scope of the cryptanalytical successes of World War II. Moreover, what is publicly known about the general logic underlying cryptanalytical activities clearly cuts against Lacqueur's argument.

Indeed, a significant variation exists in the quality (and therefore also vulnerability) of the cryptographic systems used by the various countries. Similar variation also exists in the quality of cryptographic systems used by the same country for different purposes and in different instances. But in principle at least, even the most secure cryptographic communications systems have inherent weaknesses and vulnerabilities due to objective limitations in design (the "binary principle") as well as human errors in design (such as the "trapdoor effect"), production, and especially use, and betrayal of their secrets through accidents or espionage (Calvacoressi 1981:54–55; Van Der Rhoer 1978:7–8; Farago 1967:78, 398n).

In this context it is especially illuminating to observe the impact of what has recently become known as the "Walker spy case" on Soviet ability to penetrate U.S. military crytographic systems. This spy ring is currently suspected to have compromised the security of U.S. naval communications systems, and possibly other U.S. military communications systems as well, for an extended period of time (IHT 1985a, 1985b, 1985c; USN&WR 1985).

Furthermore, while technological developments in computers and other related areas have improved the complexity and sophistication of cryptographic systems they have also created and enhanced the means to deal with the new challenges posed by these systems. Finally, and perhaps most importantly, even when a cryptographic system itself cannot be successully dealt with by a rival intelligence service, the information it transmits could still be compromised by other parts of the communication system (of which the cryptographic component is only one part).

All of the above considerations make it clear that Signint in general, and cryptanalysis in particular, still are, at present, potent sources of intelligence and are probably going to remain so for the foreseeable future—the contention to the contrary by Lacqueur and others notwithstanding. Indicative of the enormous intelligence potential lying in Sigint is the size of the budget for the American government's Consolidated Cryptographic Program. This budget, while classified, is widely speculated to be in excess of one billion dollars per year (*Time* 1978). It hardly seems likely that such sums would be authorized, appropriated, and spent if, as Lacqueur suggests, successful cryptanalysis is impossible.

The upshot of the above discussion is, in my judgment, that there simply is no solid evidence to support the contention that the capacity of intelligence to warn of impending foreign threats has declined since World War II. In fact, there is a highly plausible case to be made to the effect that this capacity has actually increased in the post-World War II period. One subscriber to this view is Admiral Bobby Inman. He sees in emerging technologies the potential for the "reduction of the element of surprise for the large-scale use of force outside natural borders" and the concomitant prospect of increasing both the amount of time available to react and the speed of response (1984:51). This view is also partially shared by Klaus Knorr who wrote that "[modern warning] technology definitely helps the defender who possesses it and tends to reduce the possibilities of surprise" (1982:20). This is not to say, however, that the possibility that strategic surprise would occur is excluded.

The capacity of any intelligence service to provide high-quality, timely warning of impending strategic threats depends on more than its ability to develop and sustain sophisticated collection assets. It also hinges on its capacity to sort huge volumes of information and provide constant training and intellectual invigoration to the intelligence analysts. Thus, it is possible that intelligence would fail to acquire solid warning, or that it would prove incapable of processing and disseminating the warning in time to prevent surprise. Furthermore, even the acquisition and dissemination of timely warning, as well as the education of the consumers, does not guarantee that warning and other available threat indicators would not fail to generate a perception of threat— it only diminishes the likelihood of such a development. Nevertheless, it is my belief, on the basis of the above discussion, that the prospects for achieving complete and total strategic surprise[11] (although not necessarily unpreparedness as well) are no brighter, and are possibly even dimmer, than at any other time in the recent past.[12]

Here another important caveat is in order. While my discussion of the capability of intelligence to obtain warning has been, up to this point, rather general and abstract, there is, in fact, a significant variation in any country's capacity to detect acute foreign threats depending on the nature of the threat involved, the point in time at which it occurs, etc. Furthermore, significant differences also exist in the capability of various countries to detect similar threats. Some of the difference in both cases is probably made by the quality and quantity of any country's intelligence assets. Yet this state of affairs does not always and everywhere favor the superpowers. For while the superpowers have by far the most extensive and sophisticated intelligence assets, and also enjoy a monopoly over certain vital intelligence collection sources and methods such as reconnaissance satellites (Knorr 1982:20), there are other factors that undercut at least some of the superpowers' advantages in raw intelligence capabilities, especially in certain contexts and areas.

Since the superpowers devote a large share of their intelligence resources to monitoring and checking each other, and allocate the remainder to the protection of their other interests, which are numerous, diverse, and scattered around the globe, their intelligence assets (both collection and evaluation) are necessarily spread rather thin, at least with respect to certain areas and issues.[13] Conversely, smaller and less developed countries, which usually possess much less sophisticated intelligence assets, are usually able to concentrate their limited resources on a substantially smaller number of issues that are more geographically circumscribed. Moreover, the gap in raw intelligence capabilities between the superpowers and some of the smaller and less developed countries may have narrowed somewhat in recent years, when concomitantly with the transfer of other advanced military technology, the superpowers have also transferred to some of these countries modern sophisticated intelligence gear such as Airborne Early Warning (AEW).

A further refinement of my earlier conclusions is now possible with regard to the susceptibility of various countries (or clusters thereof) to surprise, as well as with regard to the general vulnerability of countries to different types of surprise. As for the first point, by considering raw intelligence capabilities as the sole determinant of warning and therefore also of surprise, by impounding all the other determinants of warning and surprise in a vast *ceteris paribus,* and by comparing two clusters of countries on the capabilities dimension, I am able to conclude, albeit tentatively, that surprise can neither be excluded for the superpowers nor taken for granted for the smaller and less developed countries. This conclusion would probably remain valid once we relax the *ceteris paribus* assumption, for the other determinants of surprise (other than intelligence capabilities) essentially complicate the threat perception problem for any intended target, the superpowers being no exception.

The second respect in which the conclusion can, perhaps, be refined concerns the prospects for success of different kinds of surprise attempts. Once again, a cursory examination of the evolution of intelligence collection technology appears to suggest that in today's world, certain types of surprise, or at least certain dimensions of surprise, are somewhat less likely than others.[14] The point here is that the unmatched progress in, and proliferation of, photographic and electronic reconnaissance equipment makes it less likely that surprise attempts involving large-scale military moves would go undetected. Thus, while surprise in such circumstances may still occur, particularly with respect to the assessment and/or perception of the perpetrator's true intentions and his more esoteric capabilities, the likelihood that both *complete* and *total* surprise would occur in such cases seems more remote than before.

In closing, a word of reflection may be in order. It is commonly believed that three principles must guide any intellectual endeavor: (1) the right questions must be asked; (2) recognition must be made of the importance of facts and data as the necessary basis for making claims or drawing conclusions; and (3) the extension of concepts appropriate for one limited physical domain to new realms of phenomena for which they are invalid must be avoided.[15] In the process of conducting this study I have discovered, and subsequently sought to demonstrate, that most past studies of strategic surprise have not adhered rigorously to all three principles. In the framework of this study an effort has, therefore, been made to redirect the study of surprise and reinstate it on terms that are more compatible with the three aforementioned principles. Thus, it is the success in meeting this goal, as well as the more specific theoretical and methodological insights I have been able to generate, that should serve as the basis for evaluating the intellectual contribution made by this study.

# Appendix

# Empirical Studies of Surprise: A Bibliography

*Military Surprise*
1. The European wars of 1866 and 1870 (Knorr 1983)
2. World War I——the German attack on Belgium and France, 1914 (Knorr 1983)
3. World War II——the German attack on Norway and Denmark, 1940 (Holst 1966; Knorr 1983)
   ——the German Blitzkrieg in the West, 1940 (Kirkpatrick 1969; Betts 1982b; Knorr 1983)
   ——the German attack on the Soviet Union, 1941 (Kirkpatrick 1969; Whaley 1973; Sella 1978; Betts 1982b)
   ——the Japanese attack on Pearl Harbor, 1941 (Wohlstetter 1962; Kirkpatrick 1969; Janis 1972; Betts 1982b; Morgan 1983)
   ——the German offensive in the Ardennes, 1944 (Kirkpatrick 1969)
   ——the use of the atomic bomb against Japan, 1945 (Morgan 1945)
   ——the Soviet attack in Manchuria, 1945 (Morgan 1983)
4. The Korean War——the North Korean invasion of the South, 1950 (De Weerd 1962; Janis 1972; George and Smoke 1974; Poteat 1976; Betts 1982b; Temple 1982; Doyle 1983)
   ——the Chinese intervention in Korea, 1950 (De Weerd 1962; Janis 1972; George and Smoke 1974; Poteat 1976; Betts 1982b; Doyle 1983)
   ——the American landing in Inchon, 1950 (Betts 1983)
5. The Vietnamese attack in Dienbienphu, 1954 (Betts 1983)

NOTE: This list includes only academic case studies of surprise instances. It specifically excludes historical studies that do not focus primarily on the surprise aspect of an historical episode or discuss an instance of surprise for illustrative purposes only.

6. The Sinai campaign, 1956 (Betts 1982b; Handel 1983)
7. Operation "Rotem," 1960 (Handel 1983)
8. The Cuban missile crisis, 1962 (Knorr 1964; Wohlstetter 1965; Janis 1972; George and Smoke 1974)
9. The Indian-Chinese war, 1962 (Hoffman 1972)
10. The Six-Day War, 1967 (Betts 1982b; Handel 1983)
11. The Tet offensive, 1968 (Betts 1983)
12. The Soviet invasion of Czechoslovakia, 1968 (Betts 1983)
13. The Indian-Pakistani war, 1971 (Hoffman 1972)
14. The Yom Kippur war, 1973 (Handel 1976, 1979; Shlaim 1976; Stein 1980, 1982; Betts 1982b; Lanir 1983)
15. The Falkland Island crisis (Hopple 1983)

*Diplomatic Surprise*
1. Hitler's diplomacy, 1933–36 (Handel 1981)
2. The Ribbentrop-Molotov agreement, 1939 (Handel 1981)
3. Nixon's China policy, 1968–71 (Handel 1981)
4. Sadat's first peace initiative, 1971 (Handel 1981)
5. Sadat's expulsion of the Soviet military advisers from Egypt, 1972 (Handel 1981)
6. Sadat's second peace initiative—the trip to Jerusalem, 1977 (Handel 1981)

# Notes

## 1. The Study of Strategic Surprise

1. My definition of surprise has much in common with what Lanir (1983:404) has recently called "Situational (as distinguished from Fundamental) Surprise." Unlike Lanir's, however, my definition of strategic surprise includes surprise caused by intelligence collection failures, which Lanir labels "Sensory Surprise."

2. An excellent discussion of the "vital" national interest is provided by Alexander George and Robert Keohane (George 1980:142).

3. As Klaus Knorr correctly argues (1976, 1979), strategic surprise is one particular case of international threat perception.

4. For some of the press reaction to the recent books and articles on the Pearl Harbor surprise see "Remembering Pearl Harbor", New York Times Book Review. November 29, 1981, Kahn (1982); "FBI Releases Pearl Harbor Papers in Rebuttal." Los Angeles Times, April 1, 1983; "Did FBI Have Class?" Washington Post, December 2, 1982; "Someone Had Blundered But Who?" New York Times Book Review, January 5, 1986; "Codebuster to get Medal 45 Years Late" Washington Times, December 9, 1985.

5. For an excellent, comprehensive, and up-to-date review of the various pathologies in the processing of information, see George (1980: part 1).

6. There is some evidence to suggest that this factor played an important role at Pearl Harbor (particularly with respect to the American estimate of the range of the Japanese bombers and the depth at which their torpedoes could operate), the Cuban Missile Crisis (with respect to the American estimates of the speed at which Soviet IRBMs and MRBMs could be deployed) and the Yom Kippur War (regarding the Israeli understanding of the Egyptian notion of air supremacy).

7. The mere belief in the inevitability of surprise apparently makes it more likely to occur, as one's feeling of impotence apparently causes one to be less receptive to warning. For discussions of this link between a person's feeling of influence over events and his perceptual threshold for stimulus, see Jervis (1976:373-76). Richard Betts' prescription for developing "tolerance for disaster" (1978:89) might therefore prove counterproductive.

8. Comparative case studies of surprise have surfaced only in the last few years, and so far there are only few of them (e.g. Handel 1981; Betts 1982b; Knorr and Morgan,1983). In some respects the George and Smoke study (1974) is the first such comparative case study, but it does not address itself primarily to the surprise issue.

9. For discussion of the specific requirements for case studies, see George (1982:27-29).

10. For an excellent discussion of the problems inherent in using case studies for examining the surprise phenomenon, see Chan (1979:174–76).

11. This requirement would not necessarily prove to be too restrictive in terms of the population of cases available for study of the phenomenon. Interestingly enough, the opposite may even prove true. Acknowledging the definition explicitly allows us to discover and treat several historical cases which were heretofore studied only from the perspective of the country that was the immediate victim. Cases in point are the German invasion of Norway (1940) and the Soviet Union (1941), both of which qualify for analysis from the British perspective. Britain, which had considerable interest in both countries, was surprised by the former (Hinsley 1979: ch. 4) but not by the latter (Hinsley 1979: ch. 14). It would be extremely interesting to compare the cases in order to determine what changes occurred in the interim period that caused the difference in outcomes. Hinsley's book certainly suggests some interesting hypotheses to that effect which warrant an in-depth study. It would also prove useful to compare the surprise (or absence thereof) for both the victim country and the third country in the same historical event.

12. A similar observation with respect to strategic deception was recently made by Richard Heuer. As he points out, "deception attracts both the popular imagination and the attention of historians, while the absence of deception in strategic operations does not" (1981b:304).

13. These attempts can take the form of either an initiative that is called off (due to the loss of the element of surprise) or else an initiative that is still carried out but whose effectiveness (in the absence of surprise) is reduced. While the impact of the loss of the element of surprise is clearly evident in the former case, this does not always hold true for the latter, as a situation may occur where the defender would be unable to act on the basis of the advance warning, or would act on it ineffectively (see chapter 4).

14. In the entire surprise literature, there is only one brief examination of an abortive surprise attempt (Hoffman 1972).

15. Similar criticism is leveled by Robert Jervis against statesmen and social scientists. They are said to focus only on dramatic outcomes and ignore or learn little from negative outcomes (1976:235).

16. Since cases of abortive surprise attempts that escape attention or any kind of publicity can be deemed to have been frequent, it is impossible to derive a representative sample of surprise attempts and consequently also to make any empirical generalizations regarding the probability of the success of such attempts. Making generalizations regarding the probability of success on the basis of deductive reasoning is also open to serious challenge, as this work will demonstrate in subsequent chapters.

17. For similar criticism of the strategic surprise literature, see Chan (1979:174–75).

18. This discrepancy in the finding is not merely a product of the different (more restrictive) definitions of warning that I employ—it goes much deeper than that. I would submit that its source is the erroneous assessment, in previous studies, of the warning that was available to surprise targets prior to the event. The lack of a comparative basis for assessing warning, the failure to take into account the reliability of the source of warning, and the absence of standardized criteria for measuring wasrning seem to be the causes of this assessment.

19. This conclusion, which may seem to the layman not only intuitively correct but even trivial, nonetheless runs counter to the conclusions of practically all of the studies in the field.

20. The reliability of each source is a cumulative and dynamic measure assigned by the collection agency on the basis of the source's "track record" (the accuracy of previous reports). The reliability of the source is attached to each incoming report prior to its dissemination.

21. A useful discussion of the impact of source reliability on the consumers' assessment of warning is provided by Chan (1979:172).

22. I would submit that the acquisition by a surprise target of high-quality strategic warning is not only theoretically possible but also feasible and practical, and that historically it may not have been a rare occurrence, only a less well-known one, perhaps because there are usually strong incentives for keeping it secret so as to protect intelligence sources and methods. Such an argument is explicitly made by the former head of the Israeli Military Intelligence, Major General (Ret.) Shlomo Gazit (Godson 1980:38). There is some evidence to suggest that the recent U.S. reaction to the Libyan plot against Sudan was exactly such a case; timely warning was obtained by the United States, but attempts were made to conceal the reaction to it so as not to compromise a sensitive intelligence source. "Libya Leak Threatens U.S. Agent," *San Jose Mercury News*, February 28, 1983.

23. A similar argument with respect to cognitive biases has been made by Heuer (1981:313).

24. A detailed discussion of the method of "structured focused comparison," its requirements and advantages, is provided by George (1979b, 1982).

25. I would submit that such an indiscriminate definition of warning also stands in the way of developing a typological theory of surprise.

26. For a complete definition of warning and a discussion of the role of warning and other threat indicators in producing threat perception, see chapter 4.

27. This type of evidence proved particularly important and influential on the eve of Pearl Harbor and in the Battle of the Bulge, and the Yom Kippur war, to mention just a few examples.

28. The four indicators are: articulations of decision makers; description by contemporary spectators of the state of mind of decision makers; evidence of exploration by decision makers of alternative responses to the initiative; and coping processes put into effect by decision makers in response to the initiative. For a similar operationalization of threat perception, see Cohen (1978:95).

29. For an excellent comprehensive discussion of both approaches to causal interpretation, see George (1982).

30. This possibility is similar to a spurious correlation in statistical analysis. Incisive comment on the pitfalls of correlation is provided by Tufte (1969: part 4).

## 2. Pearl Harbor Revisited

1. The book *Pearl Harbor: The Verdict of History* (Prange 1985), a sequel to *At Dawn we Slept* (Prange 1981), came out when this book was already on its way to print. It offers little in the way of new data or analysis that has any bearing on our conclusions here.

2. Recall that while Wohlstetter and other have used the term "warning" to describe signals (threatening information), I use here a more restrictive definition of warning (see chapters 1 and 4) and use instead the broader term "threat indicators" to describe what Wohlstetter and her followers originally meant by warning. This practice is essential in order to maintain conceptual clarity throughout this study. In the few places where it

proves necessary to use warning in its original meaning (as suggested by Wohlstetter) we shall therefore provide the term in quotes (i.e., warning).

3. This examination of intelligence sources follows, in part, the exemplary analysis provided by Gazit (1980).

4. The discussion of overt sources draws heavily on Ernest May's examination of U.S. press coverage of Japan (1973).

5. For evidence regarding the performance and contribution of the attachés and observers in the Far East, see Dorowart (1983:134-37, 174-76); McCollum (1973:461); Cline (1976:13-14); and PHA (1946 18:3439, 27:56).

6. The detrimental effect of the State Department's position was enhanced by the refusal of American embassy and consular officials throughout the Far East to assist the observers and attachés in their intelligence collection, by denying them such things as cover, access to secure communication facilities, etc. (Dorowart 1983:134-37, 174-76). Such an attitude was apparently evident even in the case of Ambassador Grew in Tokyo (ibid.:135,137).

7. Until December 1941, all of the commercial cable companies adamantly refused to provide the intelligence authorities in Hawaii with copies of the messages transmitted to and from the Japanese Consulate. During that period, therefore, the United States could only intercept some of the messages—those sent by radio. In early December 1941, thanks to an informal agreement with the head of RCA (David Sarnoff), the local intelligence authorities did begin to receive copies of the messages sent through his company, though with some delay (Prange 1981:357). For all practical purposes this proved too late, since the processing of the first messages received through this channel was only completed after the attack.

8. Other names used to denote this system were the "Administrative Code" and the "AD Code." For its technical features see Kahn (1967: ch. 1) and Safford (1952).

9. Other names frequently used to describe this system were "Fleet Code," "Fleet Cryptographic System," and the "5 Number (Numeral) System."

10. For a similar assessment of the intelligence collection situation on the eve of Pearl Harbor, see Dorowart (1983:135-36, 175-76).

11. The discussion of Magic warnings is based on a review of the original messages read by the United States prior to December 7, 1941. The complete collection of these messages has been published by the U.S. Department of Defense (1977).

12. This description of the information supplied by Sigint draws heavily on SRH-012 (1942).

13. I am indebted to Robert Haslach for drawing my attention to, and providing me with a copy of, this testimony.

14. The German code name for Popov was Ivan.

15. These documents refute the claims made by several previous authors to the effect either that there are no records pertaining to the Popov questionnaire in the FBI's files (Toland 1982: 260n), or that the part of the questionnaire pertaining to Hawaii was never disseminated outside the FBI (Bratzel and Rout 1982:1347).

16. In this respect, the debate recently stirred by Toland (1982) and Bratzel and Rout (1982) concerning the handling of Popov's questionnaire by the FBI is very much a tempest in a teapot.

17. This conclusion is based on a review of Haan's "warnings," which were reproduced by Toland (1982:260-61, 289-90).

18. In this context it is interesting to observe that in ONI it was commonly believed, erroneously as it turns out, that "ever since the Japanese surprise attack on the Russians in Port Arthur . . . the Japanese considered the surprise attack on the enemy's main military facility before declaring war a primary aspect of war planning" (Dorowart 1983:178).

19. Thomas Inglis, who served as the director of ONI after Pearl Harbor, offered a very similar assessment of the quality of threat indicators available to the United States prior to the Pearl Harbor attack (see Dorowart 1983:179-80).

20. Interestingly enough, there is evidence to suggest that in the fall of 1941 there already was a feeling in ONI of a "continued threat of war with Japan," and an expectation of imminent U.S. entry into war with Japan, "most likely prompted by a Japanese attack somewhere in the Pacific or in Southeast Asia" (Dorowart 1983:175-76).

21. Similar conclusions with respect to the relative unimportance of American misperceptions in the assessment of the situation have been reached by Ben Zvi (1976:84-85; 1979:143).

22. This, incidentally, demonstrates the limitations of a threat perception that emerges on the basis of threat indicators other than explicit warning.

## 3. Prelude to Midway

1. In the battle the Japanese also lost 332 planes and had 2500 casualties to only 147 and 307 respectively for the United States (Prange 1982:396).

2. For a detailed description of the Japanese plan for "Operation MI," see Morison (1949:4:ch. 6), as well as Lord (1967:6-9), and Prange (1982:8-31).

3. For some thoughts on the impact of the war on the intelligence warning task, see chapter 1.

4. For a detailed discussion of the American cryptographic activity and its success in recovering this system prior to Midway, see Safford (1952); Kahn (1967:561-73); Holmes (1979:ch. 9); Van Der Rhoer (1978:87-103); Lord (1967:17-28); Lewin (1982:85-108); and Prange (1982:17ff.). For an historical account of these developments in Japan, see Lewin (1982:301-3).

5. As a result of the Japanese advances in Southeast Asia following the outbreak of the war, both Com 16 in Corregidor and the British CI unit in Singapore had to be evacuated and relocated. Thus, in February 1942, Com 16 was moved to Belconnen in Australia and the British unit to Colombo, Ceylon (Lewin 1982:85-87, 92).

6. The change was originally scheduled for April 1 and then May 1 but eventually came into effect only on May 28. The delays were caused by Japan's difficulties in disseminating the new cipher code books.

7. One historical account, by Van Der Rhoer, suggests that the U.S. CI units had also intercepted the May 5 order of Japan's General Naval Headquarters, which specifically and explicitly instructed the occupation of the Western Aleutians and Midway Island (1978:87). This account, however, is based on personal recollection and practically all the other (and well documented) historical accounts on the issue suggest that this order was never intercepted by the United States and that it was never actually transmitted by radio (e.g., Holmes 1979:83, 88; Costello 1981:268; Lewin 1982:105).

8. The term "naval intelligence" is used here figuratively rather than literally. It refers to *all* naval personnel performing intelligence tasks—not only those affiliated with the Office of Naval Intelligence (ONI). Thus, the term naval intelligence, as used here,

includes the CI units (which formally belonged to the Office of Naval Communications but engaged in straightforward intelligence activities) as well as the intelligence officers on the staffs of CNO and CinCPac.

9. Largely as a result of his disappointment in its performance in the Pearl Harbor episode, the new CNO—Admiral King—formally relieved ONI on December 23, 1941 of any responsibility for the assessment of short-term war-related intelligence. He transferred this responsibility to his own intelligence officer (Dorowart 1983:189–93). ONI did continue, however, to participate actively in the production of Comint (especially in the translation of decoded messages) until June of 1942 (ibid.:191).

10. As Nimitz later pointed out, Layton was only "five miles, five degrees, and five minutes off" (Potter 1976:93).

11. Documenting chronologically the emergence of a threat perception is a difficult task, and one that is also highly susceptible to error even under the best of circumstances. The sources for documenting human perceptions over time are never complete and rarely objective. Moreover, many of these sources are highly suspect, not only because they provide subjective accounts of events by participants, but also because they are written with both the benefit of hindsight and the shortcoming of significant loss of memory. In view of these problems, I have tried in this case study to rely as much as possible on primary documents and multiple sources. Furthermore, for reasons of both accuracy and narrative, I discuss here only the most prominent phases in the evolution of threat perception among a relatively few of the most important pertinent policymakers.

12. Layton himself suggested in 1980 that the briefing had taken place around May 12 (Lewin 1982:103). The other sources cited, however, have led me to believe that the briefing actually occurred on or around May 8.

13. Nimitz's expectation of confirmation for the identification of "AF" as Midway was apparently based on his authorization of a clever scheme concocted by Rochefort to make the Japanese reveal the true identify of "AF." For details of the scheme, which indeed succeeded, see Holmes (1979:88–91), as well as Lewin (1982:105–6, 301–3); and Costello (1981:276).

14. Several factors made it highly unlikely that the Japanese would be practicing deception using the Operations Code system: (1) a precondition for practicing deception would have been Japan's awareness, or at least suspicion, that the system had been compromised, but the U.S. cryptanalysts did not detect any signs of such an awareness, and were cognizant of the fact that the technical complexity of the system had given the Japanese a false sense of security regarding its invulnerability; (2) the Operations Code system was at the time the primary cryptosystem of the Imperial Navy. As such, it was both highly important and indispensable, especially under wartime conditions, which made the replacement of any widely and intensively used cryptosystem extremely difficult to execute; and (3) practicing deception in such a widely and intensively used system would have been difficult to execute without a hitch, even in peacetime, yet the U.S. cryptanalysts did not detect any suspicious signs in the system, and moreover could corroborate the authenticity of at least some of the messages in the system on the basis of other sources (in particular traffic analysis and direction finding).

15. Only fragmentary data is currently available on the pertinent information exchanged between Army and Navy intelligence prior to Midway. And while the secondary sources strongly suggest tight compartmentation, at least on the Navy's side, my conclusions on this point must necessarily be considered provisional until better evidence on this issue surfaces.

16. What remains unclear, however, is whether the Army commanders in Washington, as well as the top-level civilian policymakers, were aware that the Navy had opted for the riskier course of action, and was operating on the basis of enemy probable courses of action. At least one important source, Secretary of War Stimson's diary entry of June 1, indicates considerable ignorance on his part regarding the Navy's deployment for the impending battle. The entry reveals that Stimson expected the Pacific Fleet to be deployed, and the battle with the Japanese to take place, off the southern part of the West Coast of the continental United States. What makes this account particularly instructive is the fact that the diary entry was made following a War Council meeting that included General Marshall, in which the forthcoming battle was discussed (Prange 1982:139–40).

17. A partial success of naval intelligence was scored in the Battle of the Coral Sea in late April and early May 1942. But this success was neither as complete nor as impressive as that made in Midway. For one thing, the cryptanalytical success, and therefore also the warning, were as yet incomplete. For another thing, the ambiguous outcome of the battle did not serve to underscore or draw much attention to the utility and potential of intelligence. These would have to await the success at Midway.

18. Interestingly enough, Commander Rochefort—the navy officer who deserves much of the credit for this intelligence feat—has been posthumously awarded for it the Distinguished Service Medal in late 1985(!). The recommendation for the medal, originally made by Admiral Nimitz in 1942 had not been approved until recently when Rochefort was finally cleared from any responsibility for the Pearl Harbor intelligence failure.

19. Betts has made the point in personal communication with me. He has not offered any evidence to substantiate his claims other than to make a general reference to chapter 5 of his recent book (1982b) which does not specifically address itself to the cases under discussion here.

20. Some qualitative and quantitative improvement in certain intelligence capabilities (especially Comint) had nonetheless taken place between December 1941 and May 1942. But this improvement was largely a result of developments not directly related to American efforts in this area, such as the increased use of radio communications by the Japanese. And while these developments were the result of the outbreak of the American-Japanese war, the war also led to the further demise of other intelligence sources, in particular Magic, the military observers in Southeast Asia, the Embassy in Tokyo, etc. The increase in capabilities as a result of the war was thus initially offset, at least in part, by a concomitant decline in other capabilities.

21. That this was the case it, perhaps, best illustrated by the following statistics. While the size of Com 14 had roughly quadrupled between December 1941 and May 1942 (from approximately 30 to 120 officers and men), most of the new personnel (e.g., the band of the battleship California that was sunk in the Japanese attack on Pearl Harbor), had little or no previous exposure to intelligence work and barely half of them were even beginning to get a feel for the work prior to Midway (Kahn 1967:562).

22. To use another example drawn from Com 14, despite the dramatic increase in its manpower during 1941 and 1942, in May 1942 the unit was only capable of copying 60 percent of the possible messages and only 40 percent of these were decoded (Command Summary 1942:543).

23. For evidence regarding the involvement of the political echelon in assessing the Japanese threat during the spring of 1941, see Prange (1942:27, 66, 96, 139–40, 159,

365); Lord (1967:21); King and Whitehill (1952:383–85); Buell (1980:ch. 14 and pp. 240–42); and Costello (1981:272–73).

24. See the works cited in note 23, in particular Prange (1982:159) and Costello (1981:272–73).

25. I thus reject the idiosyncratic explanations of Pearl Harbor and Midway that commonly attribute the former to a conspiracy and the latter to a miracle.

## 4. On Warning, Threat Perception, and Response

1. The same point has been made by Admiral Samuel Eliot Morison, who suggested that "to know your enemy's intentions is fine but such knowledge does not always mean that you can stop him" (quoted in Lewin 1982:93).

2. The data base on the issue, which is clearly incomplete, consists primarily of the report published by the British commission of inquiry which investigated the episode (Franks Committee Report 1983), as well as some newspaper accounts (in particular *Sunday Times* 1983; *Times* 1982a, b; *Economist* 1983a, b).

3. Incidentally, this example may also illustrate how in the absence of conclusive warning policymakers may opt to endorse the more favorable assessment—the one that does not carry with it the penalty of having to reverse an earlier decision or take some action that is otherwise undesirable (George and Smoke 1974:574; George 1980:74–75).

4. For a useful concise review of the literature on the cognitive impediments of the policymaker, see Lebow (1981:101–119).

5. A similar phenomenon may have occurred prior to the discovery of missiles in Cuba. The CIA chief, McCone, warned of the possible deployment of these missiles in Cuba quite early but the rest of the intelligence community did not share his general apprehension and tried to downplay his influence on the intelligence estimates. I am grateful to Alexander George for drawing my attention to this analogy.

6. Art and Jervis carry this point even further when they discuss the impact of the security dilemma on statesmen's behavior. They suggest that "the need to assess capabilities along with intentions, or the equivalent, to allow for a change in intentions, makes statesmen profoundly conservative. *They prefer to err on the side of safety: to have too much rather than too little. Because security is the basis of existence and the prerequisite for the achievement of other goals, statesmen must be acutely sensitive to the security actions of others.* The security dilemma thus means that *statesmen can not risk not reacting to the security actions of other states*" (1973:4, emphasis added).

7. A similar argument regarding the impact of time pressures on distortions in information processing was made by Wilensky. As Wilensky puts it, "urgency can overcome structural obstacles to the flow of good intelligence" (1967:83).

8. Another way of looking at the scenarios is as different causal paths leading to the same outcome—the notion of equifinality in general systems theory.

9. What is meant here by unpreparedness is when a nation becomes the target of *any* threatening foreign initiative with which it is not ready to cope (militarily, politically, economically, socially, etc.).

10. When the Israeli Cabinet finally made a decision to mobilize reserves, it was not immediately implemented, apparently due to a bureaucratic snafu. A few valuable hours were wasted before the mobilization process began in earnest. Similarly, the Chief of the General Staff's orders to the Commander of the Southern Command to deploy his armor units in Sinai in a way that would improve their effectiveness were not carried

out, with no less serious consequences. For details on both instances, see *Agranat Commission* (1975:23-24, 41-43); also Schiff (1974:49-55); Bartov (1978:29-35).

11. One common method for doing so is by requiring that intelligence assess enemy intentions solely on the basis of its capabilities, ignoring actual information regarding its intentions. An interesting discussion of this method and its shortcomings is provided by Garthoff (1978).

12. In a testimony before the House of Representatives Subcommittee on International Security and Scientific Affairs, Bruce C. Clarke, Jr., then director of the CIA's National Foreign Assessment Center, suggested that "both the policymaker and the intelligence managers and analysts must understand that the penalties for failing to warn are greater than the penalties for failure to be correct." He emphasized that "we must risk being wrong in order to fulfill the alerting function" (U.S. Congress 1980:79).

13. I am indebted to Dr. William Perry for drawing my attention to his analogy with radar and its origins in communication theory.

14. For discussion of this strategy see, for example, Brodie (1965:241-48), Schilling et al. (1973:25-29), Kahan (1975:209), and Betts (1982b:247-48).

15. For interpretations of the U.S. leaders' failure to translate threat perception into effective response, see Lebow (1981:ch. 6) as well as George and Smoke (1974:ch. 7).

16. An interesting application of this strategy is provided by Betts (1982b:270).

17. The concepts of "enhanced survivability," "damage limitation," "war fighting," and "assured destruction" are extensively debated in the context of nuclear strategy. For a sample of the literature on the ability to fight, survive, and terminate nuclear wars see Kahn (1962:120; 1965:154-62), Kahan (1975:ch. 4), Betts (1982b:249-50).

18. One possible manifestation of the strategy is in the conception of strategic depth. In the Israeli context, the lack of strategic depth as well as the asymmetry in manpower resources in relation to the Arabs have traditionally been perceived as overriding considerations against the adoption of such a defensive strategy. Thus, prior to June 1967, Israel was committed to a purely offensive military doctrine combining preemption (prevention) and moving the war into enemy territory.

19. While strategy 3 is really one of not having to respond to warning at all (by nature of possessing a strong war fighting/war winning capability), some utilization of warning could still help in fighting and winning a war initiated by the opponent, if only by reducing costs.

20. For a discussion of the implementation of one such formula in the American context see the testimony of Anthony Lake, former director of the Policy Planning Staff at the State Department, before the House of Representatives Subcommittee on Security and Scientific Affairs (U.S. Congress 1980:127-28).

## 5. Strategic Surprise in Perspective

1. For an extensive discussion of the method of "structured, focused comparison" and its merits, see George (1979b). Further refinement of this research strategy is presented in George (1982:25ff.).

2. For extensive discussion of this "(negative) method of difference", see George (1982:7-13).

3. The definition of excellent warning is based on its intrinsic characteristic as apparent in *real time*. Thus, it refers to warning that is timely, comprehensive, conclusive,

coherent, and originating in a reliable source or sources, but does not necessarily refer to its accuracy, since accuracy can only be determined in retrospect.

4. The reliability of a source is determined on the basis of its track record and an access to the kind of information it provides.

5. While a source's assessed reliability commonly provides an adequate real-time measurement of the accuracy of the information it supplies, this is not always the case. Thus, in some cases when the assessed reliability does not correspond with the accuracy of the information supplied but still influences the reaction to that information, both erroneous perception of threat (false alarm) and surprise may ensue.

6. For an insightful account of the British experience, see Hinsley (1979, 1981). Useful accounts of the American and German experience are provided by Lewin (1982) and Kahn (1978), respectively. Additionally, Kahn's monumental *The Codebreakers* (1967) provides a most comprehensive review of the cryptographic experience of most of the key participants in World War II.

7. For a discussion of numerous other historical examples see Kahn (1967). A particularly fascinating analysis of another impressive intelligence success during the American War of Independence is provided by Thompson (1981).

8. A succinct discussion of some of the modern intelligece collection technologies and their application is provided by Phillips (1982). See also a discussion of some of these issues by the former Undersecretary of Defense for Research and Engineering, "Billions Targeted for 'Star Wars' Defense Systems," Richard De Lauer, *New York Times*, May 17, 1983.

9. These developments have made the manipulation of the target sources more difficult by making the activities required to achieve success in this area much more expensive, time-consuming, and technically complex.

10. Lacqueur is by no means the only one to make such a claim. For another salient example, see Kahn (1979:145, 147–148); Hilsman (1985:20).

11. By "complete" surprise I refer to surprise that occurs on all possible dimensions, while by "total" surprise I refer to the degree of surprise within each dimension.

12. A similar assessment regarding the current probability of an "absolute surprise attack"—the "bolt out of a blue scenario"—is made by Admiral Bobby Inman (1983:126).

13. For a discussion of the America's problems in this area, see Tighe's (1983) interview with Admiral Bobby Inman.

14. For a short discussion of the efficacy of American intelligence with respect to different threat scenarios, see Phillips (1982) and Tighe (1983).

15. I am indebted to Dr. Sidney Drell for drawing my attention to these principles.

# References

*Agranat Commission.* 1975. *The Agranat Commission Report* (Hebrew). Tel Aviv: Am Oved.

Allison, Graham. 1971. *Essence of Decision.* Boston: Little Brown.

Art, Robert and Robert Jervis eds. 1973. *International Politics.* Boston: Little Brown.

Barnes, Harry. 1972. *Pearl Harbor After a Quarter of a Century.* New York: Arno Press.

Bartov, Hanoch. 1978. *Daddo—48 Years and 20 More Days* (Hebrew). Tel Aviv: Maariv Book Guild.

Belden, Thomas. 1977. "Indications, Warning, and Crisis Operations." *International Studies Quarterly* 21(1):181-98.

Ben Zvi, Abraham. 1976. "Misperceiving the Role of Perception: A Critique." *Jerusalem Journal of International Relations.* 2(2):74-93.

—— 1979. "The Study of Surprise Attacks." *British Journal of International Studies* 5(2):129-49.

Betts, Richard. 1978. "Analysis, War, and Decision." *World Politics* 31(1):961-88.

—— 1980. "Surprise Despite Warning." *Political Science Quarterly* 95(4):551-72.

—— 1982a. Personal communication. March 22.

—— 1982b. *Surprise Attack.* Washington, D.C.: Brookings Institution.

—— 1983. "Strategic Surprise for War Termination: Inchon, Dienbienphu, and Tet." In Klaus Knorr and Patrick Morgan, eds., *Strategic Military Surprise: Incentives and Opportunities,* pp. 147-72. New Brunswick, N.J.: Transaction Books.

Bratzel, John and Leslie Rout. 1982. "Pearl Harbor, Microdots, and J. Edgar Hoover." *American Historical Review* 87(5):1342-51.

Brodie, Bernard. 1965. *Strategy in the Missile Age.* Princeton: Princeton University Press.

Buell, Thomas. 1980. *Master of Sea Power.* Boston: Little Brown.

Calvacoressi, Peter. 1981. *Top Secret Ultra.* New York: Ballantine.

Carr, Edward Hallett. 1961. *What Is History?* New York: Vintage.

Chan, Steve. 1979. "The Intelligence of Stupidity." *American Political Science Review* 73(1):171-80.

Chihiro, Hosoya. 1973. "The Role of Japan's Foreign Ministry and Its Embassy in Washington." In Dorothy Borg and Shumpei Okamoto, eds., *Pearl Harbor as History*, pp. 165–98. New York: Columbia University Press.

Clausewitz, Karl Von. 1968. *On War*. New York: Penguin.

Cline, Ray. 1976. *Secrets, Spies, and Scholars*. Washington, D.C.: Acropolis.

Cohen, Raymond. 1978. "Threat Perception in International Crisis." *Political Science Quarterly* 93(1)93–107.

Command Summary. *See* U.S. Navy 1942b.

Corson, William. 1977. *The Armies of Ignorance*. New York: Dial Press.

Costello, John. 1981. *The Pacific War*. New York: Rawson Wade.

Critchley, Julian. 1978. *Warning and Response*. New York: Crane, Russak.

Daniel, Donald and Catherine Herbig. 1982. *Strategic Military Deception*. New York: Pergamon.

Dayan, Moshe. 1976. *Story of My Life* (Hebrew). Tel Aviv: Dvir.

—— 1981. *Shall the Sword Devour Forever* (Hebrew). Jerusalem: Edanim.

De Rivera, Joseph. 1968. *Psychological Dimensions of Foreign Policy*. Columbus, Ohio: Merrill.

De Weerd, H. A. 1962. "Strategic Surprise in the Korean War." *Orbis* 6(3):434–52.

Dorowart, Jeffrey. 1983. *Conflict of Duty: The U.S. Navy's Intelligence Dilemma, 1919–1945*. Annapolis, Md.: Naval Institute Press.

Doyle, Michael. 1983. "Endemic Surprise? Strategic Surprise in First World-Third World Relations." In Klaus Knorr and Patrick Morgan, eds., *Strategic Military Surprise: Incentives and Opportunities*, pp. 77–110. New Brunswick, N.J.: Transaction Books.

Eckstein, Harry. 1975. "Case Study and Theory in Political Science." pp. 79–138 in Fred Greenstein and Nelson Polsby, eds., *Handbook of Political Science*, vol. 7. Reading, Mass.: Addison-Wesley.

*The Economist*. 1983a. London. January 22.

—— 1983b. London. April 10.

Farago, Ladislas. 1967. *The Broken Seal*. New York: Bantam Books.

FBI. *See* U.S. Department of Justice 1941.

FCR (Franks Committee Report). 1983. Committee of Privy Counsellors (Lord Franks, chairman). "Falkland Island Review." London: HMSO.

Friedman, William. 1945. "Expansion of the Signal Intelligence Service from 1930 to 7 December 1941." (SRH-134). Washington, D.C.: Modern Military Section, U.S. National Archives. Declassified September 2, 1981.

Garthoff, Raymond. 1978. "On Estimating and Imputing Intentions." *International Security* 2(3):22–32.

Gazit, Shlomo. 1979. "Intelligence Estimates Versus Intelligence Forecasting." *Ma'arachot* (Hebrew), 270–71:54–57.

—— 1980. "Fraud in Her Majesty's Service." *Journal of Strategic Studies* 3(2):217–26.

George, Alexander. 1979a. "Warning and Response: Theory and Practice." In Yair Evron, ed. *International Violence: Terrorism, Surprise, and Control*, pp. 12–24. Jerusalem: Hebrew University, Leonard David Institute.

—— 1979b. "Case Studies and Theory Development: The Method of Structured Focused Comparison." In Paul Lauren, ed. *Diplomatic History: New Approaches*, pp. 43–68. New York: Free Press.

——1980. *Presidential Decision Making in Foreign Policy*. Boulder, Colo.: Westview.

—— 1982. "Case Studies and Theory Development." Paper presented at the Second Annual Symposium on Information Processing in Organizations, Carnegie Mellon University. October 15–16.

George, Alexander and Richard Smoke. 1974. *Deterrence in American Foreign Policy*. New York: Columbia University Press.

Godson, Roy, ed. 1980. *Intelligence Requirements for the 1980's: Analysis and Estimates*. New Brunswick, N.J.: Transaction Books.

Gravely, Samuel. 1982. "The Ocean Surveillance Information System." *Signal* (October) pp. 30–36.

Halperin, Morton. 1974. *Bureaucratic Politics and Foreign Policy*. Washington, D.C.: Brookings Institution.

Handel, Michael. 1976. "Perception, Deception, and Surprise: The Case of the Yom Kippur War." Jerusalem Papers on Peace Problems, no. 19. Jerusalem: Hebrew University, Leonard Davis Institute.

—— 1979. "Perception, Deception, and Surprise: The Case of the Yom Kippur War." In Yair Evron, ed., *International Violence: Terrorism, Surprise and Control*, pp. 25–75. Jerusalem Papers on Peace Problems. Jerusalem: Hebrew University, Leonard Davis Institute.

—— 1980. "Avoiding Surprise in the 1980's." In Roy Godson, ed., *Intelligence Requirements for the 1980's*, vol. 2: *Analysis and Estimates*, pp. 85–111. Washington, D.C.: National Strategy Information Center.

—— 1981. *The Diplomacy of Surprise*. Cambridge: Harvard Center for International Studies.

—— 1983. "Crisis and Surprise in Three Arab-Israeli Wars." In Klaus Knorr and Patrick Morgan, eds., *Strategic Military Surprise: Incentives and Opportunities*, pp. 111–46. New Brunswick, N.J.: Transaction Books.

Haslach, Robert. 1982. "Nishi No Kaze, Hare: The Watch on Japan." Manuscript.

Heuer, Richard, Jr. ed. 1981a. *Quantitative Approaches to Political Intelligence: The CIA Experience*. Boulder, Colo.: Westview.

—— 1981. "Strategic Deception and Counterdeception." *International Studies Quarterly* 25(2):294–327.

Hilsman, Roger. 1956. *Strategic Intelligence and National Decisions*. Glenco, Ill.: Free Press.

—— 1967. *To Move a Nation*. New York: Doubleday.

—— 1985. "International Environment, the State, and Intelligence." In Alfred
  Maurer et al., eds., *Intelligence: Policy and Process*, pp. 19–27. Boulder, Colo.:
  Westview.

Hinsley, F. H. 1979. *British Intelligence in the Second World War*, vol. 1 New
  York: Cambridge University Press.

—— 1981. *British Intelligence in the Second World War*, vol. 2 New York:
  Cambridge University Press.

Hoffman, Steven. 1972. "Anticipation, Disaster, and Victory." *Asian Survey*
  12(11):960–79.

Holmes, W. J. 1979. *Doubled-Edged Secrets*. Annapolis, Md.: Naval Institute Press.

Holst, Johan. 1966. "Surprise, Signals, and Reaction." *Cooperation and Conflict*
  1(2):32–45.

Hopkins, Robert. 1980. "Warnings of Revolutions." Intelligence Monograph.
  Washington, D.C.: Center for the Study of Intelligence, Central Intelligence
  Agency.

Hopple, Gerald. 1983. "Intelligence and Warning: Implications and Lessons of
  the Falkland Island War." Paper presented at the Annual Meeting of the
  International Studies Association, Mexico City. April.

Hughes, Thomas. 1976. "The Fate of Facts in a World of Men: Foreign Policy
  and Intelligence Making." Headline Series, no. 232. New York: Foreign
  Policy Association.

IHT (*International Herald Tribune*). 1985a.Paris. "Admiral Says Spy Ring Enabled
  Soviet to Decode Secret Naval Messages." June 12. Cited as *IHT*.

—— 1985b. "Navy Spy Loss Found More Serious." July 15.

—— 1985c. "U.S. Says Navy Spy Sold Data on Military Message System."
  August 8.

Inman, Bobby. 1983. "The Role of Intelligence." Lecture delivered at the
  Conference on Reducing the Role of Inadvertent War: Crisis Management,
  University of Texas at Austin. February 24–25.

—— 1984. "Technology and Strategy." *U.S. Naval Institute Proceedings Supplement* 46–51.

Janis, Irving. 1972. *Victims of Groupthink*. Boston: Houghton Mifflin.

Janis, Irving and Leon Mann. 1977. *Decision Making*. New York: Free Press.

*The Jerusalem Post Magazine*. 1982. "Interview with Shlomo Gazit." April 16.

Jervis, Robert. 1968. "Hypotheses on Misperception." *World Politics* 20(3):454–79.

—— 1970. *The Logic of Images in International Relations*. Princeton: Princeton
  University Press.

—— 1976. *Perception and Misperception in International Politics*. Princeton:
  Princeton University Press.

Jodice, David. 1982. "Empirical Indicators of Political Instability and Revolution."
  Paper presented at the Annual Meeting of the International Studies Association, Cincinnati. March.

Jones, R. V. 1978. *The Wizard War.* New York: Coward, McCann and Geoghegan.

Kahan, Jerome. 1975. *Security in the Nuclear Age.* Washington, D.C.: Brookings Institution.

Kahn, David. 1967. *The Codebreakers.* New York: Macmillan.

—— 1978. *Hitler's Spies.* New York: Macmillan.

—— 1979. "Cryptology Goes Public." *Foreign Affairs* 58(1):141-59.

—— 1982. "Did FDR Invite the Pearl Harbor Attack?" *New York Review of Books.* May 2.

Kahn, Herman. 1962. *Thinking About the Unthinkable.* New York: Horizon Press.

—— 1965. *On Escalation.* New York: Prager.

Kennedy, Robert. 1969. *Thirteen Days.* New York: Norton.

Kent, Sherman. 1969. "Estimates and Influence." *Foreign Service Journal* (April), pp. 16-18, 45.

King, Ernest and Walter Whitehill. 1952. *Fleet Admiral King.* New York: Norton.

Kirkpatrick, Lyman. 1969. *Captains Without Eyes.* New York: Macmillan.

Knorr, Klaus. 1964. "Failures in National Intelligence Estimates: The Case of the Cuban Missile Crisis." *World Politics* 15(3):455-67.

—— 1976. "Threat Perception," pp. 78-119 in Knorr, ed. *Historical Dimensions of National Security Problems.* Lawrence: University Press of Kansas.

—— 1977. "Military Strength: Economic and Non-Economic Bases," pp. 183-99 in Klaus Knorr and Frank Trager, eds. *Economic Issues and National Security.* Lawrence: Regents Press of Kansas.

—— 1979. "Strategic Intelligence: Problems and Remedies," pp. 69-101 in Lawrence Martin, ed. *Strategic Thought in the Nuclear Age.* Baltimore: Johns Hopkins University Press.

—— 1982. "On Strategic Surprise." Research Note No. 10. Los Angeles: University of California Center for International and Strategic Affairs.

—— 1983. "Lessons for Statecraft," pp. 247-65 in Klaus Knorr and Patrick Morgan, eds. *Strategic Military Surprise: Incentives and Opportunities.* New Brunswick, N.J.: Transaction Books.

Knorr, Klauss and Patrick Morgan, eds. 1983. *Strategic Military Surprise: Incentives and Opportunities.* New Brunswick, N.J.: Transaction Books.

Lacqueur, Walter. 1981. "The Untold Story of World War II." *The New Republic* 14, October: 17-20.

Lanir, Zvi. 1983. *Fundamental Surprise: The National Intelligence Crisis* (Hebrew). Tel Aviv: Hakibutz Ha'meuhad.

Laskov, Haim. 1976. "Thoughts on Surprise" (Hebrew). *Ma'arachot* 251-52, October:17-24.

Lauder, George. 1985. "Letter to the Editor." *Foreign Policy* 58:171-73.

Layton, Edwin et al. 1985. *"And I Was There": Pearl Harbor and Midway—Breaking the Secrets.* New York: William Morrow.

Lebow, Richard. 1981. *Between Peace and War.* Baltimore: Johns Hopkins University Press.

Lewin, Ronald. 1980. *Ultra Goes to War.* New York: Pocket Books.

—— 1982. *The American Magic.* New York: Farrar Straus Giroux.

Levite, Ariel. 1981. "The Study of Strategic Surprise: A Blind Alley or a Path to Be Blazed." Ithaca: Cornell University Press Peace Studies Program. Mimeo.

Lindbloom, Charles. 1959. "The Science of Muddling Through." *Public Administration Review* 19(2):79–88.

Lord, Walter. 1967. *Incredible Victory.* New York: Harper and Row.

*Los Angeles Times.* 1983. "FBI Releases Pearl Harbor Papers in Rebuttal." April 1.

*Maariv,* Tel Aviv (Hebrew). 1977. November 11.

MacArthur Hearings. *See* U.S. Congress 1951.

McCollum, Arthur. 1973. "Reminiscences of Rear Admiral Arthur H. McCollum, U.S. Navy (Ret.)." Oral History Series. Annapolis, Md.: Naval Institute.

Mahan, Alfred. 1957. *The Influence of Seapower Upon History.* New York: Hill and Wong.

Masterman, John. 1972. *The Double-Cross System.* New Haven: Yale University Press.

May, Ernest. 1973. "U.S. Press Coverage of Japan 1931–41." In Dorothy Borg and Shumpei Okamoto, eds., *Pearl Harbor as History,* pp. 511–32. New York: Columbia University Press.

—— 1981. "Unheeded Warning." In Paul Stillwell, ed., *Air Raid: Pearl Harbor,* pp. 79–87. Annapolis, Md.: Naval Institute Press.

Meir, Golda. 1975. *My Life.* New York: Putnam.

Millet, Alan and William Moreland. 1976. "What Happened? The Problem of Causation in International Affairs." In Klaus Knorr, ed., *Historical Dimensions of National Security Problems,* pp. 5–37. Lawrence: University Press of Kansas.

Morgan, Patrick. 1983. "Examples of Strategic Surprise in the Far East." In Klaus Knorr and Patrick Morgan, eds., *Strategic Military Surprise: Incentives and Opportunities,* pp. 43–76. New Brunswick, N.J.: Transaction Books.

Morison, Samuel. 1949. *History of the United States Naval Operations in World War II.* Vol. 4: *Coral Sea, Midway, and Submarine Action.* Boston: Little, Brown.

Nakdimon, Shlomo. 1982. *Low Probability* (Hebrew). Tel Aviv: Revivim.

*New York Times Book Review.* 1981. "Remembering Pearl Harbor." November 29.

*New York Times Book Review.* 1986. "Someone had Blundered But Who?" January 5.

NIE 2. *See* U.S. Central Intelligence Agency. 1950a.

NIE 2/1. *See* U.S. Central Intelligence Agency. 1950b.

NSC 81/2. *See* U.S. Executive Secretary to the National Security Council. 1950.

Perlmutter, Amos and John Gooch, eds. 1982. "Special Issues on Military Deception and Strategic Surprise." *Journal of Strategic Studies* 5(1).

Petrov, Vladimir. 1968. *June 22, 1941*. Columbia: University of South Carolina Press.

PHA. *See* U.S. Congress 1946.

Phillips, David. 1982. "CIA Boosts Intelligence Role Using High-Tech Electronics." *Defense Electronics* 14(2):54–66.

Popov, Dosko. 1974. *Spy, Counterspy*. Greenwich, Conn.: Fawcett.

Poteat, George. 1976. "The Intelligence Gap." *International Studies Notes*. 3(3):4–8.

Potter, E. B. 1976. *Nimitz*. Annapolis, Md.: Naval Institute Press.

Powers, Thomas. 1981. *The Man Who Kept the Secrets*. New York: Pocket Books.

Prange, Gordon with Donald Goldstein and Katherine Dillon. 1981. *At Dawn We Slept*. New York: McGraw-Hill.

—— 1982. *Miracle at Midway*. New York: McGraw-Hill.

—— 1985. *Pearl Harbor: The Verdict of History*. New York: McGraw-Hill.

Przeworski, Adam and Henry Teune. 1970. *Logic of Comparative Social Inquiry*. New York: Wiley.

Safford, Lawrence. 1952. "A Brief History of Communications Intelligence in the United States" (SRH-149). Washington, D.C.: Modern Military Section, U.S. National Archives. Declassified March 6, 1982.

*San Jose Mercury News*. 1983. "Libya Leak Threatened U.S. Agent." February 28.

Schiff, Zeev. 1974. *October Earthquake*. Tel Aviv: University Publishing Projects.

Schilling, Warner et al. 1973. *American Arms and a Changing Europe*. New York: Columbia University Press.

Sella, Amnon. 1978. " 'Barbarossa': Surprise Attack and Communication." *Journal of Contemporary History* 13(3):555–83.

Shlaim, Avi. 1976. "Failures in National Intelligence Estimates: The Case of the Yom Kippur War." *World Politics* 28(3):348–80.

Shmuel. Lt. Col. 1985. "The Imperative of Criticism: Intelligence Review." *IDF Journal* 2(3):62–69.

Simon, Herbert. 1957. *Administrative Behaviour*. New York: Free Press.

Singer, David and Michael Wallace, eds. 1979. *To Augur Well*. Beverly Hills, Calif.: Sage Publications.

SRH-012. *See* U.S. Navy. 1942a.

Stein, Janice Gross. 1980. " 'Intelligence' and 'Stupidity' Reconsidered: Estimation and Decision in Israel, 1973." *Journal of Strategic Studies* 3(1):147–77.

—— 1982. 'Military Deception, Strategic Surprise, and Conventional Deterrence: A Political Analysis of Egypt and Israel, 1971–73." *Journal of Strategic Studies* 5(1):94–121.

Steinbruner, John. 1974. *The Cybernetic Theory of Decision*. Princeton: Princeton University Press.

*The Sunday Times*, London. 1983. "Falklands: Who Blundered?" January 16.

Temple, Harry. 1982. "Deaf Captains: Intelligence, Policy, and the Origins of the Korean War." *International Studies Notes* 8, 3–4:19–23.

Thompson, Edmund. 1981. "Intelligence in Yorktown." *Defense* (October), pp. 25–28.

Thorpe, Elliott. 1969. *East, West Rain*. Boston: Gamit.

Tighe, Eugene. 1983. "View from the Top: Interview with Admiral Bobby Inman." *Military Electronics/Countermeasures* 9(1):4–12.

*Time Magazine*, New York. 1978. "Intelligence Control." February 6.

*The Times*, London. 1982a. "Why Argentina Took Tough Line After Talks." April 6.

—— 1982b. "Lord Carrington Tells Why He Resigned." April 6.

—— 1982c. "Britain Given the Invasion Plans 11 Days Ago." April 6.

Toland, John. 1982. *Infamy*. New York: Doubleday.

Tomiko, Kakegawa. 1973. "The Press and Public Opinion in Japan, 1931–41" In Dorothy Borg and Shumpei Okamoto, eds. *Pearl Harbor as History*, pp. 533–50. New York: Columbia University Press.

Trevor-Roper, Hugh. 1980. Valedictory lecture as Regius Professor of Modern History, Oxford University. May 20.

Tufte, Edward. 1969. "Improving Data Analysis in Political Science." In Edward R. Tufte. ed., *The Qualitative Analysis of Social Problems*, pp. 641–54. Reading, Mass.: Addison-Wesley.

Tversky, Amos and Daniel Kahneman. 1974. "Judgement Under Uncertainty: Heuristics and Biases." *Science* 185:1124–31.

—— 1981. "The Framing of Decisions and the Psychology of Choice." *Science* 211:453–58.

Tzu, Sun. 1971. *The Art of War*. New York: Oxford University Press.

U.S. Central Intelligence Agency. 1950a. "Chinese Communist Intervention in Korea." National Intelligence Estimate 2. November 8. Declassified April 10, 1979. Cited as NIE 2.

—— 1950b. "Chinese Communist Intervention in Korea." National Intelligence Estimate 2/1. November 24. Declassified April 10, 1979. Cited as NIE 2/1.

U.S. Congress. 1946. Joint Committee on the Investigation of the Pearl Harbor Attack. *Hearings*. 39 vols. Washington, D.C.: GPO. Cited as PHA.

U.S. Congress. 1951. Senate, Committee on Armed Services and the Committee on Foreign Relations. Hearings to Conduct an Inquiry into the Military Situation in the Far East and the Facts Surrounding the Relief of General of the Army Douglas MacArthur from this Assignment to that Area. 82d Cong., 1st Sess. Washington, D.C.: GPO. Cited as MacArthur Hearings.

U.S. Congress. 1980. House of Representatives, Committee on Foreign Affairs, Subcommittee on International Security and Scientific Affairs. *Hearings on the Role of Intelligence in the Foreign Policy Process*. 86th Cong., 2d Sess. Washington, D.C.: GPO.

U.S. Department of Defense. 1977. *The "Magic" Background to Pearl Harbor.* Washington, D.C.: GPO.

U.S. Department of Justice. 1941. Federal Bureau of Investigation, "Memorandum for Mr. Ladd Re Duson M. Popov, Confidential Informant" (6 documents). Washington, D.C.: Federal Bureau of Investigation. Declassified March-April 1982. Cited as FBI.

U.S. Executive Secretary to the National Security Council. 1950. "United States Courses of Action with Respect to Korea: Report to the National Security Council." NSC 81/2. April 14. Declassified June 24, 1975. Cited as NSC 81/2.

U.S. Navy. 1942a. " The Role of Radio Intelligence in the American Japanese Naval War" (SRH-012), vol. 1. Washington, D.C.: Modern Military Section, U.S. National Archives. Declassified May 26, 1978. Cited as SRH-012.

U.S. Navy. 1942b. "Command Summary: Admiral C. W. Nimitz." Book 1, vol. 2. Washington, D.C.: Operational Archives, U.S. Navy. Cited as Command Summary.

USN&WR. *U.S. News and World Report,* New York. 1985. "Interview with John Lehman." June 24. Cited as *USN&WR.*

Van Der Rhoer, Edward. 1978. *Deadly Magic.* New York: Scribner's.

*Washington Post.* 1982. "Did FBI Have Class?" December 2.

*Washington Times.* 1985. "Code Buster to Get Medal 45 Years Late." December 9.

Weizman, Ezer. 1981. *The Battle for Peace* (Hebrew). Jerusalem: Edamim.

Whaley, Barton. 1969. "Stratagem, Deception, and Surprise in War." Cambridge: MIT. Mimeo.

—— 1973. *Codeword Barbarossa.* Cambridge: MIT Press.

—— 1975. "The Causes of Surprise in War." Paper delivered at the Conference on Strategic Issues, Hebrew University, Jerusalem, Israel.

—— 1982. "Toward a General Theory of Deception." *Journal of Strategic Studies* 5(1):178–92.

Wilensky, Harold. 1967. *Organizational Intelligence.* New York: Basic Books.

Winterbotham, F. W. 1974. *The Ultra Secret.* New York: Harper and Row.

Wohlstetter, Roberta. 1962. *Pearl Harbor: Warning and Decision.* Stanford: Stanford University Press.

—— 1965. "Cuba and Pearl Harbor." *Foreign Affairs* 43(4):690–707.

*Yediot Ahronot* (Hebrew), Tel Aviv. 1977. November 15.

# Index